HEBREWS

ABINGDON NEW TESTAMENT COMMENTARIES

HEBREWS

VICTOR C. PFITZNER

Abingdon Press
Nashville

ABINGDON NEW TESTAMENT COMMENTARIES:
HEBREWS

Copyright © 1997 by Abingdon Press

This book is printed on recycled, acid-free, elemental-chlorine–free paper.

Library of Congress Cataloging-in-Publication Data

Pfitzner, V. C. (Victor C.)
   Hebrews / Victor C. Pfitzner.
     p.   cm.—(Abingdon New Testament commentaries)
   Includes bibliographical references and index.
   ISBN 0-687-05724-8 (pbk. : alk. paper)
   1. Bible. N.T. Hebrews—Commentaries. I. Title. II. Series.
BS2775.3.P355 1997
227' .8707—dc21   97-37867
                                                CIP

97 98 99 00 01 02 03 04 05 06—10 9 8 7 6 5 4 3 2 1

MANUFACTURED IN THE UNITED STATES OF AMERICA

*For John Hall Elliott
Scholar and Friend*

CONTENTS

FOREWORD

The *Abingdon New Testament Commentaries* series provides compact, critical commentaries on the writings of the New Testament. These commentaries are written with special attention to the needs and interests of theological students, but they will also be useful for students in upper-level college or university settings, as well as for pastors and other church leaders. In addition to providing basic information about the New Testament texts and insights into their meanings, these commentaries are intended to exemplify the tasks and procedures of careful, critical biblical exegesis.

The authors who have contributed to this series come from a wide range of ecclesiastical affiliations and confessional stances. All are seasoned, respected scholars and experienced classroom teachers. They take full account of the most important current scholarship and secondary literature, but do not attempt to summarize that literature or to engage in technical academic debate. Their fundamental concern is to analyze the literary, socio-historical, theological, and ethical dimensions of the biblical texts themselves. Although all of the commentaries in this series have been written on the basis of the Greek texts, the authors do not presuppose any knowledge of the biblical languages on the part of the reader. When some awareness of a grammatical, syntactical, or philological issue is necessary for an adequate understanding of a particular text, they explain the matter clearly and concisely.

The introduction of each volume ordinarily includes subdivisions dealing with the *key issues* addressed and/or raised by the New Testament writing under consideration; its *literary genre, structure, and character;* its *occasion and situational context,* including its wider social, historical, and religious contexts; and its *theological and ethical significance* within these several contexts.

In each volume, the *commentary* is organized according to literary units rather than verse by verse. Generally, each of these units is the subject of three types of analysis. First, the *literary analysis* attends to the unit's genre, most important stylistic features, and overall structure. Second, the *exegetical analysis* considers the aim and leading ideas of the unit, deals with any especially important textual variants, and discusses the meanings of important words, phrases, and images. It also takes note of the particular historical and social situations of the writer and original readers, and of the wider cultural and religious contexts of the book as a whole. Finally, the *theological and ethical analysis* discusses the theological and ethical matters with which the unit deals or to which it points, focusing on the theological and ethical significance of the text within its original setting.

Each volume also includes a *select bibliography,* thereby providing guidance to other major commentaries and important scholarly works, and a brief *subject index.* The New Revised Standard Version of the Bible is the principal translation of reference for the series, but the authors draw on all of the major modern English versions, and when necessary provide their own original translations of difficult terms or phrases.

The fundamental aim of this series will have been attained if readers are assisted, not only to understand more about the origins, character, and meaning of the New Testament writings, but also to enter into their own informed and critical engagement with the texts themselves.

Victor Paul Furnish
General Editor

PREFACE

A commentator should make an ancient document no more difficult than it really is. The message of Hebrews is hard enough to comprehend without the addition of technical data. Origen's famous answer to the question of the author's identity, "God only knows," can all too easily become the answer to the Letter's final meaning as the student becomes lost in a maze of scholarly details.

My aim in revisiting Hebrews has been to show as simply as possible what questions must be asked and to suggest reasonable responses, without presuming to know final solutions. I have attempted to help readers—including those without knowledge of Koine Greek—to appreciate the writer's literary skill, and to understand his message within his own terms of reference, allowing them to gain their own access into the writer's mind. Whether his argument would hit the mark today is not the question. At issue is the coherency of a pastoral appeal at a certain time and place.

The format of this series rightfully encourages students to examine blocks of material before analyzing verses and dissecting words. Those who know the literature will see where I am indebted to those who have studied the structure and rhetoric of Hebrews, especially Albert Vanhoye and George Guthrie. It will be equally apparent how much I owe to recent commentators, especially to Harold Attridge and William Lane, and to the study of the Letter's religiohistorical setting by L. Hurst. I hope this volume will make a contribution to the study of Hebrews by indicating the coherency of the author's argument as a theology of worship.

I gratefully acknowledge the encouragement of the general editor, Victor Paul Furnish; the help of Pheme Perkins in reducing an over-long manuscript to prescribed proportions; and the patient communications across the Pacific by the editorial staff of Abingdon Press. It is my delight to dedicate this work to one of the series editors, Jack Elliott, a fellow doctoral student in Germany long ago, a sharer of wisdom, and a true friend.

Victor C. Pfitzner

LIST OF ABBREVIATIONS

1 [2] Clem.	*First [Second] Clement*
1 Enoch	Ethiopic *Book of Enoch*
1QH	*Thanksgiving Hymns* (Qumran Cave 1)
1QS	*Rule of the Community* (Qumran Cave 1)
1QSa	Appendix 1 *(Rule of the Congregation)* to 1QS
2 Apoc. Bar.	Syriac *Apocalypse of Baruch*
2 Enoch	Slavonic *Book of Enoch*
4QDeut	*Deuteronomy* text (Qumran Cave 4)
4QFlor	*Florilegium* (Qumran Cave 4)
4QShirShabb	*Songs of the Sabbath Sacrifice* (Qumran Cave 4)
11QMelch	*Melchizedek* text (Qumran Cave 11)
11QTemple	*Temple Scroll* (Qumran Cave 11)
AB	Anchor Bible
Abr.	Philo, *On Abraham*
ACNT	Augsburg Commentary on the New Testament
AnBib	Analecta biblica
Ant.	Josephus, *The Antiquities of the Jews*
Apost. Const.	*The Apostolic Constitutions*
AT	Author's translation
Barn.	*Barnabas*
Bib	*Biblica*
CBQ	*Catholic Biblical Quarterly*
CBQMS	Catholic Biblical Quarterly—Monograph Series
ConBNT	Coniectanea biblica, New Testament
Congr.	Philo, *On the Preliminary Studies*

CR:BS	*Currents in Research: Biblical Studies*
De Prov.	Seneca *On Providence*
Dial. Trypho	Justin Martyr, *Dialogue with Trypho*
Did.	*Didache*
Diss.	Epictetus *Dissertations*
Ebr.	Philo, *On Drunkenness*
EKKNT	Evangelisch-katholischer Kommentar zum Neuen Testament
Heres	Philo, *Who Is the Heir of Divine Things?*
Herm. Man	*Hermas, Mandate(s)*
Herm. Vis.	*Hermas, Vision(s)*
Hist. Eccl.	Eusebius, *The History of the Church*
HNT	Handbuch zum Neuen Testament
HNTC	Harper's NT Commentaries
HTR	*Harvard Theological Review*
ICC	International Critical Commentary
Ign. *Magn.*	Ignatius, *Letter to the Magnesians*
Ign. *Rom.*	Ignatius, *Letter to the Romans*
Ign. *Pol.*	Ignatius, *Letter to Polycarp*
JB	*The Jerusalem Bible*
J.W.	Josephus, *The Jewish War*
JSNT	*Journal for the Study of the New Testament*
JSNTSup	Journal for the Study of the New Testament— Supplement Series
Jub.	*Jubilees*
KNT	Kommentar zum Neuen Testament (Zahn)
Leg. All.	Philo, *Allegorical Interpretation*
LXX	Septuagint
Mart. Isa.	*The Martyrdom of Isaiah*
Mart. Pol.	*Martyrdom of Polycarp*
MeyerK	H. A. W. Meyer, Kritisch-exegetischer Kommentar über das Neue Testament
Migr. Abr.	Philo, *On the Migration of Abraham*
NCB	New Century Bible
NICNT	New International Commentary on the New Testament

NIGTC	The New International Greek Testament Commentary
NIV	*The Holy Bible, New International Version*
NJB	*The New Jerusalem Bible*
NovTSup	Novum Testamentum, Supplements
NRSV	New Revised Standard Version
NTS	*New Testament Studies*
Odes	*The Book of Odes* (appended to Psalms in the LXX)
Phil.	Polycarp, *To the Philippians*
Praem.	Philo, *On Rewards and Punishments*
Pss. Sol.	*Psalms of Solomon*
REB	*The Revised English Bible*
Ref. Haer.	Hippolytus, *Refutation of All Heresies*
RSV	Revised Standard Version
SBLDS	SBL Dissertation Series
Somn.	Philo, *On Dreams*
Sib. Or.	*Sibylline Oracles*
SNTSMS	Society for New Testament Studies Monograph Series
T. 12 Patr.	*Testament of the Twelve Patriarchs*
T. Levi	*Testament of Levi*
T. Zeb.	*Testament of Zebulon*
TDNT	G. Kittel and G. Friedrich (eds.), *Theological Dictionary of the New Testament*
TEV	*The Bible in Today's English Version* (Good News Bible)
THKNT	Theologischer Handkommentar zum Neuen Testament
TNTC	Tyndale New Testament Commentary
Vita Mos.	Philo, *The Life of Moses*
WBC	Word Biblical Commentary

INTRODUCTION

HEBREWS AS CHALLENGE

Interpreting Hebrews presents many challenges. We are reading part of a dialogue without any communication from the other party to help situate the letter. Its interpretation requires a careful search for clues to anchor the document in historical and social reality, and a sensitive ear for hints at an agenda that was perfectly clear to the recipients, if not to us.

The writer assumes that his audience holds common traditions, reads the Old Testament as he does, and shares a view of reality and store of symbols with which to express it. He assumes that people know where he is standing on common ground, and where he is moving into new territory. He expects them to follow the logic of his rhetoric, so that subtle nuances in his argument will not be lost on them.

Hebrews was written to challenge a community that the author saw as being in a perilous situation. He urges it to remain faithful to its confession (3:1; 4:14; 10:23), warning against drifting away and neglecting salvation (2:1, 3), losing confidence in God's promises (3:6), falling away from God (3:12), and being rebellious and unbelieving like Israel in the past (3:16-19). His hearers have not progressed to Christian adulthood (5:11–6:2). Having experienced God's saving gifts in Christ they may finally reject him (6:4-6; 10:29; 12:25). Sluggishness (6:12) could lead to something far worse: apostasy (10:26).

Why the readers are regressing is not clear. There are hints at a persecution once endured with joy and concern for others. Now there is a lack of confidence (10:32-39). The writer's tactic is not merely to appeal for renewed commitment. All appeals are grounded on gospel affirmations. The recipients are to set their sights on Christ (2:10; 12:2) who is the ultimate revelation of God

(1:1-2). As faithful Son and High Priest (3:6; 2:17), he has opened up access into God's holy presence so that those sanctified by him can offer up sacrifices that are pleasing to God (12:28; 13:15).

Neglect of worship (10:25) is symptomatic of external pressure and inner fatigue. That helps to explain why the Letter (meant to be read in worship; see 13:24-25) is full of cultic language taken from Old Testament texts that must have played a role in the community's worship. Hebrews asserts the certainty of faith in the context of the Christian cultus, viewed primarily not as what God's people do but as the cultic enactment of divine blessing.

LITERARY GENRE, RHETORICAL DEVICES, AND STRUCTURE

Literary Genre

Hebrews lacks the normal epistolary opening identifying the writer and recipients. It does have a letter ending, with personal references and greetings (13:20-25). Suggestions that an original opening has been lost, that 13:18-25 was added to a discourse by a later hand, or even that the whole of chapter 13 is an addition, fail to convince (see Attridge 1989, 13; Lane 1991, lxviii). The last chapter forms the essential conclusion to the Letter; it elaborates on the call to worship in 12:28.

The author describes his message as a "word of exhortation" (13:22), a term used in Acts 13:15 for a synagogue address in the Jewish diaspora. Such exhortation probably involved an exposition of Old Testament texts (see Wills 1984). Whether "word of exhortation" was a technical expression or not, the author considers his letter to be sermonic.

With its recurring pattern of formal introduction, scriptural quotation, exposition, and application (e.g., 3:1-6; 3:7-11; 3:12–4:13; 4:14-16), Hebrews is the prime example of extended exhortation in the New Testament. As a sermon in epistolary form, Hebrews conforms closely to the kind of hellenistic-Jewish synagogue address represented by 4 Maccabees. Both are passionate appeals for enduring faith; both use authoritative examples to draw lessons that form the basis of appeals.

Rhetorical Devices

The Letter directs passionate appeals to a community in danger of surrendering the distinctiveness of its faith. The writer knows the situation of his addressees (see 5:11-12; 6:9; 10:33-34), yet he does not let his own person (see 11:32; 13:19, 22-23) intrude into the argument. He lets his argument speak for itself.

The writer's polished Greek is matched by his literary skill. He shows facility with a variety of devices used for aural impact (see Attridge 1989, 20-21). He is not concerned with literary niceties as such, but with formulating a persuasive argument. In ancient rhetoric, effective composition and arrangement of material was conditioned by the setting of a speech. *Judicial* (or forensic) rhetoric belonged to the courtroom; it aimed to accuse or defend before a judge or jury. The purpose of *deliberative* rhetoric was to persuade a public assembly to take some action (or, conversely, to dissuade it from the same). Speakers used *epideictic* rhetoric on public memorial occasions to confirm communal values by praise or censure. Although it has often been described as either deliberative or judicial, Hebrews conforms more closely to epideictic oratory (For the three classes see Kennedy 1984, 19-20; Mack 1990, 34-35; Cosby 1988, 94.):

(1) Epideictic speech extolled the greatness of a person and promoted the values that followers should espouse. It was thus suitable for funeral orations. Hebrews extols Jesus who once died but is now the enthroned Son and High Priest who calls his followers to decisive action. Epideictic oratory is suited to exhortation in the context of worship.

(2) Amplification by means of comparison was a standard feature of epideictic oratory (Aristotle *Rhetoric* 1.9, 38-40). Much of Hebrews is amplified comparison; the author compares Jesus Christ to angels, Moses, Levitical priests, and to Melchizedek; the new covenant to the old; the new holiness to the old cultic purity.

(3) Epideictic speech dealt with praise and blame. Blame in Heb 5:11–6:8 is followed immediately by praise in 6:9-12. Blame alone

would be harsh; praise by itself would be dishonest. Heard together they serve a final purpose: warning.

(4) Epideictic speech was concerned with reinforcing beliefs and attitudes already held by those being addressed. Hebrews aims to reinforce Christian faith as the basis for renewed perseverance.

Structure

The homiletical craft of Hebrews has never been disputed. Less clear is how the discourse as a whole should be structured in order to elucidate the logic of its argument. A simple thematic arrangement tends to result in a reading in which doctrinal themes (e.g., the superiority of Christ) gain independent significance, with parenesis seen as adjunct material. This thematic arrangement also tends to ignore the devices that are designed to help the *hearer* to make the necessary connections.

Another approach seeks to structure Hebrews according to patterns of ancient oratory. Assuming that Hebrews is forensic rhetoric, a four-part scheme has been proposed, using the technical terms for each section (see Lane 1991, lxxvii, for this analysis by F. von Soden):

(1) 1:1–4:16   *exordium* (Gk. *prooemium*)—prologue (1:1-4) with *prothesis* or thematic statement (1:5-4:16)

(2) 5–6   *narratio* (Gk. *diēgēsis*)—statement of facts and treatment of the argument's plausibility

(3) 7:1–10:18   *probatio* (Gk. *apodeixis*)—proof of the argument

(4) 10:19–13:25   *peroratio* (Gk. *epilogos*)—conclusion

A third approach attempts to trace the letter's structure by means of literary analysis. Albert Vanhoye noted five literary devices that the writer of Hebrews uses to mark off sections in his argument. (1) Thematic announcements state the subject of the next section. The theme of Jesus as "merciful and faithful" High Priest in 2:17-18 is developed in reverse order in 3:1–4:14 ("faithful") and 4:15–5:10 ("merciful"). Again, 5:9-10 announces Jesus as the "source of eternal salvation" and as "priest according to the order of Melchizedek," themes that are treated, again in reverse order, in chapter 7 and in 8:1–10:18. (2) Hook words tie one section to another. The word "angel" links 1:1-4 with 1:5–2:18, just as the term "high priest" in 2:17 and 3:1 links two sections. (3) Changes in genre take place as the writer switches between exposition and exhortation, usually with transitional words like "since" or "therefore" (2:1; 3:7; 4:14; 10:19; 12:1). (4) Repetition of a term (e.g., "angels" in 1:5–2:18) marks off a section. (5) Inclusions in the form of parallel words or phrases mark the beginning and end of sections. For example, the extensive parallels between 4:14-16 and 10:19-23 indicate an *inclusio* that links major sections of the letter.

These criteria have proven useful in determining the structure of Hebrews. In particular, Vanhoye's broadly chiastic outline has found wide acceptance:

(1) 1:5–2:18 the name superior to the angels (eschatology)
(2) 3:1–5:10 Jesus faithful and compassionate (ecclesiology)
(3) 5:11–10:39 the central exposition (sacrifice)
(4) 11:1–12:13 faith and endurance (ecclesiological parenesis)
(5) 12:14–13:19 the peaceful fruit of justice (eschatology)

The text-linguistic approach recently proposed by George H. Guthrie seeks to provide a more comprehensive method of plotting the structure of Hebrews. The expository material is shown to have the following shape (G. Guthrie 1994, 117):

I. The Position of the Son in Relation to the Angels (1:5–2:18)
    A. The Son Superior to the Angels (1:5-14)
        1. The Superior Son for a Time . . . Lower Than the Angels (2:5-9)
    B. The Son Lower Than the Angels . . . to Suffer for the Sons (2:10-18)
II. The Position of the Son, Our High Priest, in Relation to the Earthly Sacrificial System (4:14–10:25)
    Opening: We Have a Sinless High Priest Who Has Gone into Heaven (4:14-16)
    A. The Appointment of the Son as Superior High Priest (5:1-10; 7:1-28)

    1. We Have Such a High Priest Who Is a Minister in
        Heaven (8:1-2)
  B. The Superior Offering of the Appointed High
      Priest (8:3–10:18)
  Closing: We Have a Great High Priest Who Takes Us into
      Heaven (10:19-25)

Two discourses are developed in two smaller embedded discourses. The second discourse is framed by parallel opening and closing statements (4:14-16; 10:19-25). In section I the spatial movement is from heaven to earth, from glory to humiliation. In section II the movement is from the High Priest's appointment and suffering to his exaltation.

By contrast, the hortatory material does not develop a step-by-step argument, but draws warnings and encouragement from the exposition at key points. Even so, the parenetic material from 3:1-6 to 12:1-2 shows a chiastic structure, as does the final macrodiscourse when parenesis and exhortation are welded together (G. Guthrie 1994, 136, 144).

The distinction between exposition and exhortation is helpful, but the whole Letter has a parenetic thrust; some sections are a blend of both (see 3:1–4:11, and chap. 11). The central discourse on Christ as High Priest is framed by two exhortations that form an *inclusio* (4:14-16; 10:19-25). These sections are more than overlapping transitions; preceded (4:12-13) or followed (10:26-31) by warnings, they form the author's central appeal: to hold fast to the confession and to claim priestly access into God's presence.

IN SEARCH OF A HISTORICAL CONTEXT

Hebrews in the Early Church

Echoes of Hebrews are first heard in the *West*, in *1 Clement* (c. 96 CE). Both cite Num 12:7 to recall that "Moses was faithful in all God's house" (Heb 3:2, 5; *1 Clem.* 17:5; 43:1), state that God cannot lie (Heb 6:18; *1 Clem.* 27:2), and call Jesus "high priest" (Heb 2:18; 3:1; 4:14-16; *1 Clem.* 36:1; 64).

The *Shepherd of Hermas* (between 120 and 140 CE) seems to know Hebrews. He offers sinners a second chance to repent of manifest sin after conversion, but insists that this offer cannot be repeated (*Herm. Vis.* 2.2.4, 5; *Herm. Man.* 4.3.1, 2). His polemic against those who teach otherwise suggests knowledge of Hebrews 6:4-8. Circulation of Hebrews in the western church by the late-second century is indicated by Irenaeus in Gaul, Gaius in Rome (Eusebius *Hist. Eccl.* 5.26.3; 6.20.3), and by Hippolytus (*Ref. Haer.* 6.30.9), yet all three did not recognize the Letter as Pauline. Rejection of Pauline authorship in the West partly explains its neglect of Hebrews for three centuries, but the Letter's statement in 6:4-6 surely contributed to its unpopularity.

The situation was different in the *East* (it was probably there that the Letter gained its misleading name "To the Hebrews," perhaps on the assumption that it was a document of the church's mission to Jews). Ignatius of Antioch seems to reflect Heb 13:9-10 in *Magn.* 7:2–8:1, and there are allusions in Polycarp *Phil.* 6:3 and 12:2. By the end of the second century the Letter was widely known, and the tradition of Pauline authorship established.

Origen (c. 185–254 CE) is aware of the differences between the polished Greek of Hebrews and Paul's "rudeness in speech." He views the Letter's thoughts as equal to those of Paul, but the style and diction suggest a pupil, such as Clement of Rome or Luke, who made notes of what the apostle said. "But who wrote the epistle, truly God knows" (*Hist. Eccl.* 6.25.11-14).

From the early third century, Hebrews was consistently listed in the Pauline corpus, though in differing positions (Ellingworth 1993, 6-7). By the late-fourth century, the eastern church's view of Hebrews as Pauline and fully canonical prevailed also in the West.

The Search for an Author

Early tradition reveals on what shaky foundations the theory of Pauline authorship of Hebrews stands; internal evidence renders such a position untenable. (1) Paul insists on his authority as an eyewitness of the risen Lord; the author of Hebrews claims to be no more than a recipient of apostolic witness (2:3). (2) While Paul can write the smooth prose that is typical of Hebrews, his normal style is diatribal, argumentative, and often filled with anacolutha (abrupt midsentence shifts to a different grammatical construction). (3) Though Hebrews uses the athletic image that is common in Paul's letters (10:32; 12:1, 4; see 1 Cor 9:24-27; Phil 3:12-16), it has its own distinctive imagery. (4) The vocabulary of Hebrews is distinctive (Ellingworth 1993, 7-12), containing over 150 words found only here in the New Testament. (5) Central theological concepts and themes are markedly different. The explication of the person and work of Christ by analogy with the Old Testament cult and its sacrificial ritual is not typical of Paul.

Early traditions linking Hebrews with one of Paul's associates may point in the right direction, but no evidence has been adduced to show which associate *must* be identified as the author. Two candidates deserve some consideration. Barnabas (linked with a "Hebrews" by Tertullian; *Hist. Eccl.* 6.14.2-4) was a disciple of Paul. As a Greek-speaking Levite (Acts 4:36) he was probably well versed in the priestly ritual of the old covenant. But Hebrews bases its argument on the Scriptures, not on familiarity with the temple ritual. Further, Luke pictures Paul as more eloquent than Barnabas (Acts 14:12), whereas the rhetoric of Hebrews would suggest the opposite if Barnabas were the author. That there is a play on the name Barnabas ("son of encouragement," Acts 4:36) at Heb 13:22 ("word of encouragement" [NRSV: "word of exhortation"]) is a clever rather than convincing idea.

The argument for Apollos is marginally stronger. Also an associate of Paul, he was Jewish by birth, an educated Alexandrian—an "eloquent man, well-versed in the scriptures" (Acts 18:24). His instruction by Aquila and Priscilla (v. 26) gave him contact with Rome, the probable destination of Hebrews. Some find in the affinity between the thought of Hebrews and Philo of Alexandria another pointer to Apollos. Yet the Philonic connections can be debated. At best, nothing excludes Apollos as author.

The Relationship Between Author and Audience

There are hints at the kind of person who wrote Hebrews—that it was a male is inferred from a Greek masculine participle (NRSV: "tell") in 11:32. The way in which he argues (his *logos*) tells us something about his character and standing (his *ethos;* see Aristotle *Rhetoric* 1.2, 1356) with the readers.

The author prefers to identify with his readers when making appeals ("let us . . . "), addressing them as "brothers [and sisters]" (3:1, 12; 10:10; 13:22), and as "beloved" (6:9). That says little, since such language is typical of early Christian appeals. Though the writer and readers have common acquaintances, the references to Timothy and "those from Italy" in 13:23-24 are unclear. We naturally assume that this Timothy is the person encountered elsewhere in New Testament writings, and that he has been "released" from some confinement. The writer adds personal references at the end of his message to cement his relationship to the addressees until he is again with them in person (13:19, 23).

This relationship is not expressed in a Pauline way. The writer expects his message to be heeded, but never bases his authority on a special office or exercise of divine power. The first person plural in 5:11, 6:9, and 8:1 does not denote apostolic or collegial authority as it often does with Paul. Unlike Paul, the writer never claims a special possession of the Spirit (see 1 Cor 7:40; 2 Cor 3), never refers to his relations with other authorities (Gal 1:11-20; 1 Cor 15:5-11), and never adopts the stance of an authoritative link in the passing on of sacred tradition (1 Cor 11:23; 15:3; 1 Thess 4:1, 2; 2 Thess 2:15; 3:6). Nor does he ask the readers to imitate him as a model (1 Cor 4:16-17; Phil 3:17; 1 Thess 1:6; 2 Thess 3:7-9).

The writer's way of arguing suggests that he is, first, a *catechist and teacher of wisdom.* He can castigate the readers' slowness to learn, and recall their elementary instruction (5:11–6:3). He can reproach and encourage because he has been a teacher in the community. He cannot claim to be their "father" (see 1 Cor 4:14-21), yet he speaks as a teacher of wisdom in picturing God as a father who disciplines his children (Heb 12:5-11).

Second, the author is an *expositor* of the Scriptures, a biblical preacher. Much of his sermon is direct quotation or allusion to the sacred text—at least half of Hebrews is "textual" in this sense.

Third, the author is a *pastoral guide.* Lack of confidence and flagging zeal are not final problems. They point to the real issue, expressed in the heart of the Letter: neglect of worship that can lead to apostasy (10:19-31). The argument of Hebrews is cultic not merely because Israel's worship is the constant point of reference, but because every climactic point in the Letter is a statement about worship (4:16; 10:19-25; 12:22-24; 13:15-16). For the writer, certainty of faith in Christ as Son and High Priest has meaning only if it leads to the priestly sacrifice of praise.

The Situation of the Audience

Given the lack of precise internal evidence, any reconstruction must remain in the realm of probability. The constant movement from Christology to parenesis (2:1-4; 3:7–4:16; 5:11–6:12; 10:19-39; 12:1–13:25) suggests that neither christological heresy nor failure to come to grips with sin and guilt (Lindars 1991) is the problem. Christology serves as a springboard to exhortation. It is the practical significance of confessing Christ that is the issue.

The recipients seem to be located in an urban rather than rural setting. They are to look for a "lasting city" (13:14). Maritime imagery may suggest their closeness to a port, or at least to the sea (2:1; 6:19). Specific injunctions in 13:1-6, applicable in any setting, make better sense in an urban environment. The readers are expected to understand refined language and rhetorical conventions. Sharing with the writer the heritage of hellenistic Judaism and a view of Christ informed by hellenistic-Jewish wisdom traditions (1:3), the group probably had its roots in an urban synagogue. They are second generation believers (2:3) who probably include some Gentile Christians (see Ellingworth 1993, 22-26).

The readers form a local group with leaders, past and present (13:7, 17, 24). They are, most likely, members of a house-church, though the description of the church as house (3:6; 10:21) has other connotations.

The problem of the "Hebrews" begins with social pressure, not with doctrine. Loss of confidence is here the end product of suffering for the faith (10:32-39; 11:24-28, 32-38; 12:1-11), which may have already caused some defections from the group (10:25), though no one has suffered martyrdom (12:4). At some time in the past, the community has endured abuse, persecution, imprisonment, and confiscation of property (10:32-34). It is implied (see 11:26; 13:13) that the community is still under threat.

There is no clue as to when the first trials began. Public humiliation and abuse (10:33; 13:13) were probably instigated by the local populace, though imprisonment and confiscation of property indicate involvement of local authorities. We can only conjecture what caused the members of this community to be maligned. One possibility is that they were regarded with suspicion as a new and strange oriental sect. Christianity's claim to be a separate religion could be challenged on the basis of external observations: Where were its temples, its priesthood, its sacrifices, its cultic ritual? Hebrews certainly provides a detailed answer to each of these questions.

The contrast between old covenant and new is no mere rhetorical device, but points to a real problem: the relationship between Christianity and Judaism. The call to suffer with Christ "outside the camp" (13:13) does not imply attacks on the readers by Jews. Yet separation is the clear message of the writer. The passionate appeal of Hebrews to hold on to the new surely hints at the temptation to move back, in some sense, to the old. Without fully realizing the dangers involved, and without wanting to give up their confession, the readers are possibly tempted to seek security under the cover of Judaism, which has an identity and some status in Roman society. The argument of Hebrews is thus not anti-Jewish, but is designed to prove the distinctiveness of Christian faith and worship for a group of Jewish Christians. Even Judaism can provide no secure haven for those called to suffer for Christ!

Whatever its origin, social pressure on the community means that group identity, cohesion, and solidarity are under threat. This has led to a diffident approach to worship (10:25), to deafness to the word (see the warnings in 2:1-4; 4:12-13; 6:4-8; 10:26-31; 12:25-29), and to a waning of those acts of kindness that demonstrate group identity and solidarity (see 10:24, 32-36; 13:1-5). Without restoration of confidence, the ultimate outcome would be the total loss of faith, though the author maintains high hopes for the community (6:9-12).

Parallels can be drawn between the social situation of the audiences addressed in Hebrews and in 1 Peter. Both writings are directed to maligned communities. The readers of Hebrews may, like those addressed in 1 Pet 1:1 and 2:11 (see Elliott 1981, 21-73), be aliens and temporary dwellers in this world (11:13) in more than one sense.

First Peter reminds its readers of their privileged status as the elect, holy, priestly people of God. Similarly, Hebrews reminds its readers of their status as people who have been sanctified for priestly access into God's presence; they have joined the heavenly hosts in worship (12:22-24). Those who have suffered loss of possessions and face further deprivation are reminded of what they "have": an eternal High Priest (4:14-15; 8:1; 10:21), a sure hope (6:18-19), confidence to approach God (10:19), better possessions (10:34), and a lasting home (13:14; see also the further property metaphors of sharing in 2:14; 3:1; 6:4; and of inheritance in 1:14; 6:12; 9:15; 11:7-9; 12:17).

Destination and Date

The recipients of Hebrews have been located in a variety of places. Variants of the thesis that the audience was in Palestine (diaspora Jews on pilgrimage in Jerusalem; converted priests [cf. Acts 6:7]; converts from Qumran) are highly improbable. According to 6:10, the readers have distinguished themselves in supporting other needy Christians, whereas the saints in Jerusalem were, rather, on the receiving end of such support. A persecution in Jerusalem (see 10:32-34) poses difficulties, and we would expect "apostles" rather than "leaders" in 13:7 if Jerusalem were the Letter's destination. Finally, the athletic image (10:32; 12:1-4) is limited to hellenistic-Jewish sources outside of Palestine (see Pfitzner 1967, 16-72).

A Roman destination has both external and internal support. (1) A Roman document, *1 Clement,* first attests the existence of Hebrews. (2) "Those from Italy send you greetings" (13:24) could imply that the Letter is sent from Italy or to Italy. The second is the more likely interpretation (see Acts 18:2). (3) The term used to describe the "leaders" of the community (Heb 13:7, 17, 24) appears in other early Christian documents connected with Rome (*1 Clem.* 21:6; *Herm. Vis.* 2.2.6; 3.9.7.). (4) Hints at the support given to other saints by the audience (Heb 6:10; perhaps 10:33-34) find echoes in later tributes to the generosity of Roman Christians (Ign. *Rom.*, Opening; *Hist. Eccl.* 4.23.10). (5) Romans 16:3-15 attests the existence of a number of house-churches in Rome. Hebrews could have been directed to one with which the writer had a special relationship (Heb 13:24).

William L. Lane (1991, lviii; lxiii-lxvi) has suggested that the sufferings referred to in Heb 10:32-34 are consistent with the experience of Jews expelled from Rome by the edict of Claudius in 49 CE (see Acts 18:2). Suetonius (*Claudius* 25.4) records that the emperor "expelled Jews who were continually causing a disturbance at the instigation of Chrestus." This can be interpreted to mean that Jewish Christians who proclaimed *Christ* caused such dissension among the Jews that the emperor was forced to take action.

Whether Jews or only Jewish Christians were ejected from Rome is not clear. Yet a connection between this event and Heb 10:32-34 remains possible. It would provide a historical setting for the imprisonments and confiscation of property in the past, and partly explain the ongoing threat to the community. Since the edict of Claudius may not have distinguished between Jews and Jewish Christians, a situation could have arisen where Christians, faced with pressure from non-Jewish sources, sought to align themselves, socially and politically, with Jews.

Outer limits for the dating of Hebrews are easier to set if it was sent to a house-church in Rome. Some time has passed since the audience received the gospel and suffered its first trials (2:1-4; 5:12; 10:32-34; 13:7), so the Letter can be dated as early as the late fifties. Debate on the upper limit has focused on two events: the destruction of the temple in 70 CE and the Neronian persecution in 64 CE (the use of Hebrews by *1 Clem.* in about 96 provides the absolute upper limit).

Use of the present tense to describe the Old Testament cultus does not prove that the temple of Jerusalem was still standing. Writing later, Josephus also describes aspects of the temple's appointments and ritual in the present tense (*Ant.* 4.6-9). Yet there is reason to believe that the author of Hebrews was writing before 70 CE. If writing later, he would surely not have ignored the actual destruction of the temple as proof that the old cult and its sacrificial system were obsolete (8:13). If we are right in placing the recipients in Rome, the Letter must be dated before 64 CE when some Christians did die for the faith (cf. 12:4). A date somewhere from the late fifties to the early sixties is indicated. An early rather than late dating is supported by the writer's expectation of an imminent parousia (10:25, 36-39).

THE THEOLOGY OF HEBREWS

Whether we regard the writer as an original and imaginative thinker will depend on an assessment of his dependence on cultural and intellectual presuppositions that he shared with his readers, and on gauging the degree to which he was indebted to early Christian traditions. That he was influenced by hellenistic thought is beyond dispute. Less agreement exists in determining other cultural and religious influences.

Hebrews' World of Thought

The Greek Scriptures

Though Hebrews alludes to deuterocanonical writings (Wisdom and 1–4 Maccabees), the constant point of reference and the only text quoted is the Old Testament in a Greek version, though not always that of the LXX. Occasionally, the text varies widely from the Hebrew (e.g., in Heb 10:5; 11:21; 13:6). Frequently, two texts are associated through the linking of etymologically related words (e.g., Ps 95:11 and Gen 2:2 are connected in Heb 4:3-11 by the word "rest"; Pss 110:1 and 8:6 in Heb 1:13 and 2:8 are linked because of the common motif of subjection under the feet). In constructing their homiletical *midrashim* (running commentaries), the rabbis also used this linking technique (Heb. *gezerah shawah*), as well as the "stringing of pearls" into a chain quotation (*haraz;* see Heb 1:5-13).

Over a third of the Letter contains either quotations of, or allusions to, the sacred text. The Christology is drawn primarily from the Psalms, while the Letter's soteriology is developed with reference to the Pentateuch. The author views the text as living oracles of God through which the Spirit still speaks (see 3:7; 10:15; G. Hughes 1979, 35). There is no interest in the location of texts or their original setting. Quotations are prefaced with general introductions (e.g., "someone has testified somewhere," 2:6; see also 1:6-8; 3:15; 4:3; 5:6; 7:17; 8:8).

Scripture is prophetic (1:1) because it is united in its witness to Christ. Texts not only speak *about* Christ; some are spoken *by* Christ (e.g., Ps 40:6-8 in Heb 10:5-7). Hebrews treats the Old Testament typologically, that is, past events, institutions, and persons are seen as foreshadowings of even greater realities in the future. This reading of Scripture gives full weight to past revelation within history.

Philo and Hellenistic Judaism

A few scholars have continued to suggest that Alexandrian Judaism (Sowers 1965) or the dualism of Middle Platonism (Thompson 1982) provide the formative religious and cultural milieu for an understanding of Hebrews, but most remain skeptical about direct links. Similarities between Philo and Hebrews in diction, imagery, interpreting texts, and general worldview suggest no more than a common hellenistic milieu (see Williamson 1970).

Some contrasts in Hebrews seem to be typically hellenistic, for example, between external and internal (9:9-14; 10:2-4, 22), heavenly and earthly, eternal and temporal, unseen and seen, intangible and tangible, immutable and changing, and permanent and fleeting (e.g., 1:8, 11-12; 11:1-3, 27; 12:18-28). But the author of Hebrews is not interested in a dualistic metaphysic. His final concern is to point to the goal of God's dealings. There is an age to come beyond this passing world (1:6; 2:5; 6:5), a remaining, heavenly rest after the temporary, earthly rest (4:1, 8). A linear view of history and a typological use of Scripture have little in common with Philo whose allegorical approach aims to describe contrasting "vertical" worlds.

Qumran

Points of contact between Hebrews and sectarian movements such as Jewish Merkabah Mysticism and Samaritanism have been proposed (see the critical assessment by Hurst 1990, 75-85). More significant are proposed connections with the Qumran scrolls, beginning with Yigael Yadin's proposal in 1958 that the letter was written to converts from the Qumran sect. Some commentators (e.g., Buchanan 1972; P. Hughes 1977) find in the Dead Sea Scrolls the conceptual background for an understanding of Hebrews. However, despite linguistic or conceptual parallels, earlier enthusiasm for direct connections has given way to a reluctance to see in the Scrolls the thought world of Hebrews.

Topics common to Hebrews and the Scrolls (angels; messianism; concern for true worship) do not prove that the author was either polemicizing against the Qumran community or using its teaching as the starting point for his own message (see Hurst 1990, 43-66; Ellingworth 1993, 48-49; Lane 1991, cviii). The Qumran sect claimed to have both the true priesthood and the correct temple specifications (in 11QTemple). Hebrews does not lay claims to a legitimate priestly class, but insists that all Christians have priestly access to God through the one High Priest who brought the earthly highpriestly office to an end. Qumran aimed to reform old institutions; Hebrews points to their replacement. Qumran was a closed community.

The Scrolls have a developed angelology; Hebrews deals with angels (1:4–2:16) only to demonstrate the superiority of the Son. Terms used for angels in the Scrolls, for example, "sons of heaven" (1QS 4.22; 11.8; 1QH 3.22) or "gods" (4QDeut 32.43; 11QMelch 10), would be impossible for the author of Hebrews (see Heb 1:4, 8). One concept has clear parallels in the Scrolls. According to Heb 12:22-24, believers participate in a heavenly worship with angels as their partners. For the Qumran covenanters also, heavenly and earthly worship do not merely run parallel; human beings join with angels in a priestly sacrifice of praise (1QH 3.19-23; 11.11-12, 25-26; 18.23; 1QSa 2.3-11). But such a parallel does not prove direct dependency on Qumran. That worship involves angelic presence is an idea not far removed from the picture of cosmic worship in Ps 148, and one that could have developed simultaneously in both Jewish and Christian circles.

The famous Melchizedek fragment from Cave 11 at Qumran (first published in 1965) yields little of direct relevance for the interpretation of Hebrews 7 (see Horton 1976; Hurst 1990, 52-60; Pearson 1990, 108-23). The gaps in the existing twenty-six lines allow varying reconstructions, but Melchizedek seems to be an angelic figure sent to exact eschatological judgment on Belial and his followers. Although the writer sees Melchizedek as "resembling the Son of God," and as a priest who remains forever (7:3), the argument for the superiority of his priesthood over the Levitical (Heb 7:4-10) would suggest that the author regarded Melchizedek as a human figure.

Gnosticism

Ernst Käsemann in 1939 rejected an exclusively apocalyptic reading of Hebrews, arguing that its Christology is based on the Gnostic myth of the Primal Man (with Melchizedek seen as an incarnation of this *Urmensch*), sent to earth to rescue those enslaved in matter. Its soteriology reflects the Gnostic motif of the soul's pilgrimage from bondage in this world to its original heavenly home.

Working with added material from the Nag Hammadi library, recent studies have lent support to the view that a variety of Gnostic traditions grew out of syncretistic Judaism, probably among disaffected Jews in Alexandria (see Pearson 1990, 133-35). These traditions, including that of the Gnostic redeemer, were not systematized until the second century. It cannot be maintained that the writer of Hebrews, or any other New Testament writer, was involved in polemic against a Gnostic group, or in deliberate adaptation of a Gnostic system (see Perkins 1993, 4).

Hebrews does not reflect a dualistic worldview, with matter seen as essentially evil. The world was created through the Son (1:2), not by any demiurge. Angels are God's agents in the service of humanity (1:14), not emanations hostile to it. The wilderness wandering of Israel (3:7–4:13) and the motif of access into the heavenly sanctuary (10:19-22) hardly represent adaptations of a

Gnostic pilgrimage or ascent of the soul. Entry into the heavenly rest (4:9-11), into the "city that is to come" (13:14), points to a final consummation. But the author's stress on *present* access into God's presence suggests that the heavenly rest can be enjoyed *now*, not merely after some Gnostic-like ascent. Faith in Hebrews is not an intellectual *gnosis* (knowledge) that carries the soul upward, but a clinging to the divine promise of unseen, future realities that reach into the present.

Early Christian Traditions

Intended to restore stability to a community, the theology of Hebrews is in no sense speculative. The message enlarges on the faith already known and confessed, drawing on early Christian credal and catechetical traditions. The origins and exact scope of these traditions are not always easy to determine.

Hebrews and Acts 7

In 1951 William Manson proposed that Hebrews echoes views held by Greek-speaking Jewish Christians in Jerusalem and preserved in Stephen's speech in Acts 7. These Hellenists adopted a broad vision of salvation history that included mission to the Gentile world in the name of a universal Messiah (1951, 25-46). They saw Israel's history as the story of God's dealings with a *disobedient* people. Israel's wandering in the wilderness typified God's call to live as a pilgrim people, dependent on his presence and promises. The portable shrine showed that God was not tied to any one place, not even to the temple (Acts 7:2, 4-7, 22-25, 44-50).

Some of Manson's proposed links between Stephen's speech and Hebrews have not survived critical assessment (see Hurst 1990, 89-106; Lane 1991, cxlvi-cl; Isaacs 1992, 65-66), yet there are some points of contact. Both Stephen's speech and Hebrews trace a pattern of disobedience in Israel's past (Acts 7:35, 39, 51-52; Heb 4:11). Both see the earthly sanctuary—"made with [human] hands" (Acts 7:48; Heb 9:11-24) but at God's direction (Acts 7:44; Heb 8:5; referring to Exod 25:40)—as provisional (Acts 7:44-50; Heb

9:11-14, 23-28), thereby rejecting the view that God's presence can be confined to any earthly sanctuary. Both see God's people as called to leave earthly security and to be a people of pilgrimage (Acts 7:2-6, 29, 43; Heb 3:7–4:11; 11:8-38; 13:11-13). Both speak of a nonearthly rest on the background of Joshua's leading of Israel into the earthly land of promise (Acts 7:45, 49; Heb 4:8, 9). Both describe God's word as living (Acts 7:38; Heb 4:12) and see angels as mediators of the Law (Acts 7:53; Heb 2:2). Such agreements suggest that the author of Hebrews and Luke dipped into common traditions, but different accents in Acts 7 and Hebrews speak against any kind of literary dependence.

Other New Testament Writers

Points of contact between the theology of Hebrews and Paul were obvious enough to allow the early church (at least in the East) to affirm Pauline authorship of the Letter. These similarities include their use of Psalm 8 (Heb 2; 1 Cor 15) and of hymnic traditions (Heb 1:2-4; Phil 2:5-11), and in their understanding of faith (Hurst 1990, 110-24). However, differing accents and the uniqueness of Hebrews argue strongly against literary dependence on any of Paul's letters.

Similarly, echoes of the wisdom Christology of John 1 in Heb 1:2-3, and parallels between the thought and language of Hebrews and 1 Peter, point to common traditions rather than to direct borrowing. In short, the building blocks that make up the impressive theological edifice of Hebrews are diverse in content and origin.

Christology in Outline

The "Confession"

Without introduction or explanatory comment, Hebrews speaks of the "Jesus of our confession," later issuing an appeal to hold fast to that confession (see 3:1; 4:14; 10:23). A formal confession to Christ as *High Priest* could be suggested by the use of the title in the three passages.

To confess the name of Jesus is to proclaim its saving power, so confession and liturgical praise are inseparably linked in Hebrews (12:28; 13:15). However, we cannot be sure that 13:15 is referring to a specific christological formulation or precise act of confession. The "name" could be *Kyrios* (Lord; see Rom 10:8-9; 1 Cor 12:3; Phil 2:9-11) or *Son*. If the writer is thinking of the former, the reference could be to the eucharistic acclamation of Christ as Lord (see the *maranatha* of 1 Cor 16:22; also Rev 22:20; *Did.* 10:6). Yet even if the sacrifice of praise in Heb 13:15*a* is a specific liturgical confession, it need not be identical with the confession of 3:1; 4:14; and 10:23.

Though "Son" and "High Priest" appear with equal frequency in Hebrews, the first title to be adduced and developed is "Son" (1:2). Christ's sonship is the constant point of reference for the author's Christology as the following observations show. (1) Only at the end of the argument for the superiority of the Son over the angels is Christ referred to as High Priest (2:17). All texts cited in 1:1-16 deal with him as Son. (2) "High Priest" occurs in the immediate context of all three references to the confession, but the author always returns to his primary title. The "high priest of our confession" is the Son (3:1, 6); the "great high priest" (4:14) is immediately identified as "Jesus, the Son of God"; to reject the confession of Christ as High Priest is to spurn the "Son" (10:21, 23, 29). (3) When the author finally describes Christ's qualifications as High Priest in 5:1-10 he cites Ps 2:7 (Son) before Ps 110:4 (priest). In the same passage, the mention of the Son precedes the description of Christ as High Priest (5:8-10). (4) The Son is the first point of reference even in chapter 7; Melchizedek resembles the Son of God (v. 3). At the end the writer speaks of the appointment of a perfected "Son" (v. 28)—even though 5:10 has pictured the perfected Son as being designated High Priest! Thus, although both titles are vital for the Christology of the Letter, the primary title is "Son."

Hymn and Text

Two other "sources" contributed to the Letter's portrayal of Christ. In two places we have what appears to be a *hymnic statement* on Christ (1:3-4; 5:8-10). Elevated language traces the path of the Son from preexistence, suffering on earth, to final exaltation with the giving of a name. Much of the vocabulary of these statements can be ascribed to the author, so these statements cannot be seen as fixed formulations, simply quoted by him.

Second, the author cites two key *texts* to support central christological statements: Pss 2:7 and 110:4. Both texts speak of the exaltation of Christ: as Son, and as "priest forever." That the scope of hymnic statement and text are not the same can be seen from the way in which they are woven together in Heb 5:5-10. A consistent exaltation Christology is expressed in verses 6 and 10. Christ's enthronement in glory is the moment of his installation as heavenly (High) Priest. There is not the same consistency in the two statements about the Son. Verse 5 speaks of the Son's exaltation, yet verse 8 speaks of the Son having to learn obedience through suffering. The paradox of that statement becomes clear only when we take "Son" to refer to his preexistence. The Son's learning of obedience in suffering (cf. Phil 2:8) must be seen in contrast to his former and later glory (preexistence and exaltation). Whereas the text speaks only of final exaltation, the hymnic statement alludes to the Son's preexistence.

Hebrews 1 has the same interplay between statements about the Son's eternal being (vv. 2c-3a), his earthly existence (2a, 3b), and his exaltation (2b, 3c-4). The texts that follow (1:5-13) all serve the latter theme, just as the exaltation motif that predominates in 5:5-10 is served by first citing Old Testament texts.

This uneven combination of christological motifs can be explained only on the presupposition that the author is weaving together various strands of tradition. Instead of adopting a timeless concept of sonship, the author works with the inherited picture of Christ as the Davidic Son exalted at God's right hand. This latter phrase is adduced from Ps 110:1 already at Heb 1:3 (see also 1:13; 8:1; 10:12; 12:2). The early Christian combination of Pss 2 and 110 to picture the messianic dignity of the exalted Christ (cf. Acts 2:34-35; 4:24-26; 13:33) is the bedrock of Hebrews' Christology.

The Saving Work of the High Priest

The confession of Christ as Son is the witness of Scripture, and the content of the church's confession and liturgical sacrifice of praise. Why then does Hebrews go to such lengths to develop a picture of Christ as High Priest? The reasonable answer is that the confession to the exalted Son depicts his messianic dignity, but does not fully explain his past and present work that makes him the "source of eternal salvation" (5:9). This *priestly* work is explained in two ways: as completed sacrifice, and as ongoing intercession.

The motif of *intercession* always follows a statement about the High Priest's exaltation (2:17-18; 4:14-16; 7:20-25; cf. Rom 8:34). The author explicates what he sees as the key phrase in the exaltation statement of Ps 110:4: the High Priest lives "forever" to intercede (5:6; 6:20; 7:17, 21, 24, 28; 13:8).

The treatment of Christ's qualifications to be heavenly High Priest (see how chap. 7 is framed by 6:20 and 8:1) presupposes his installation. Thus, every reference to Christ as "High Priest" refers to his *present* status and function. He *now* intercedes for those who cry for help. While salvation can still denote final rescue at the Second Coming (9:28), the main emphasis is on present rescue from the trials and temptations that reveal human weakness (2:18; 4:15).

Both Ps 110:4 and Gen 14:17-20 (the basis of the Melchizedek typology) speak only of a priest. In speaking of Christ as *High* Priest in 2:17; 3:1; 4:14; 5:1-10; 6:20; and 7:26-28, Hebrews is anticipating the later argument in chapters 8–10 where the earthly work of Christ is explained by analogy with the office and work of the Levitical high priests.

The picture of Christ's *sacrifice* has a double focus. First, it is the presupposition for his enthronement as heavenly High Priest, since his self-sacrifice becomes effective with the offering of his blood in the heavenly sanctuary (9:11, 12, 23-25; 10:12). Second, his death is the establishment of the new covenant (8:6-13) in which he mediates direct access to God through the perfect removal of sin (9:13, 14, 26-27). These two points appear side by side in the central appeal of 10:19-22.

The cultic interpretation of Christ's sacrifice in Hebrews assumes that the Old Testament covenant and its institutions, especially the

Day of Atonement ritual, are promissory in character. They are the prefigurement of something better (10:1). The "shadow" is not mere symbol of timeless realities, nor is it a humanly devised system, later replaced by one divinely ordained. Typology presupposes continuity of revelation (cf. 1:1-2). So the description of the heavenly sanctuary as the "true tent" (8:2), and the judgment on the old covenant as "obsolete" (8:13) do not imply that the old earthly sanctuary and its cultic regulations were false; they were ordained by God to prepare for something better.

Christ's highpriestly office and work are not merely the fulfillment of an ideal. On the one hand there is correspondence with Old Testament institutions. Like other high priests, Jesus must be appointed by God (5:1-4). He must make a sacrifice for sin, and offer it in the inner sanctuary of God's holy presence. From here on the typology is one of contrast (Isaacs 1992, 74-75). Both Melchizedek and Christ are outside the Levitical priesthood (7:4-14). Christ mediates a new covenant based on better promises (8:6). His sacrifice was the offering up of himself in a single event that does not need to be repeated (9:11-12, 25-26). His was a perfect sacrifice since he was sinless (4:15; 7:26-27). So the presentation of his blood in the heavenly sanctuary is perfectly efficacious for the removal of sin; it leaves the consciences of sinners clean (9:14; 10:2, 22), whereas the blood of animals could effect only an external cleanness (9:9-10).

There is a realism in the author's portrayal of Christ's death that fully reflects Old Testament thought. The ritual of Yom Kippur (Lev 16) required the selection of a victim, its slaughter, and the application of its blood. It was the blood as the bearer of life (Lev 17:11) that effected atonement; it cleansed the people and sacred things from impurity, and made them holy. (The importance of the blood explains why Hebrews ignores the scapegoat [it was not slaughtered but sent into the wilderness; Lev 16:8, 20-22], but does include the ritual of the red heifer whose blood was spilled [9:12-13]).

In Hebrews "blood" is not simply shorthand for the reality of death. The author clearly distinguishes between Christ's death and the offering of his blood in the heavenly sanctuary (9:11-12, 23-24). He knows that the ritual of the Day of Atonement culminated in the *application* of holy blood sprinkled on the mercy seat, incense altar, and main altar (Lev 16:14-19). He recalls how the Sinai covenant was inaugurated by the application of blood (9:18-22).

The distinction between the death of a sacrificial victim and the application of its blood is important for an understanding of 9:22*b*. The one Greek word usually translated with "shedding of blood" (*haimatekchysia* occurs only in Christian literature) can also be rendered with "sprinkling/pouring out of blood" (see Lindars 1991, 94, note 96; Pursiful 1993, 69-70). That the application of blood is intended is supported by 12:24 where the Greek phrase, "blood of sprinkling" can be translated with "blood for sprinkling." While Christ's offering of blood in the heavenly sanctuary is a finished, unrepeatable event, the blood remains as atoning power, as much as the High Priest himself remains "forever." So "the blood of the eternal covenant" still has power to cleanse (reading 13:20*b* with v. 21; cf. 1 John 1:7).

Hebrews does not specifically state how the blood of Christ is now appropriated. Yet there are hints at an answer. Baptismal language is used in 10:22 to call the readers to approach God with "hearts *sprinkled* clean . . . and our bodies washed with pure water." A case can also be made for eucharistic allusions at several points. The adapted words of Moses at the inauguration of the Sinai covenant, "this is the blood of the covenant" (9:20), combined with the "shedding/pouring out of blood" for the "forgiveness of sins" (v. 22), recall the words of institution: "This is my *blood of the covenant,* which is *poured out* for many for the *forgiveness of sins*" (Matt 26:28, emphasis added; cf. Mark 14:24). Hebrews 9:20-22 has stronger eucharistic allusions than other passages (10:25, 29; 13:10, 20).

That the "heavenly things themselves need better sacrifices" (9:23) must be understood in the context of the heavenly High Priest's ongoing work. This is more than an aside, meant to complete the analogy between the annual entry of the high priest into the inner sanctuary and Christ's final entry into the heavenly sanctuary (as in 9:11-12). That completed event is in view (see the past tense in vv. 24 and 26), but the past entry is the basis of the continuing process of purification (the NRSV rightly has the present tense in 9:23). In the old covenant, the cleansing effected by sacrificial blood reached its goal in the purification of people (9:13, 19). The "heavenly things" that continue to be purified for service by Christ's better sacrifice are, finally, the hearts and consciences of the faithful (9:14; 10:22). Christians are the house of God in which Christ *now* functions as faithful Son and High Priest (10:21)—the Greek text of 3:2 and 6 should be translated with the present tense (*"is* faithful"), in keeping with the statement of 4:14 and 8:1 that "we have a great high priest."

Eschatology: Participating in Perfection

It is in worship that the people of the new covenant experience the present work of their heavenly High Priest. By purifying believers through his life-giving blood, he provides them with access into God's holy presence (2:17; 7:25*a;* 10:19-22). Second, he mediates their prayers before the throne of grace (2:18; 4:15-16; 7:25*b*). Third, he sanctifies them so that they also can function as God's "proleptic priests" (Scholer 1991) in offering up the sacrifice of thanksgiving and praise (12:28; 13:15-16; the verb "draw near/approach" in 4:16; 7:25; 10:1, 22; 11:6; 12:18, 22 has priestly connotations). Finally, as "mediator of a new covenant," he joins their earthly worship with that of the coming world (2:5) into which he has entered. The people participate in the heavenly worship of angels and of those who have already completed their course (12:22-24).

This reading of Hebrews as a *call to worship* (10:25) provides us with a framework for understanding both the eschatology and the parenesis of Hebrews. The Letter views sin in two ways. It is *defilement* that prevents access to a holy God (1:3; 9:14, 22-23; 10:22; 12:15; 13:4). This is removed by the all-sufficient sacrifice of Christ. Second, sin is *unfaithfulness* and disobedience (2:1-4; 3:6-19; 4:11; 6:4-6; 10:21-31, 35-39; 12:1-3, 25). The solution to this problem is to look to Jesus "the pioneer and perfecter of . . . faith" (12:2), and so to endure to the end where there is a perfect sabbath rest for God's pilgrim people (4:1-9). Also the call to faithfulness is a summons to worship, to hear and obey the word (2:1-2; 3:7-11; 4:12; 12:25-29).

To hold fast the confession (4:15; 10:23) is to claim the perfection that is offered now in worship, and to endure until the final perfection. The language of *perfection* in Hebrews indicates the double eschatology that provides the framework of its parenesis. Hebrews speaks of perfection not as a moral quality but rather as God bringing a plan, system, or person to an intended goal. Christ himself has been perfected through suffering and glorification. These events brought God's plan for him to completion (2:10; 5:9-10; 7:28—the Greek word *telos,* meaning "end" or "goal," is the root of the verb *teleioun,* "to perfect"). That perfection means reaching an *end* is indicated by the way in which the writer can, in the same context, speak of a *beginning.* Christ is the "pioneer and perfecter" of faith, literally, the "beginner and ender" (12:2).

Statements about Christ's perfection are always descriptions of a finished salvation in the light of his installation as eternal High Priest (5:9-10; 7:28—the LXX uses the verb "to perfect" for the consecration of priests; see Exod 29:9, 19, 23; Lev 8:33; 16:32; Num 3:3). In this office he now offers salvation as a completed gift (Heb 1:14; 2:3, 10; 5:9; 6:9). He has been perfected to perfect others by leading them safely to his own glory (2:9-10). This involves past, present, and future. Christ's sacrifice "*has perfected* for all time those who are sanctified" (10:14), so they can now join "the spirits of the righteous made perfect" (12:23; cf. 11:40) in anticipation of final salvation (9:28). The parenesis of Hebrews calls its readers to claim the gift of salvation now. Faith, understood primarily as hope, clings to God's promise that the future will affirm the reality of the present (3:6, 14; 6:11-19).

Hebrews assures its readers that there is a final rest (4:9). It contrasts the eternal world with the transient (1:10-12). It holds up the sure hope of a final reception of what God has promised. But the Letter's response to suffering, uncertainty, and loss is not an exclusively futuristic eschatology. Access to God in worship is possible now (4:16; 10:19-22; 12:22-24). The heavenly High Priest who is the same yesterday, today, and forever (13:8) has drawn the sanctified into the realm of the eternal as they live in the world of transience. The realized eschatology of Hebrews is based on an understanding of worship as bringing the future into the present.

Looking to Jesus who has finished his course (12:2-3) means more than looking to the future. The Christian runs toward Jesus, but also with Jesus. That is why Christ can never be merely a model of faith. He is author of salvation at every stage of faith's pilgrimage—from beginning to end (5:9; 7:25).

COMMENTARY

GOD'S FINAL REVELATION IN THE SON (1:1–2:18)

The opening two chapters form a unified discourse. An opening statement (1:1-4) climaxes in the assertion of the Son's superiority *over* angels that is documented in a chain of scriptural quotations, framed by rhetorical questions (1:5, 13). The description of angels as serving those who receive salvation (1:14) provides the link to the exhortation not to neglect salvation (2:1-4). The following exposition deals with the Son's subjection *under* the angels (2:5-9), paving the way for the first major conclusion of the Letter that links the Son to his brothers and sisters (2:10-18). The opening of the section placed the Son with God; the conclusion identifies him with humanity.

The section's unity is served by its focus on the Son (1:2, 5; in 2:10-14), yet God is the prime subject as the author of past and final revelation (1:1-2a). The Son's glory is first described in terms of his relation to God (heir; exact imprint; right hand; 1:2b-3). It is God who testifies to the Son in Scripture (1:5-13), confirms the preaching of the gospel (2:4), and makes the Son lower than the angels (2:9-10).

The opening discourse is marked by contrasts: of past with final revelation (1:1-2; 2:2-3); of the Son with angels; of the preexistent and exalted Son with the subjected Son. The former is defined in terms of glory, power, honor (1:3; 2:9), God's majesty (1:3, 13), throne, scepter and power (1:8), and superiority and greater excellence (1:4). The latter is characterized as lower (2:9), flesh and blood (2:14), and as suffering fear of death, bondage, temptation, and death itself (2:9-10, 15, 18).

All contrasts serve to extol the exalted Son. The elevated language in 1:1-4, the citing of Scripture, the picture of angels as "ministering spirits" (see 1:14), the focus on the holy name that is to be adored and proclaimed (1:4; 2:12), and the picture of Christ as representative of both God and humanity (2:10-18), make this opening a fitting prelude to the Letter as a call to worship.

The Thematic Statement (1:1-4)

The opening *exordium* (one sentence written in Greek) has striking literary features. The opening statement consists of two parallel lines, the first marked by alliteration. To show the effect we may paraphrase thus: In *p*lural ways God *p*reviously spoke to the *p*atriarchs by the *p*rophets.

More striking is the structure of the passage. Though the subject changes from God (vv. 1-2) to the Son (vv. 3-4), it has a concentric symmetry (see Lane 1991, 6-7):

> **A:** God spoke to our ancestors by prophets . . . to us by a Son (vv. 1-2*a*)
> > **B:** whom he appointed heir of all things (v. 2*b*)
> > > **C:** through whom he also created the worlds (v. 2*c*)
> > > **C':** as the reflection of God's glory and exact imprint of God's very being, he sustains all things by his powerful word (v. 3*a, b*)
> > **B':** when he had made purification for sins, he sat down at the right hand of the Majesty on high (v. 3*c*)
> **A':** having become as much superior to angels as the name he has inherited is more excellent than theirs (v. 4).

The framing statements (A/A') outline the superiority of the Son over other agents of revelation (angels; prophets). Further framing statements (B/B') picture the royal status of the Son with allusions to the Letter's key psalms (Pss 2:8; 110:1). Core statements (C/C') speak of the divine Son as the Wisdom-agent of creation. Including the brief reference to "purification for sins" in B', the four central statements picture Christ as royal Son, divine Wisdom, and royal Priest.

The abrupt change of subject and rare vocabulary in verse 3*a* and 3*b*, the elevated language of verses 3-4, and the christological pattern of preexistence-humiliation-exaltation, reflected elsewhere in the New Testament (Phil 2:6-11; Col 1:15-20; 1 Tim 3:16; 1 Pet

3:18-22; see also Heb 5:8-10), have given rise to the suggestion that these two verses are based on an early credal hymn (see Attridge 1989, 41-42; Ellingworth 1993, 96-98). But much of the language is so typical of Hebrews that it is impossible to distill the exact form of an original hymn or creed.

◊ ◊ ◊ ◊

A clear message results from reading verses 1-2a and 3c-4 as one statement: final revelation has come with the Son who suffered to purify us from sin, but is now exalted in heaven. The reference to the Son as medium of creation (v. 2c) is also clear, but do the statements that speak of the Son being appointed as heir (v. 2b) and as reflecting God's glory and being (v. 3a, b) refer to his preexistence or to his exaltation? And why do these verses climax with a comparison between the exalted Son and angels?

1-2a: Despite beginning with an elaborate contrast, the Letter connects past and present revelation. Past revelation was not defective; it was the penultimate, not the ultimate word from God. There is also continuity between the ancestors and the audience. The former are the patriarchs and all in Israel's history who received the word of promise and held to it in faith (Heb 11). Those in the past had nothing but the promise; the present generation has the promise realized as it hears God speaking the climactic word in Christ (see 11:39-40). The phrase "last days" recalls the prophetic vision of God's decisive intervention in Israel's history (Isa 2:2; Jer 23:20; 49:39) and the common Jewish and early Christian distinction between two ages of redemptive history. With the Son's coming, a new age has begun (Heb 9:26).

The contrast between communication "in many and various ways by the prophets" and revelation "by a Son" is made more striking by the brevity of the second phrase. Revelation through prophets was promissory in character; it was incomplete, not faulty. By contrast, God's ultimate word through the Son is unique and final. As in 7:23-24, the contrast is between the many and the one. The Old Testament speaks of many sons/children of God: Israel (Exod 4:22); angels (Gen 6:2); the king (Ps 2:7). "A Son" does not imply that he is one among many children (as in 2:10-14). The absence of the definite article draws attention to the generic difference between a Son and any other agent of revelation, especially angels (2:2).

4: Structural analysis has shown that verse 4 forms a closing bracket, with elements running parallel to verses 1-2*a*. The implied contrast between the excellent and more excellent in verse 1 now becomes explicit, with angels replacing the prophets as agents of revelation. The common motif of revelation is underlined by the mention of the "name" given to the exalted Son. Thus, the purpose of verse 4 is not to denigrate the angels. The rhetorical function of the comparison is to extol the Son. The suggestion that the author is rejecting a heretical Christology that viewed Christ as an angelic figure lacks any support from the rest of Hebrews (see Lane 1991, 8; Attridge 1989, 51-52). Another proposal, that the author wishes to counteract the worship of angels, has to propose some connection between the Colossian heresy (see Col 2:18) and Hebrews. Yet the Letter makes no negative statement about angels; it simply affirms the tradition that the acquisition of a new name places Christ above the angels (Eph 1:20-21; Phil 2:9-10; 1 Pet 3:22).

The superiority of Christ is represented in the more excellent name received at his exaltation. Since the next verse cites Ps 2:7, the name must be "Son" (as in Heb 5:5), not "high priest" (5:10), or "Lord" (Phil 2:9-11). The author sees no tension between the identification of the Son with preexistent Wisdom (Heb 1:2*c*-3*b*) and his acclamation as Son at his exaltation. The inheritance of the "name" marks the completion of his messianic mission. God's holy name was once revealed in order that Israel could call on it in worship, prayer, and praise (Exod 3:14-15; Heb 2:12); now the revelation of the Son's name means new worship. Those who acknowledge his name offer the new sacrifice of praise to God (13:15), one that angels also offer (1:6; 12:22).

2*b*, 3*c*: These intermediary phrases (= B/B') express the Son's uniqueness. Only he has been appointed "heir of all things" (v. 2*b*). Since verse 5 cites Ps 2:7, the writer here has verse 8 of that psalm in mind: "Ask of me, and I will make the nations your heritage."

The writer sees Ps 2 as referring to the exaltation of the messianic King to whom everything has been subjected (2:5-9).

This first description of the Son's dignity, with reference to Ps 2, corresponds to verse 3c, which picks up a motif from Ps 110:1. God says to the king: "Sit at my right hand until I make your enemies your footstool" (cf. Heb 1:13; 5:5-6 again links Pss 2 and 110 as enthronement texts). The early church confessed that the risen and exalted Lord sat down at God's "right hand" (Heb 8:1; 10:12-13; 12:2; see also Rom 8:34; Eph 1:20; Col 3:1). "Right hand" and "Majesty" are respectful circumlocution for God's power and person (cf. Heb 8:1).

In other hymnic formulations (5:7-8; Phil 2:7-8), Christ's suffering and death figure prominently. The point of this *exordium* is the superiority and uniqueness of the Son as preexistent Wisdom and exalted King, so his earthly ministry is touched on with pointed brevity: "he . . . made purification for sins." This short phrase, detailed in 8:1–10:18, is left undeveloped since its main function is to provide a link to what follows. Christ's death and exaltation are linked in that the sacrifice of his life is completed with the offering of his blood in the heavenly sanctuary (9:12; 10:12). His resurrection (see 13:20) and session in glory declare his death and blood to be effective (13:20).

2c-3b: These core statements (C/C') show how the Son's exaltation fittingly corresponds to his eternal power. They describe the Son as the creative word, identified with preexistent Wisdom (cf. Heb 11:3; John 1:3; Col 1:16). Behind this identification lies the picture of divine Wisdom as God's agent in creation (Prov 8:22-31). Wisdom traditions also lie behind the description of the Son as "reflection of God's glory" and "exact imprint of God's very being." Wisdom is "a pure emanation of the glory of the Almighty . . . a reflection of eternal light, a spotless mirror of the working of God, and an image of his goodness" (Wis 7:25-26).

Changing the metaphor, the Son bears the stamp of God's own divine being as the imprint on a seal or coin corresponds exactly to the die. While not calling Christ the "image of God" (see Col 1:15), Hebrews asserts that only the Son who bears the very being and essence of God can serve as agent of creation and revelation (cf. John 1:1-3, 18). The agent of creation shares God's providential care of the world: he "sustains all things" (cf. Col 1:16-17).

◊ ◊ ◊ ◊

With its rich depiction of Christ as God's agent in creation, providence, revelation, and redemption, the *exordium* is a fitting prelude to the entire Letter. It sounds the theme of revelation. Since the Letter is a scriptural argument, it must establish that God has spoken in the past through the prophetic word. New revelation does not invalidate all that was revealed in the past, but puts it into proper perspective as word of promise. Christ is the hermeneutical key to the Old Testament, so it is important for the author to establish both continuity and discontinuity in revelation.

The second dominant theme is the exaltation of Christ. Descriptions of his preexistent power and glory serve to confirm the appropriateness of his present rule. The rhetorical movement in the opening two chapters takes the audience from the dignity bestowed on the Son at his heavenly enthronement, to his lowliness in suffering and death. Yet the writer is not concerned merely with the powerful effect created by contrasting Christ in glory and in suffering. His concern is pastoral. The heavier brushstrokes in his portrait of Christ depict his *present* status, for it is the exalted Son and High Priest on whom the audience can call *now* (4:14-16).

Finally, the *exordium* sounds the theme of worship. Adoration is the fitting response to one who reflects divine glory, who is eternal Wisdom and King of all. The "name" (v. 4) is the revealed Son who is to be proclaimed and adored (cf. 2:12; 13:15). The readers are to cling without wavering to this name, and can do this in the knowledge that he sustains them (v. 3).

The Son's Superiority over the Angels (1:5-14)

To support the thesis of verse 4, seven Old Testament texts are cited—five from the writer's favorite book, the Psalter. Parallel rhetorical questions preface the first and last quotations (vv. 5, 13) to form an *inclusio*, indicating that all texts in this chain of quotations illustrate the one theme: God's own pronouncements show the superiority of the Son over the angels.

The *catena* presents three pairs of texts and one concluding text. The first pair deals with the Son's status (v. 5), the second with the function of angels (vv. 6-7), the third concerns the conditions of the Son's eternal reign (vv. 8-12). A final text recalls the Son's session at God's right hand, thus linking the end of the quotation chain (v. 13) with the letter's opening statement (v. 3; see G. Guthrie 1994, 61).

A concluding statement by the writer provides a link between the *catena* (v. 14 restates v. 7) and the exhortation in 2:1-4 (the link word in 1:14 and 2:3 is "salvation"). There are also links with the opening *exordium*. The first and last quotations cite the coronation psalms (Ps 2:7 in v. 5; Ps 110:1 in v. 13) that have been alluded to in 1:2, 3. Also the core statements of the *exordium* are echoed in the quotations: the Son is agent of creation (v. 2c = v. 10); his glory and being are eternal (v. 3a, b = vv. 11-12). However, the bracket formed by quotations from Pss 2 and 110 in verses 5 and 13 shows that *all* texts refer to Christ as enthroned King.

◊ ◊ ◊ ◊

The texts contain God's own confession to the messianic King. Though the ultimate word is *through* the Son (Heb 1:1), prior revelation speaks *about* the Son. The *first pair* of texts (Ps 2:7 and 2 Sam 7:14 are linked also in the Qumran scrolls; see 4QFlor 10.11, 18-19) forms a neat chiasm (Son/Father/Father/Son). Psalm 2:7 is an ancient recognition formula, originally addressed to a king as heir to the Davidic covenant expressed in 2 Sam 7:12-16. Our author is interested only in its application to the messianic King in the "today" of his exaltation (Heb 1:3-4, 13). He is surely aware that angels are called "sons of God" (Gen 6:2, 4; Pss 29:1; 89:7; Job 1:6), but the rhetorical question in verse 5 reminds his audience that no angel has ever been *addressed* by God as "my son."

Psalm 2:7 finds varied application in the New Testament. Combined with Isa 42:1, it lies behind the acclamation of Jesus at his baptism (Mark 1:11 and par.) and transfiguration (Mark 9:7 and par.). The psalm is also linked with Jesus' resurrection (Acts 13:33;

cf. Rom 1:4). Hebrews links it with the heavenly enthronement of the Son (Heb 1:3) as God's public proclamation that the King has completed his mission.

The *second pair* of texts (vv. 6-7) states the divinely ordained function of angels: they serve; the Son rules (vv. 8-9). The first quotation bears some resemblance to the Greek version of Ps 97:7 (LXX: 96:7): "Worship him, all his angels," but is more closely related to Deut 32:43 LXX: "Let the sons of God *worship him.* Rejoice, you nations, with his people, and *let all* the *angels* of God ascribe strength to him." Possibly the author quoted it from the popular version of the "Hymn of Moses" in the book of *Odes* (2:43), which was appended to the Greek Psalter (a similar wording appears in 4QDeut 32:43).

In the original text the angels are summoned to worship God; here they are called to worship the "firstborn" Son who can be addressed as both God (Heb 1:8) and Lord (Heb 1:10). A messianic interpretation of Deut 32:43 (= *Odes* 2:43) may have been suggested by the last line that speaks of the Lord purifying the land of his people; purification is also the work of the Son (Heb 1:3).

The NRSV correctly places a comma after "again" in verse 6*a,* since Hebrews commonly uses the word to link quotations (see 2:13*a, b;* 4:5; 10:30). The enthronement setting established by the *inclusio* of verses 5 and 13 must apply also to verse 6. The angels adore the Son at his exaltation (Phil 2:10-11).

In Ps 89:27-29 the title "firstborn" is given to the king who is promised a kingdom that will last as long as the heavens endure. The connection with Ps 2:7 and 2 Sam 7:14 (Heb 1:5) is clear; the theme of the eternal kingdom, contrasted with the temporary heavens, will be developed in 1:8-12. It is thus unlikely that the author is alluding to Deut 6:10 and 11:29, which speak of God "bringing" firstborn Israel (Exod 4:22; Hos 11:1; Jer 31:9) into the promised land. The Son of Heb 1 is the final heir of the Nathan prophecy, not a new Israel.

Given the enthronement setting, the "world" that the Son enters must be the heavenly realms or the "coming world" of the messianic age, inaugurated with his exaltation (the Greek word for "world" in 1:6 and 2:5 is the same: *oikumenē*). It does not refer to the plane of human history that he enters at his incarnation (Spicq 1952–53, 2.17; Montefiore 1964, 45), for the Son enters this world (Gk. *kosmos*) to be made lower than the angels (2:7, 9; 10:5).

The fourth quotation (v. 7) further describes the angels' function, paving the way for a final contrast: between their limited service and the eternal rule of the Son (vv. 8-12). Despite their exalted position, angels are merely servants, messengers at God's beck and call. Psalm 104:4 speaks of the natural elements of wind and fire as God's agents, but early Judaism could use the text to picture the speed and power of angels in carrying out God's commands (see Lane 1991, 29). Hebrews follows the LXX, which speaks in pictorial language of angels *as* winds and flames of fire. They, like the whole of creation, are mutable, ephemeral forms with limited function; the Son's rule is eternal and unchanging.

The *third pair* of texts (vv. 8-12) provides God's testimony to this unchanging rule. In Ps 45:6-7 the anointed king is addressed as heir to the prophecy of an eternal kingdom (2 Sam 7:13). The text probably came to the writer's mind because he had already cited the Nathan prophecy (Heb 1:5), and because Ps 45:6 uses the key phrase of Ps 110:4: "forever" (see Heb 5:6; 6:20; 7:17, 21, 24, 28; 13:8). Psalm 45:6 could be translated: "God is your throne forever and ever" (i.e., "God is the basis of your eternal rule"). A vocative reading ("O God") is surely intended because of the address "Lord" in verse 10.

What was never true of human kings is fully true of the King who shares God's deity (Heb 1:8 goes beyond 1:3). His rule shares features of God's own reign: righteousness and justice (see Ps 89:14; Isa 9:7; 11:5). He is the "king of righteousness" (Heb 7:2). Oil (v. 9) is the symbol of richness and prosperity that prevail throughout his rule. The companions of the king in Ps 45:7 are rulers of other nations; here it is the angels who are the Son's companions. Like him, they do God's will (vv. 7, 14), but they are not the Anointed King!

The second text in this final pair (Ps 102:25-27 cited in vv. 10-12) belongs to a prayer of an afflicted saint who cries for help. He contrasts the brevity and transitory nature of human existence with the abiding and eternal nature of God. Creation will grow old; even the heavens will be rolled up like a cloak when they have served their purpose. The permanence and immutability of the Son's rule is thus confirmed.

The quotation of Ps 110:1 in verse 13 forms a closing bracket to the whole *catena*. Alluded to in 1:3, this key text of the letter is now cited to show that the Son took his place at God's right hand at God's direct command. With its image of the footstool, the text underlines the absolute sovereignty of the Son. The subjugation of the King's enemies under his feet (see the same motif in 2:8) implies that all, including angels, are subjected to him. The writer is not interested in further identifying the King's enemies (e.g., death or the devil; 2:14).

A final rhetorical question (v. 14) picks up the description of angels in verse 7 as "spirits" and "servants" (Gk. *leitourgoi*), now calling them "serving *[leitourgika]* spirits." Christ is himself the "minister" *(leitourgos)* who presides over a new "ministry" *(leitourgia)* that replaces worship under the old covenant (8:2, 6; 9:21; 10:11). Hence the angels have only a subordinate ministry. And since their mission is to serve those who are heirs of salvation, they are in one sense lower than humans (see 2:16), though partners with them in worship (12:22).

Hebrews 1:14 sees salvation as a future inheritance. It can be grasped now in hope (or neglected; 2:3), but will become a full possession (i.e., as an eternal rest; 4:1-11) only after following the pioneer of salvation to the end that he himself has reached (2:10). The exaltation of the Son is a promise of the believer's own glorification. It is an eternal inheritance through him who was appointed heir of all things (1:2) and who inherited a more excellent name (v. 4).

◊ ◊ ◊ ◊

Proposition (1:1-4) and proof (1:5-14) form an argument meant to be persuasive in its entirety, not in any single element. The parenetic conclusion in 2:1-4 shows that chapter 1 is a recitation of christological themes born of pastoral concern. It reiterates the common faith of the audience, explicating it so that only one conclusion can be drawn. Those who find themselves in a changing, hostile world are reminded that they have an unchanging exalted Lord, that even the angels are their servants.

The proposition concerning the Son's transcendent dignity was expressed in terms of a comparison: his name is greater (v. 4). The chain of seven texts serves as exemplary elucidation, and is meant to say no more. So the writer is not polemicizing against a cult of the angels or against an angel-Christology. All we hear is that the angels worship the Son and serve believers (vv. 6, 14). The entire argument is presented with such magnificent symmetry that it has the effect of an *encomium;* it is itself a song of praise.

The author has shown that final revelation through the Son results in the worship of the Son (1:1-4). He then recalls God's own pronouncements concerning the Son in order to sing the Son's praises. Using texts from the Psalter (apart from v. 5b), with one passage (v. 6) cited from the later liturgical tradition of Judaism, he invites his audience to join him in the fitting response to the Son's enthronement: worship.

First Warning: Do Not Ignore the Son's Message (2:1-4)

The switch from exposition to exhortation brings a marked change in style. Hymnic cadences, allusions to Scripture and the church's confession (1:1-4), and biblical quotations (1:5-13) are replaced by the writer's own polished prose. A short opening assertion (v. 1) is expanded in one long sentence (in the Greek): an opening conditional statement in the form of an *a fortiori* argument climaxes in a rhetorical question (vv. 2-3a), followed by dependent clauses that elaborate on the "great salvation" that the addressees have received (vv. 3b-4).

There are obvious links with the preceding verses. "It was declared . . . through the Lord" (v. 3b) picks up the motif of revelation from 1:1-2; the reference to the serving role of angels (v. 2) echoes the theme of their subservience in 1:4-14; and the key word "salvation" (v. 3) picks up the last word of 1:14. This brief exhortation draws a conclusion from the argument of chapter 1, but also connects the two great themes of the opening discourse: the transcendent dignity of the Son over the angels (1:1-14), and his subjection of them (2:5-18).

◊ ◊ ◊ ◊

The letter has portrayed Christ's relationship to God, to the world, and to angels, elaborating on the community's confession to Christ in 1:1-4. Now the community is asked to draw the conclusion from its own profession of faith. An inclusive form of address ("we") softens the appeal.

The appeal to heed what the Son has revealed is expressed with the help of two images, one nautical, the other legal. The verb *prosechein* (NRSV: "pay attention") in verse 1 is an idiomatic term for listening carefully, but can also mean to bring a ship to port. More explicit is the verb "to drift away"; it suggests the image of a ship without moorings. Salvation is an event, but it has come to the readers as a message to be "heard." Failure to listen will result in the loss of a secure anchorage (see 6:19), in the surrender of the stability provided by faith and hope (see 3:6, 14; 4:16; 6:11; 10:19, 22, 35). The writer later (12:5-6) cites Prov 3:11-12 to show that wisdom teaches discipline. Here in 2:1 he may have Prov 3:21 LXX in mind: The student of wisdom is not to allow himself to "drift away" from understanding.

Legal imagery is prominent in verse 2. Promulgation of a law makes it legally "valid" or binding; any "transgression" is an offense requiring a "just penalty." That was the case with the giving of the Law at Sinai. Intertestamental Judaism developed the thought that God gave the Law through the agency of angels (see *Jub.* 1:27-29; 2:1; 5:1-13; *Ant.* 15.136; cf. Acts 7:38, 53; Gal 3:19). This idea that stresses the transcendence of God, and thus the need for intermediaries, was possibly based on Deut 33:2: "The LORD came from Sinai. . . . With him were myriads of holy ones."

The logic of comparison, as elsewhere in Hebrews (see 9:13-14; 10:28-29; 12:9, 25), is clear. What angels once revealed had built-in sanctions and warnings, blessings and curses (Lev 26; Deut 11:26-28). The word spoken by the Son is no less binding. Neglect of his message by deliberate transgression or by disobedience (failure to hear properly; see v. 1) places one under the living God who sees all and judges justly (3:12; 4:13; 6:10; 10:31). Greater revelation requires keener hearing—and sterner punishment where it is disregarded. The fate of the Israelites who heard but did not obey serves as a warning (3:16-19).

The validity of the message of salvation is expressed in three statements. They echo the legal language of verse 2 ("attested"; "added his testimony") in outlining the way in which the sacred tradition has reached the addressees (vv. 3b-4). Salvation was first declared by God (implied in the circumlocutory passive) "through the Lord" in Jesus' earthly ministry (see 1:3; 9:14; 10:7, 10). The proclaimer then became the proclaimed in the preaching of those who heard him (in Hebrews "apostle" is reserved for Christ alone; 3:1). They in turn guaranteed or confirmed ("attested") the validity of the message for their listeners.

God's tangible witness to the gospel's truth and power—the phrase "according to his will" qualifies the whole of God's corroborating evidence in verse 4—was threefold. (1) "Signs and wonders" is a fixed phrase for God's mighty acts of deliverance, especially in the exodus (Exod 7:3; Deut 4:34; 6:22). Miracles accompanied the preaching of the gospel in the early church (Acts 2:22, 43; 2 Cor 12:12). (2) The "various miracles" (literally, "deeds of power") were evidence of God's power at work, as in Jesus' ministry (Matt 7:22; 12:28; Mark 6:2; Luke 11:20). (3) Gifts of the Spirit (discussed at length by Paul; Rom 12:6-8; 1 Cor 12-14; Eph 4:11, 12) are not mentioned again in Hebrews. Nor does the author again refer to miracles in the experience of the community. His concern is not the supernatural, but the certainty of the message of salvation.

◊ ◊ ◊ ◊

Hebrews 2:1-4 contains a theology of preaching in miniature. The message of salvation is word from God, the proclamation of Christ, the continuation of primal testimony, and is accompanied by the Spirit's powerful working. The whole letter, as proclamation, calls on its audience not to neglect the word. To do so would be to deny the speaking and acting of God, of the Son, and of the Spirit, though verses 3-4 are hardly meant to develop a trinitarian theology. Hebrews rarely mentions the Spirit (cf. 3:7; 6:4; 9:8; 10:15); its concern is to proclaim Christ.

For the first time there are hints at a historical setting. Repeated appeals to listen and cling to the word show concern about a real threat to the life of the readers: spiritual indifference. What they have received is firmly attested; their hold on the word is less than firm.

Perhaps "the positive role assigned to angels and the appeal to the normative character of the Mosaic law in v 2 tend to suggest" that the readers "continued to maintain emotional and intellectual ties with the Jewish community" (Lane 1991, 36). Yet the writer does not refer to the revelation on Sinai as "law" but as the "message declared." He means the Torah, but speaks of the Law only in chapters 7–10 where it refers to the cultic requirements and regulations of the old covenant, seen as prophetic foreshadowings of the new worship instituted by Christ.

The Temporary Abasement of the Son (2:5-9)

This section opens with the Son's superiority over angels, but only to introduce his temporary lowliness under them. First, the nature of his abasement is developed in a quotation and midrashic application of Ps 8:4-6. Further texts are cited to amplify the salvific purpose of the Son's identification with humanity (2:10-16). A final statement confirming Christ as "merciful and faithful high priest" (vv. 17-18) concludes the argument and provides a link to the next two major discourses of the Letter that expand on the meaning of this phrase.

Christological exposition brings the author back to scriptural argument. An *inclusio* implying the superiority of the Son over angels bracketed the first set of quotations (1:5, 13). In parallel fashion, references to angels (2:5, 16; see also 2:7, 9) bracket the four texts cited to show the nature and necessity of the Son's temporary lowliness.

Links between 2:5-9 and the preceding sections are provided by the reference to angels (v. 5), the motif of the subjection of everything under the Son's "feet" (v. 8 picks up elements of 1:2-4 and 1:13), and the reference to the "coming" world that is the locus of future salvation (the connection between 1:14 and 2:5 is clear in the Greek, which repeats a verb expressing futurity).

◊ ◊ ◊ ◊

The assertion that "God did not subject the coming world . . . to angels" (v. 5) assumes that they were given some dominion. According to Deut 32:8-9 (cited in Heb 1:6), God gave the angels oversight of the world's nations, reserving for himself the care of Israel (cf. Dan 10:13, 20). Our author asserts that angels have a ministry directed to the future (1:14), but only the exalted Son is regent over the "world to come." This is the *oikumenē* in which the angels adore the Son at his enthronement (1:6). It corresponds to the coming age of salvation (6:5).

This final assertion of the Son's superiority over angels introduces the great paradox: The glorified King was once a lowly human being (v. 9). Psalm 8:4-6, which speaks of God's act of "subjecting" all things under humanity, illustrates the paradox.

The combination of Pss 110:1 (cf. Heb 1:13) and 8:6 is natural because of the common theme of subjection "under the feet." These texts are linked elsewhere in the New Testament to depict the results of Christ's exaltation (1 Cor 15:25, 27; cf. Eph 1:20, 22; 1 Pet 3:22). There is no evidence that Judaism understood Ps 8 in a messianic sense, so the author is probably reflecting an early church tradition that applied both texts to Christ. Yet the application of Ps 8:4-6 in Hebrews is unique (see Hurst 1990, 110-13). Though the motif of "glory and honor" is also applied to Christ, the focus is on the phrase "made . . . a little . . . lower" (Heb 2:7, 9).

Psalm 8 praises the majestic name of God by recalling, in amazement, the exalted status of human beings as creatures who are little less than angels in being given dominion over God's other creatures (cf. Gen 1:26-28). A specific application of Ps 8:4-6 to Christ in his incarnation is facilitated by the LXX where the phrase "a little lower than God" can be understood as "a little *while* lower than the angels." The text thus becomes a prophecy of Christ's temporary humility before his glorification.

The twin themes of temporary lowliness and final glory were enough to suggest a christological application of the text for the writer. The first verse says, literally: "What is *man* that you are mindful of him, and the *son of man* that you care for him." Though some argue to the contrary (Bruce 1990, 72-74; Buchanan 1972, 38-51), the author does not develop a Son of Man Christology. He surely knew that "man" and "son of man" were synonymous expressions for a human being (the NRSV, using inclusive language, has "human beings" and "mortals").

That the psalm quotation must be read as first referring to humanity becomes clear in the initial comment on the text in verse 8*b*. God made no exceptions in giving humans universal dominion. Yet human experience of finiteness, of subjection to death and the fear of death (2:14-15), belies its divine mandate to rule. That we do "not yet" see humanity's dominion suggests that there will be a time when it will be apparent. Mortals will reign with the Son in glory (2:10; cf. 1 Cor 4:8; 2 Tim 2:12; Rev 5:10; 22:5).

The lack of literal fulfillment suggests to the writer that the text's final meaning must be found elsewhere (cf. 4:1-11). For the present, Christ is the only one to whom the psalm fully applies (v. 9)—not as "Son of Man" in terms of a christological title, but as representative Human Being (note the phrase "for everyone" at the end of v. 9). Placed late in the Greek text, the name "Jesus" receives special stress (as in 3:1; 6:20; 7:22; 10:19; 12:2, 24; 13:20). Only of this human being is it true that he "was made" (God is the subject, as in v. 7) lower than the angels, though lowliness was not his natural state (see 1:3). By placing the phrase "for a little while" before the verb (v. 9), the author stresses the momentariness of humiliation.

Only of this Jesus can it also be said that he is "now crowned with glory and honor." The names he bears prove that (1:4-5; 5:5-6, 10; cf. 3:3). Humanity's hope for dominion over creation in an age to come (see Kistemaker 1981, 103-4) is already fulfilled, but only in the Son. His coronation was the fitting reward for perfect obedience in suffering (5:8; 12:2; Phil 2:8-9). Thus, his sufferings do not mark him as representing mortal humanity in a merely typical sense. He is uniquely representative.

This is made clear in the purpose clause at the end of verse 9. Humility, suffering, and death were part of a divine plan grounded in the "grace of God." Jesus "tasted death"—a Semitic expression (see Mark 9:1; John 8:52)—for everyone in a vicarious sense. His enthronement as universal ruler corresponds to the universal significance of his suffering.

There is a famous textual variant to "by the grace of God" in 2:9. "Apart from God" is a reading attested as early as the third century. Manuscript evidence is slight, but the reading has some patristic support (see Lane 1991, 43). An experiential separation from God in Christ's suffering and death could be suggested by 2:7. The reading "apart from God" possibly arose as a marginal gloss with 1 Cor 15:27 in mind: "everything" subjected under the Son does not include God! Few recent commentators accept the variant (Ellingworth 1993, 156, does so "with some hesitation").

◊ ◊ ◊ ◊

Despite the mention of angels in 2:5-9, the writer is no longer comparing the Son with angels. His point in adducing Ps 8 is to draw an initial contrast between human beings and the Son. Only the Son has unlimited dominion by virtue of his heavenly enthronement (1:2, 8, 13). The contrast paves the way for the picture of the Son's total identification with humanity, in his incarnation (2:10-16), and role as exalted High Priest (2:17-18). Highlighting the phrase "for a little while" forestalls any objection that the incarnation detracts from Christ's heavenly glory. His temporary humility is, in fact, the prelude to even greater glory and honor as the Son is now the object of worship.

Hebrews's picture of Christ as the representative of humanity brings us close to the Pauline concept of Christ as the last Adam (Rom 5:12-19; 1 Cor 15:45-50). The second representative Adam has everything subjected under him, including death (1 Cor 15:25-28). With Paul, Christ's resurrection is the key to understanding his present lordship. Hebrews, in an even bolder application of Ps 8, argues that Christ represents humanity also in his incarnation!

The final phrase "for everyone" (v. 9) hints at the Letter's next argument. It is not yet clear how the Son has come to represent humanity in both his humility and his glory. A lesson yet to be drawn is that the Son has endured suffering so as to identify with sufferers before leading them to glory (2:10, 18).

The Son's Solidarity with Humanity (2:10-18)

These verses belong to the second chain of texts bracketed by the *inclusio* of 2:5 and 2:16. The first text (Ps 8:4-6) was cited to depict the Son as representing humanity in his temporary abasement and present glory. Three more texts show that such representation is based on total identification with mortals. Links between verses 9 and 10 indicate that a prior argument is being continued: God is again the subject in verse 10, though identified with a circumlocution; "everyone" in verse 9 is restated with "many children"; the key words "glory" and "suffering" are repeated.

That 2:10-18 forms a unified statement is clear from the way in which four features of verse 10 are echoed in verses 17-18: the Son's identification with humanity is seen as fitting and appropriate; the Incarnation is seen in the light of what happened finally to Christ; those with whom he has identified are called "children" and "brothers and sisters"; and the Son's sufferings find their counterpart in the sufferings of the readers (see G. Guthrie 1994, 77-78).

The movement in 2:10-18 corresponds to that in 2:5-9: from suffering to glory. Future glory is mentioned in verse 10, but the accent immediately falls on the past event of the Son's identification with humanity. At the end comes a statement of what the exalted Son is now: "merciful and faithful high priest . . . able to help" (vv. 17-18).

◊ ◊ ◊ ◊

Two statements draw conclusions from verse 9 and set the agenda for what follows. In saying that it was "fitting" for God to bring the Son to glory through suffering, the writer draws a theological conclusion about the appropriateness of God's actions in the light of verse 9 (see 7:26 for similar logic). Humanity has not yet reached its glorious goal, expressed in Ps 8:4-6 (Heb 2:6-8); the Son has. But the confession of the Son's progress from suffering to glory implies a soteriology that is in keeping with God's nature ("grace . . . for everyone", v. 9).

The circumlocution for God, the one "for whom and through whom all things exist," sounds like a liturgical phrase (cf. Rom 11:36; 1 Cor 8:6; Col 1:16; Rev 4:11), possibly borrowed from the Greek-speaking synagogue.

The Son is not symbolically representative of humanity; he became as fully human (v. 14) as the "many children" ("everyone," v. 9). The author does not recall Paul's doctrine of adoption through the indwelling of the Spirit (Rom 8:14-17, 23; Gal 4:4-7). Rather, human beings are affirmed as God's children because the Son identifies with them (vv. 11*b*-13).

It is difficult to render in English the wordplay behind the description of Jesus as "pioneer" (for various meanings of *archēgos,* see Attridge 1989, 87) who has been made "perfect." The Greek noun and verb are built on root words meaning "beginning" (*archē* in compounds implies "first") and "end" *(telos).* To complicate matters, there is a further wordplay that involves the notion of "leading." We can recapture the total effect by paraphrasing thus: "in *leading* the children to glory, God brought the *first leader* to his *end/goal* through suffering." Two thoughts are combined. The translation "pioneer" rightly suggests that Jesus went ahead to blaze the trail from suffering to glory. Thus 6:20 calls him the "forerunner." Second, because he has completed his course from beginning to end, he is the "source of salvation" (cf. 5:9) in the sense of its beginning or origin. That is why he can be called the "pioneer of salvation" or the "pioneer and perfecter of our faith" (12:2). He who has been "perfected" brings others to faith's goal. His course is the way that believers must follow (10:20; 12:1).

It was both in and through suffering that the Son was perfected. He reached the goal that God had set for him by being installed as the heavenly High Priest (5:9-10; 7:28), but only after he had been equipped for this role in the school of suffering (5:8). Having suffered, he can sympathize with others (2:18; 4:15).

Since the Son's "perfection" has cultic connotations, it is natural that his solidarity with God's children should be expressed in cultic terms (v. 11*a*). In the Pentateuch, God identifies himself as "the one who sanctifies" (see Exod 31:13; Lev 20:8; 21:15; 22:9, 16, 32). Here it is the Son who sanctifies through his self-sacrifice (10:10, 14; 13:12), so that people are consecrated and "perfected" (10:14) for priestly access to God and the sacrifice of praise (10:19-26; 13:12-15).

At this point, the accent lies on the solidarity of the sanctifier with the sanctified; they are, literally, "all of one." This phrase could mean that the Son and the many children "all have one Father" (vv. 10-11). But this weakens the letter's argument for the uniqueness of the Son, and detracts from the point being made: the Son's solidarity with humanity. The writer means that the Son and the children belong to the human family (RSV; NJB; it is unlikely that the author is referring to either Abraham [v. 16] or Adam [see Acts 17:26] as a common father). The texts cited in verses 12-13 do not speak of "children of God" but of human beings who are declared to be the Son's siblings because he shares their humanity (v. 14).

The texts cited in 1:5-13 constituted God's confession to the Son. In 2:12-13 we have the Son's confession to his human siblings. Not being "ashamed" suggests eagerness to acknowledge or accept; God was not ashamed to be called the God of the patriarchs (11:16), while Moses was ashamed, that is, refused to be identified as the son of Pharaoh's daughter (11:24).

The Son's first confession (Ps 22:22) is part of a suffering saint's cry for help. He recalls occasions when God has come to his rescue, and changes his song of woe to one of praise. He proclaims God's name to his "brothers and sisters" (the NRSV always translates the one Greek word "brother" inclusively). Probably two factors prompted the writer to place these words in the Son's mouth: (1) In the passion tradition, Jesus identified himself with the psalmist by taking on his own lips the opening words of this psalm: "My God, why have you forsaken me?" (Matt 27:46; Mark 15:34). (2) The Greek word for "assembly" (ekklēsia) is the normal word for "church." The reference to the descendants of Abraham in Heb 2:16 may well echo Ps 22:23: the offspring of Jacob are to praise God.

The next text (Isa 8:17-18 in Heb 2:13) is divided into two separate statements by the insertion of "and again" (similarly, 10:30). This division is less odd when we note that the LXX has the first statement also in 2 Sam 22:3, enabling it to be viewed as a separate text. Like the psalmist, Isaiah speaks as one who has endured suffering—in his case, rejection by the people. He sees himself and his children (including his disciples) as signs of hope at a time when foreign invasion looms large on the horizon.

Hebrews sees Christ using this text to declare his solidarity with those who are called to a life of faith. He deserves to be called the "forerunner" of hope (6:19-20) because he is the first of God's children to show perfect trust in God (5:7-8). That is why he is a trustworthy ("faithful") High Priest (2:17). Second, the description of the children as God's gift suggests the final purpose of his solidarity with them: to lead them from suffering and death to glory (vv. 10, 14-15). The "children" are such not merely by virtue of belonging to the human family, but because they belong to the family of faith (Attridge 1989, 91).

The identification of the Son with the children is expressed in parallel symmetry (v. 14a; see Lane 1991, 53): "the children/share flesh and blood"; "he himself likewise/shared the same things." "Flesh and blood" is a Semitic expression for mortal humanity (Matt 16:17; 1 Cor 15:50; Gal 1:16; Eph 6:12). The tense of the verb in the second line suggests that the Son assumed his humanity at a point in time (as in John 1:14), but the writer is interested in the human state of Jesus, not in his human story.

The goal of this identification is expressed in a chiastic formulation (v. 14a): through his *death* Christ *disempowered* the one who has the *power* of *death* (the parenthetical naming of the devil falls outside the neat structure). Death's advent into God's good world is traced back to the devil also in Wis 2:24: "Through the devil's envy death entered the world" (cf. 18:15). Hebrews does say how Christ's victory over death and the devil was effected. There are no more than hints at the widespread picture of the Messiah's victory over demonic forces in Jewish apocalyptic and in early Christianity (see Attridge 1989, 92). The writer presupposes that Christ's perfect sacrifice has effectively removed sin as the root cause of human mortality (4:15; 5:8; 7:26; 9:14). Though he speaks explicitly of Christ's resurrection only in 13:20, he presupposes that the power of death has been overcome by the power of an indestructible life (7:16).

The experience of mortality means subjection to a lifelong slavery to fear—as often noted in Greek literature (see Attridge 1989, 93) and in the Old Testament Wisdom traditions (Job 4:12-21; Sir 40:1-9). The Son's identification with humanity included even that experience (5:7). But by remaining the trusting and obedient Son (2:13; 5:8; 10:7), he delivered his siblings from the fear of death, and remains their champion when life-threatening situations tempt them to surrender their trust (2:18; 4:15).

Though verse 16 seems to interrupt the flow of the argument, it is important for two reasons. Forming an *inclusio* with verse 5, it marks the end of a scriptural argument. Second, it again identifies the beneficiaries of the Son's work of deliverance, and does so in a final comparison involving the angels who are not "flesh and blood" (v. 14). That the Son "takes hold to help" (the literal meaning of the Greek text of v. 16) the descendants of Abraham is hardly an allusion to Jer 31:31-32 where God takes Israel by the hand (*pace* Lane 1991, 64). It recalls Isa 41:8-10 LXX: Israel, the seed of Abraham, is not to fear; it is God's servant whom he has not forsaken, but will always help. The summons not to fear and the reminder of God's help are echoed in the portrayal of Christ (Heb 2:15, 18).

Abraham is the bearer of divine promises, the model of faith and obedience (6:13; 7:1-10; 11:8-10, 17-19). All who inherit the promises of God (see 4:1-11) and trustingly cling to them are descendants of Abraham. The Son's rescue of his siblings who are also Abraham's family shows God's continuing care of those who, like himself, trust in God (see 2:13).

The concluding statement on the necessity of the Son's incarnation (vv. 17-18) recalls the logic of verse 10. That the Son "had to" become human does not denote a divine necessity, dictated by God's immutable will, but a moral obligation deduced from the human predicament outlined in verses 14-15. It was to save all humanity that the Son took on full humanity. Like Paul who speaks of Christ being "born in human likeness" (Phil 2:7) and coming "in the likeness of sinful flesh" (Rom 8:3), our writer picks his words carefully. Terms such as "made like" and "likeness" (the Greek noun occurs in 4:15) could be wrongly taken to mean that the Son only appeared to be human. This possibility is removed by the clause "in every respect" (cf. 4:15; the Son's sinlessness that sets him apart from humanity comes later; see also 7:26).

The eternal Son (1:2-3) had to "become" the heavenly High Priest by following the path from suffering to glory (2:10). He was equipped for his office by suffering, and was installed into it at his exaltation (5:8-10). His present ministry is marked by mercy in representing God to humanity, and by faithfulness in representing humanity to God (5:1). The High Priest's faithfulness (see 1 Sam 2:35: "I will raise up for myself a faithful priest") will be dealt with in 3:1-6. Here, his ability to show compassion is stressed (v. 18). Only one who has fully known human suffering and the temptation to lose trust in God in the face of suffering and death (2:13-15) can help those who go through the same experience (see also 4:15; 5:2, 7).

Somewhat problematic is the phrase that the NRSV renders "to make a sacrifice of atonement" (v. 17c). The Greek text does not speak of Christ's "sacrifice" in the past, nor does it separate the statements about Jesus becoming a High Priest and his function: "to atone" (the comma in the NRSV is misleading). It rather implies that Christ's installation as High Priest (see 2:10; 5:9-10) is the basis for an ongoing ministry of atonement, just as it is the basis of his present mediatorial activity (v. 18; cf. 4:15-16). Every reference in Hebrews to Christ's once-for-all sacrifice and entry into the heavenly sanctuary is part of a statement about his ongoing work as exalted High Priest (see 7:26-28; 9:11-14, 24-28). Even where Hebrews stresses the efficacy of Christ's single sacrifice in removing sin (10:10-14), it presupposes that atonement has been effected by the blood that he offered *after* he entered the heavenly sanctuary (9:12-14).

This interpretation of verse 17c finds support in 3:2, 6 where the author speaks of the *present* faithfulness of the High Priest and Son. It also corresponds to the typology developed in chapters 8–10: on the Day of Atonement the high priest sacrificed an animal, then sprinkled the blood on and in front of the mercy seat to "atone for" the sins of the people (Lev 16:11-16). The exalted High Priest, through the application of his blood, provides continual cleansing from sin, and can do so because he lives forever (5:6; 7:25). Thus, the high-priestly title is adduced in 2:17 to introduce the two features of his present work: cleansing from sin, and intercession for sinners.

◊ ◊ ◊ ◊

Some (see Lane 1991, 56-57; Aune 1991) have proposed that the Christology of 2:10-15 reflects the widespread myth of the divine hero who descends to the plane of mortals to become their champion. It recalls, in particular, the picture of the legendary Hercules as "champion" (Gk. *archēgos*, which the NRSV in 2:10 translates with "pioneer") and "savior." One of his famous labors, wrestling with Death, is alluded to in the picture of Jesus as the one who rescues mortals from oppression (2:14-15).

It is possible that people, even of Jewish background, may have drawn a parallel between the picture of the deliverer Jesus and the hero Hercules. Yet the intention of the writer is to develop his Christology not on any mythological model, but on the basis of a shared confession, the testimony of Scripture, and historical recollection.

The word *archēgos* in 2:10 is best interpreted in connection with the idea of the Son's perfection. His "end" in God's plan confirms his role as the "beginner" of faith's course and as the source of salvation (see 5:9; 6:20; 12:2). That the *archēgos* had to go through suffering to deliver others from death (2:10, 14-15) does not determine the meaning of the term; it is used elsewhere in the early hellenistic church without suggesting the picture of the divine hero (see Acts 3:15; 5:31).

The portrayal of Christ as deliverer in Hebrews is decidedly nonmythical. He is no demigod who tangentially enters human existence, or only typifies the human predicament. He suffers as a human, and rescues through his humanity. Yet the human Son shares God's own being (1:3, 8). It is natural, then, that his role as deliverer should reflect the Old Testament concept of God as Israel's champion (Heb. *gibbor*). William L. Lane himself rightly draws attention to Isa 42:13 and 49:24-26: Yahweh is the "mighty one" who snatches his people from the grasp of tyrants. Jewish apocalyptic extended the image to include rescue from satanic power (*T. Zeb.* 9:8; see Jesus' saying about the strong one being despoiled by someone stronger in Luke 11:21-22), and even linked the hope of rescue from the devil's tyranny with the coming of a new priest who would "remove the threatening sword against Adam" (*T. Levi* 18:10-12).

The stress on the Son's humanity at this point has a dual purpose. It allows the author to introduce the high-priestly title for the first time. In Hebrews the confession to the Son accents Christ's relationship to God, both in his preexistence and exaltation. In this scheme, the Son's incarnation must be seen as a paradox (5:8). By contrast, the confession of Christ as High Priest embraces his total ministry for humanity, beginning with his death.

The presentation of the Son's abasement is applied Christology for people who know suffering and the enslaving fear of death (2:15). Their hope of future glory is anchored not in a general principle: after suffering must come glory. They are to fix their eyes on Jesus (3:1; 12:2) who has passed from suffering to glory. Because he has completed the course *for* them, he can also be *with* them as they struggle along the way of faith.

THE SON, AS FAITHFUL HIGH PRIEST, CALLS TO FAITH (3:1–4:13)

Apart from 2:1-5, the opening chapters have been expository. This next discourse is predominantly exhortation, though its appeals are based on scriptural exposition. Its opening in 3:1-2 recalls the phrase "faithful high priest" in 2:17. Where the unit ends is a more difficult question. An *inclusio* is formed in 3:1 and 4:14 with the repetition of four key terms: "Jesus," "high priest," "heavenly/heavens," "confession." Yet 4:14-16 echoes the whole of 2:17–3:1, and is best seen as a transitional exhortation that introduces a new sequence of thought by focusing on the first epithet for Christ in 2:17: "merciful." Further, 4:14-16 points the audience forward, rather than simply recapitulating what has been said; it forms a major *inclusio* with 10:19-23.

The thematic unity of 3:1–4:13 centers on the concepts of faithfulness and disobedience. A new comparison, between the Son and Moses (3:1-6), serves to demonstrate the superior faithfulness of the Son. A call for the hearers to remain faithful (v. *6b*) leads to the portrayal of Israel's disobedience (3:7-19) and an appeal to cling to God's promise (4:1-11). A description of God's powerful word brings the appeal to a conclusion (4:12-13).

The Superior Faithfulness of the Son (3:1-6)

Despite the hortatory overtones of the opening imperative and closing conditional clause, these verses are expository. The argument is now based on scriptural allusions rather than direct quotations, as in chapters 1–2. The key words, "faithful," "priest," and "house," recall Num 12:7 and 1 Sam 2:35.

The rhetorical technique of comparison is again adopted to exalt Christ, not to denigrate his counterpart. The writer structures his argument as follows: (1) an opening appeal establishes the terms of reference for a comparison between Jesus and Moses (vv. 1-2 are one sentence in the Greek); (2) the superiority of Jesus is asserted in terms of an analogy: the relationship of the builder to what he has built (vv. 3-4), and (3) in terms of Christ's status as Son (vv. 5-6*a*); (4) a conclusion with parenetic implications is drawn (v. 6*b*).

◊ ◊ ◊ ◊

A comparison with Moses is totally in place. He is the chief representative of the prophets through whom God spoke in the past (1:1-2). Though angels were the mediators of revelation at Sinai (2:2), Hebrews recognizes the unique mediatorial role of Moses in establishing the Sinaitic covenant (7:14; 8:5; 9:18-20; 10:28; 12:18-21). In Jewish tradition, Num 12:7 (alluded to in Heb 3:2*b*, 5) was used to prove that Moses was granted greater rank and honor than angels (D'Angelo 1979, 95-131). So it is natural that the argument for the Son's ranking above angels should be followed by one that shows his superiority to Moses. Furthermore, the portrait of Christ as deliverer (see 2:10, 15) invites a comparison with Moses who led Israel out of Egypt (3:16; 11:28).

There are priestly features in the Old Testament picture of Moses. Although called a priest only in Ps 99:6, he was the son of a Levite couple (Exod 2:1-4), interceded in priestly fashion for Israel (Exod 32:31-32), and functioned at the altar (Exod 24:4-8; Heb 9:19-21). Thus, Philo can call Moses a high priest (see Lane 1991, 74).

The Appeal (vv. 1-2): The readers are brothers (and sisters) in that they share a common faith relationship through the Son (2:10-14). Hebrews uses this form of address only in appeals (cf. 3:12; 10:19; 13:22) where it is meant to capture attention, to invite response, and, perhaps, to soften an appeal. Those addressed are holy because they have been cleansed from sin and consecrated for service (2:11). They are, literally, "sharers in a heavenly calling" because they "share in Christ" (see 3:14) who leads them from suffering to glory (2:9-10; 4:14).

Faith focuses on Jesus who has completed the course. The earthly name recalls that he became human to be like his siblings (2:10-18). He remains Jesus also in his exaltation, no matter what titles are given to him (see 4:14; 6:20; 7:22; 12:2, 24; Rom 10:9; 1 Cor 12:3; Phil 2:11).

The precise content and original setting of the "confession" in 3:1; 4:14; and 10:23 are not stated. It may have included a reference to Christ as High Priest, but had its focus in the Son (v. 6; see the introduction, p. 38). The titles "apostle" and "High Priest" belong together since both suggest divine authorization and appointment. Hebrews never uses the term "apostle," that is, "one who is sent," to denote the specially commissioned witnesses of the risen Lord (see Acts 1:21-22; 1 Cor 9:1; 15:7-9) or other emissaries (see 2 Cor 8:23). The Son is *the* authoritative emissary who has revealed God's will in the last times (1:2). It may be that Christ is called "apostle" to complete the analogy with Moses who was "sent" by God to Pharaoh (Exod 3:10; for other theories see Lane 1991, 75). "Apostle" comes first, probably because it describes the movement from God to humanity, whereas "high priest" embraces the movement from earthly suffering to heavenly installation.

Despite the use of the present participle in the Greek of verse 2, translators and commentators consistently read "he was faithful." Both the appointment of Christ (v. 2a) and the faithfulness of Moses (v. 2b) belong in the past. Yet a case can be made for translating "is faithful" here and in verse 6 where a verb has to be supplied. We have argued that 2:17-18 focuses on what the Son is *now* doing as the exalted High Priest: atoning for sins and interceding for those who suffer. That same focus should be carried over into this section.

Verse 2 alludes to texts where God is the speaker. In 1 Sam 2:35 God promises to raise up for himself a "faithful priest. . . . I will build him a sure house. . . ." In 1 Chr 17:14 LXX, the Nathan prophecy of an eternal throne for David's descendants includes the words "I will entrust him in my house." Finally, there is an allusion to Num 12:7: "My servant Moses . . . is entrusted with all my house" (the allusion becomes a quotation in Heb 3:5). In answer to Aaron and Miriam, jealous of their brother, God points to Moses' special role as recipient of revelation and spokesperson for God. God speaks to him face-to-face, not in riddles or through dreams and visions (Num 12:1-8). Only the first of these three texts uses the word "faithful," but faithfulness is implied in the verb "entrust," which also suggests appointment.

The Analogy of the Builder (vv. 3-4): Great as Moses was, a greater one with a greater mission has appeared. Consequently, more glory has been ascribed to him by God than to Moses (2:9). An analogy, suggested by the word *house*, shows this to be entirely fitting. First a truism is asserted (vv. 3*b*-4*a*): a builder who designs and erects a house deserves greater honor than the construction itself. The central theological assertion (not a side comment as in the NRSV) then follows: God, as Creator, is the builder of all things, including the house of Israel.

The Argument Concerning Status (vv. 5-6*a*): The reference to Num 12:7 now becomes explicit: Moses was faithful *in* God's house as a *servant*. He was a trusted and faithful intimate of God, yet he remained only a servant of the household. Like the angels, he was a servant of future generations who would hear the final word spoken through the Son (v. 5*b*; cf. 1:1-2, 14). By contrast, Christ (the title appears here for the first time in Hebrews) is—not "was"—faithful *over* God's house as a *Son*.

The Conclusion (v. 6*b*): The sense in which the audience is God's house is determined by the picture of Christ as royal priest and by what follows in 3:5-11. Two of the texts speak of the establishment of a new priestly house and a new royal house, both of which will last forever (1 Sam 2:35; 1 Chr 17:14). Christ fulfills both hopes in that he is now installed as High Priest and Son (Heb 5:5-6). The house of "Israel" over which he is faithful (Num 12:7) is the new wandering people of God (3:7–4:11).

Verse 6a anticipates the confession in 10:21: "We have a great priest over the house of God," just as verse 6b anticipates 10:22-23 with its call to draw near to God. Confidence and hope are essential marks of God's purified and consecrated people. The first term (Gk. *parrēsia*), originally suggesting the freedom of citizens to speak their mind, is associated in Hebrews with the confession to Christ (4:14, 16; 10:19, 23) who has opened access to the heavenly sanctuary, allowing God to be addressed freely and confidently. "Pride that belong[s] to hope" means "the content of boasting that gives hope." That the author is again thinking in cultic terms is clear from 6:18-21: hope follows Christ as High Priest into the inner shrine of God's presence. The inference is clear: cling to the confession of Christ as faithful Son and High Priest!

◊ ◊ ◊ ◊

Familial terminology in 2:10-18 (children; brothers and sisters; descendants) is echoed by household terminology in 3:1-6 (cf. 12:5-11). Whatever the connotations behind the phrase "God's house" the audience would have seen in it an apt description of their own situation as members of a house-church. "House" describes a concrete reality, as well as an image. It suggests intimacy, protection, solidarity, and unity. Loss of confidence and hope means losing that which binds the family of God together. That is why 3:1-6 is a fitting prelude to the minisermon of 3:7-13 with its appeal for faithfulness.

The Faithlessness of Israel in the Wilderness (3:7-19)

The comparison of the Son with angels concluded with an appeal to listen to God's word of warning and promise (2:1-4). The comparison with Moses is followed by a similar appeal (note the opening "therefore" in 2:1 and 3:7). A homiletical midrash on Ps 95:7-11, which itself interprets the exodus story in the light of Num 14, gives the negative example of Israel's faithlessness. An implied exhortation in 3:6 becomes explicit. Though the parenesis continues to 4:14, it seems 3:7-19 is a distinct literary unit. It contains the quoted text (vv. 7-11) and a commentary that is bracketed in verses 12 and 19 by the repetition of the words "see" and "unbelief" (the NRSV translation of v. 12 obscures the *inclusio*).

◊ ◊ ◊ ◊

7-11: The text is introduced as a message that *is* (not "was") spoken by the Spirit (cf. 9:8; 10:15). What was once spoken of the desert generation applies immediately to the present readers. Psalm 95 contains an invitation to worship God (vv. 1-7a), followed by a call to hear his voice and not disobey (vv. 7b-11). Hebrews cites only the verses that recall the sad story of Israel's rebelliousness.

At Rephidim the people provoked God to anger by complaining about the shortage of water. Psalm 95:8 recalls how Moses named the place Massah and Meribah, but the LXX translates these Hebrew names with "rebellion" and "testing" (Heb 3:8; see Exod 17:1-7; Num 20:2-13). The main focus of the psalmist, and of our writer, is on the rebellion at Kadesh. God's answer to the rebellion was that none of those who had *tested* his patience by not listening to his *voice* (Heb 2:7-8), despite seeing his glory and signs of deliverance in the exodus (his *works;* 3:9), would enter the land that he *swore* to them (v. 11; the allusions are to Num 14:11, 21-23, 30, 35). Of the host of people who left Egypt, only Caleb and Joshua survived to enter the land. In formulating God's complaint, "they always go astray in their hearts" (v. 10), the psalmist is thinking of Israel's persistent refusal to accept his directions and promises (see Num 14:11, 22). Numbers 14:30 speaks only of God's resolve not to allow the desert generation to enter the "land in which I swore to settle you." The psalmist has reformulated this verse, relating the oath to the prohibition of entry, and replacing "land" with "rest," used elsewhere in the Pentateuch for the promised land (Deut 12:9).

Disregarding minor changes, Hebrews alters "this" to *"that generation"* in verse 10, thereby making it clear that the Spirit is talking about God's anger against Israel in the past. The promised rest can still be claimed in the present (4:1-11). Second, the writer links the "forty years" not with God's anger (v. 10), but with Israel

seeing God's works in the desert (v. 9), though he later returns to
the original connection in verse 17. By first linking the forty years
with God's signs (v. 9), the author probably wants to highlight
divine grace that leaves the promise of verse 11 open.

First Application (vv. 12-15): Heeding the Spirit's warnings is a
matter of familial responsibility (see 3:1), so continuous mutual
encouragement is needed. Concern for each individual (cf. 4:1, 11;
10:25; 12:15-16) reflects concern for the integrity of the whole
group, which will be affected if anyone "turns away" from God
(the noun formed from the verb is *apostasis,* but "apostasize" is
too strong a term here). The characterization of God as "living"
points to the ultimate concern: divine judgment (see 10:31; Jer
10:10).

The brief application in verses 12-13 picks up key terms of the
psalm quotation ("harden"; "hearts"; "today"), but also has Num
14 in mind. The concept of unbelief (vv. 12, 19; the word does not
appear again in Hebrews) reflects Israel's refusal to believe (Num
14:11), while the heart as "evil" recalls the description of Israel
itself as wicked (Num 14:27, 35). Repeating the opening word
"today" (vv. 7, 13, 15; 4:7), the writer stresses that the word of
warning and promise still applies in the present day of salvation
(see 9:27-28; 10:37-39; 13:8).

Those who have become "partners of Christ" (v. 14; "partners
in a heavenly calling" in 3:1) are under obligation. (For the con-
tractual and legal connotations of the terms "partners," "confidence," and "firm," see Lane 1991, 87; Attridge 1989, 119.)
Christ's faithfulness (3:2, 6) commits them to faithfulness (3:14*b*
recalls 3:6*b*). Partnership with Christ exists only where there is the
certainty of faith ("confidence" in v. 14 translates the same Greek
word as "assurance" in 11:1). The text speaks, literally, of the need
to cling to the "beginning" of confidence until the "end," thus
suggesting the path that Christ himself has followed as the pioneer
and perfecter of faith (see 12:2; 2:10). Perseverance and patient
endurance are required to reach the promised rest (3:6; 6:11-20;
10:36; 12:1).

Rhetorical Conclusion (vv. 16-19): In three rapid questions and answers, the people referred to in the psalm are identified. The response in each case recalls Num 14. Each response invites the audience to draw a conclusion. Those who received the promise but still rebelled (vv. 7-9) were all who were saved out of Egypt. As in 1 Cor 10:1-5, the inference is that those who experienced rescue in the past should have shown faithfulness to the end. Second, those who angered God were those who sinned (v. 10), and thus died in the wilderness without seeing the promised land (Num 14:27-29; 1 Cor 10:8-10). The inference is that God will always punish failure to heed his promises. Those who were banned from entering the land of rest (v. 11) were guilty of disobedience. Israel's rebellion, sin, and disobedience are summed up with the one word: unbelief (v. 19; cf. v. 12). God was not at fault, nor were the promises unreliable. So the promise of rest is still valid.

◊ ◊ ◊ ◊

This midrashic homily illustrates the author's understanding of God's word as living and dynamic (see 4:12-13). He applies to the present the message of Ps 95, which is itself an application of Num 14. Scripture is the voice of the prophetic Spirit that must be spoken "today" (3:7).

Exodus typology is a common feature in early Christian writings. It was natural to relate the Christ-event to the central saving event of the Old Testament. Jesus' departure becomes his "exodus" (Luke 9:31); his death is seen in terms of exodus events (the brazen serpent, John 3:14; the Passover victim, 1 Cor 5:7; 1 Pet 1:19; John 1:29, 36; 19:36). The church saw in the wilderness generation a type of its own pilgrim existence in which it heard both warning and promise (see 1 Cor 10:1-13; Jude 3). The exodus motif underlies the letter's continual references to the cult and its regulations.

This suggests that the audience is in transition. Its situation is marked by impermanence and social insecurity that could, in the writer's view, lead to a "falling away." His response is first to warn of the dire results of hardness of heart. But that is only half of the answer. The following section focuses on the promise.

This section makes clear what the writer understands by sin. It is not the acts of ignorance and weakness that the heavenly High Priest readily understands (4:15; 5:2; 7:28), but the deliberate rejection of God's promises. The story of Israel in the Exodus is thus a prelude to the warning of 6:4-8. Apostasy is the only unforgivable sin.

The Promise of Final Rest (4:1-11)

Warning now turns into promise; imperatives (3:12-13) give way to cohortatives ("let us"; 4:1, 11) at the beginning and end of the section. Though continuing his homiletical midrash on the psalm, the writer adds a new dimension by linking the promised rest in Ps 95:11 with God's own rest in Gen 2:2.

An *inclusio,* formed in verses 1 and 11 (not 3 and 11, as G. Guthrie 1994, 79, suggests) by the cohortatives and the phrase "to enter the rest," marks this section as a complete statement. Its two parts are delineated by the same technique: verses 1-5 and 6-11 are framed by varying forms of the key phrase "to enter the rest," with "disobedience" (only here in Hebrews) underlining the second *inclusio* in verses 6 and 11. In addition, each subsection begins with the reminder that God's promise is still "open" (vv. 1 and 6). At the center of each subsection (vv. 3 and 7) stands a quotation from Ps 95.

1-5: Behind the positive application of Ps 95 lie two basic assumptions: (1) God's promises remain valid despite human faithlessness, and (2) God's word can never remain unfulfilled. This second principle was operative in the author's application of Ps 8:4-6—since the promise of glory for human beings remains unrealized, it must be fulfilled in Jesus. Similar logic applies here. The promise of rest was not made invalid by Israel's disobedience and unbelief (Heb 3:18-19); it was simply not claimed. That it remains an open promise is deduced from the opening words of the psalm quotation (3:7-8) and from Num 14:22-24, 31, where the promise of entering Canaan is extended to the children of the wilderness generation. Special diligence is needed now to ensure that not one person (see the same concern in 3:12; 4:11) should lose out on what the promise effects as a creative word.

Though the verb "to announce good news" occurs twice (4:2, 6), the noun "gospel" *(euangelion)* never appears in Hebrews. It is replaced by the etymologically related word "promise" *(epangelia)*, which appears for the first time in the Letter in 4:1. The good news is seen as promissory: it holds out the prospect of a future inheritance (1:14; 6:12, 15, 17; 9:15; 10:36) that can be claimed now by faith.

Faith was the condition for appropriating the promise in the past; it remains the one condition in the present (v. 2). Simply hearing a message does not ensure appropriation. Israel received the good news of a promised rest but forfeited the land through disobedience, that is, lack of faith (v. 6). That is the general meaning of verse 2b, though the Greek text is uncertain. The reading adopted by the NRSV would suggest that the unbelieving Israelites were not united with Joshua and Caleb who did listen (see Num 14:6). Another possible reading, supported by Heb 4:3 and 11:40b, suggests that the unbelieving Israelites were "not united" with "us" who have believed.

As the center of the subsection (vv. 1-5), verse 3 serves two purposes. It develops the contrast between "we who have believed" and the unbelieving generation that God debarred from entering the promised land. The repetition of Ps 95:11 serves a second purpose: the definition of the rest as God's *own* rest that he enjoys since the "foundation of the world."

This new thought could give rise to an objection: If the rest is that into which God has entered, and not the land of Canaan, surely it was not yet available to Israel! That objection is countered in verses 3b-5 by linking Ps 95:11 with Gen 2:2, which speaks of God resting from his work of creation on the seventh day. The point is not that the promised rest is one of God's finished "works," but that God's own resting from the work of creation is an archetype for the final rest promised to Christians (see vv. 9-10).

The two texts, linked through the common word "rest," were already associated in the sabbath liturgy of the Greek-speaking synagogue; Ps 95:1-11 and Gen 2:1-3 were readings on the sabbath eve (see Lane 1991, 100). Hebrews can interpret the rest spoken of in Ps 95 in the light of God's own primordial rest since Jewish tradition saw the sabbath as a symbol of eschatological salvation (see Attridge 1989, 129). Clearly, the author is locking into a long tradition in which the term "rest" has acquired new meanings. In the context of the Exodus, Canaan was God's promised rest after the toil of the desert wanderings (Deut 12:9, 10; Josh 21:44). In 1 Kgs 8:56 the word "rest" is associated with the new temple of Solomon. An eschatological extension of the term is implied already in Ps 95:11, so Jewish apocalyptic could develop the image of a final land or city of rest, while hellenistic Judaism, particularly Philo, could speak of a state of rest in spiritual realms beyond any earthly land (see the excursus in Attridge 1989, 126-28).

It is a common early-Jewish and Christian argument that an original situation retains validity over that which comes later. The priesthood of Melchizedek is above that of Levi since it precedes it (Heb 7:4-10; for similar logic see John 1:30; 8:58; Gal 3:17). The argument of Heb 4:3b-5 is similar: God's own original, archetypal rest determines how the promise of eschatological rest for his creatures is to be understood. And since God's rest precedes human history, the final eternal rest cannot be on the plane of normal human history, for example, as a restored home in an earthly land (*pace* Buchanan 1972, 63-65, 71).

6-11: The repetition of three thoughts shows verse 6 to be transitional: Since Israel lost the land of rest through disobedience (3:18), despite receiving the promise as good news (4:2), it is open to others to enter God's rest (4:1). There is no suggestion that all in the past failed to live by faith in God's promises (see chap. 11). Rather, the sweeping condemnation of a past generation's disobedience is meant to show the availability of the promise to another generation. Heavenly rest is not a gift for a select few, but for the whole "people of God" (v. 9). Israel's disobedience did not change God's promise, only the time when it could be claimed in full.

Uniquely in Hebrews, verse 7 gives a name in connection with a quotation of Scripture. David is specified as the agent of the prophetic word in order to stress the great time gap between the Exodus and the "today" that falls "much later." Since his words are a revalidation of God's promise of rest, the further reference to Israel's rebellion is dropped. A distinction is drawn between the "day of testing" in Ps 95:8b and the "today" of verse 7b. This other day cannot refer to the capture and settlement of Canaan under Joshua, for David spoke long after these events. David, a person of faith (Heb 11:32), must therefore have been speaking about a day in the future, one that has now arrived in the salvation offered in Christ. Though the name Joshua (4:8) in Greek is "Jesus," the author does not offer a comparison between the Joshua who did not lead the people to their final rest, and Jesus who now does. That typology was developed only later (see *Barn.* 6:8; *Dial. Trypho* 113, 132).

The conclusion drawn in verse 9 parallels the statements in verses 1 and 6, but with an important change. So far the writer has used a word for "rest" *(katapausis)* that has land associations. He now uses a new word *(sabbatismos* occurs here for the first time in Greek literature) that implies the observation of sabbath rest as an act of worship in praise of God (see Exod 20:8-10; 2 Macc 8:27; *Jub.* 50:9). Those who enjoy this rest have a sabbath celebration that conforms to God's own resting (4:10).

The analogy with God's own rest is complete in itself; it does not require us to identify the "labors" from which believers rest, whether the trials and temptations of life generally, or persecution specifically. Final rest will mean the end of all striving (cf. 12:1). Meanwhile, concerted effort is required to ensure that such a joyful prospect is not lost by disobedience. Verse 11 returns to the theme announced in verse 1, and recalls 3:18 and 4:6.

◊ ◊ ◊ ◊

Nowhere in Hebrews is the concept of rest precisely defined, though sabbath connotations (4:3-5, 9-10) suggest a state of being rather than a location. Clearly, the writer is working with a concept that has acquired varying associations within a long tradition of Old Testament and Jewish thought. Rest has become synonymous with the eternal inheritance of salvation to which believers look in hope (1:14; 9:15). Not to trust God's promise of rest is the same as neglecting salvation (2:3; 4:1, 11). As the consummation of Christian hope, the final rest is the believers' glorification with Christ

(2:10), their perfection (11:40; 12:23), their citizenship in an abiding city (13:14), in a heavenly country (11:16), and an unshakable kingdom (12:28).

These images, the stress on rest as promised (4:1), and the appeal for effort to enter it (4:11) suggest that rest is a future reality. Yet 4:3 says that believers *now* enter it (see Kistemaker, 1981, 109). This tension between present fulfillment and future realization is not resolved, but becomes more understandable when we note the worship themes that underlie the author's thinking.

The picture of entry into heavenly rest anticipates the author's later teaching on Christ's entry into the heavenly sanctuary. That event provides believers with access into God's presence so that, as sanctified priests, they can now join the heavenly beings in worship (10:19-24; 12:22-23; 13:15). It is in worship, as the experience of God's saving presence, that rest is celebrated as present and future reality. "A foretaste of the eschatological sabbath festivity may be actualized in the worship of the community" (Attridge 1989, 131, who recalls how, in Rev 6:11; 14:13, the souls resting in God constantly sing God's praise). Hebrews 4:9-10 anticipates "the festival of the priestly people of God in the heavenly sanctuary, celebrating in the presence of God the eternal Sabbath with unceasing praise and adoration" (Lane 1991, 102).

Second Warning: Do Not Reject the Word of God (4:12-13)

A note of warning has permeated the homily on Ps 95:7-11 (Heb 3:12-13; 4:1, 11). What follows is the climax to the whole sermon, not only to 4:1-11. Since the homily has been based on the word that must he heard (4:2; NRSV: "message"), it is natural that the author should conclude with a characterization of the word. As a warning not to neglect the word, 4:12-13 corresponds to 2:1-4.

Both sentences are finely honed pieces of expressive prose, employing vivid imagery and a creative play on words—the word is "more cutting than any two-cutting sword" (v. 12 AT). The word is the subject only in verse 12; in verse 13 God is the subject. *Logos* ("word") appears at the beginning and end, but has a different meaning in each case.

◊ ◊ ◊ ◊

God's word is powerful in effecting what it promises; it also effectively judges disobedience. In making this point, the author uses descriptions of the word derived from the Old Testament and from Wisdom traditions (see Wis 18:15-16). Four statements in verse 12 offer complementary epithets and graphic images for God's powerful word:

(1) It is living because it comes from the living God (Heb 3:12; 9:14; 10:31; 12:22). Since Hebrews speaks of the living God as judge, the point here is not the life-giving power of the word (see Deut 32:47), but its ability to expose and judge sin. The complementary epithet "active" underlines the innate energy of the word as performative utterance.

(2) Though the wordplay is the author's own creation, the image of the word as a sharp sword is traditional. The mouth of the prophet is made "like a sharp sword" (Isa 49:2). Divine Wisdom personified is itself sharp, and wields the sword of God's command (Wis 7:22, 24; 18:15-16). Paul pictures the word as the sword of the Spirit (Eph 6:17; for the two-edged sword see Rev 1:16; 2:12).

(3) The word penetrates into a person's innermost being (Wis 1:6) in a way that no knife or sword can do. The division of "soul from spirit" and "joints from marrow" is not meant to define the psychological and physiological composition of humanity, but to picture the deep recesses of people's spiritual and physical being into which the word can penetrate.

(4) It judges in the sense that it critically discerns secret thoughts and intentions; God alone knows human hearts (Acts 1:24; 15:8), and can separate genuine from false.

The author easily moves from the word to God in verse 13, since the word bears God's own attributes. That nothing is hidden from God is acknowledged in apocalyptic and Wisdom literature. "All lies open and bare in your sight" (*1 Enoch* 9:5); the spirit of God "knows what is said, therefore those who utter unrighteous things will not escape notice" (Wis 1:7-8; cf. Rom 8:27; 1 Cor 4:5). "Laid bare" suggests the graphic image of the prisoner or sacrificial victim whose throat is exposed to a sharp blade. God's all-seeing eye renders all creatures exposed and defenseless. People must give account (literally, "word") to God who speaks the word to them.

The last phrase in verse 13 reflects the language of commerce (see Luke 16:2; Rom 14:12; 1 Pet 4:5). In this instance, giving account allows for no deception.

◊ ◊ ◊ ◊

For the author of Hebrews, all theology as speaking *about* God and speaking *to* God begins with the Word. By including himself in the warning of verse 13 he shows awareness of his own accountability, so any unfaithfulness on his part will incur the judgment of the word. Yet the main focus is on those who are the object of his pastoral concern. Forceful language and graphic imagery, as in other warnings (2:1-4; 6:4-8; 10:26-31; 12:25), betray deep concern that the readers have reached a crisis point. The word of promise can become the word of judgment.

THE SON AS MERCIFUL HIGH PRIEST (4:14–7:28)

The previous discourse pictured Christ as *faithful* High Priest and Son, and called the readers to faithfulness. Now the writer turns to the first epithet in 2:17 to demonstrate how Christ qualifies as *merciful* High Priest. This theme reaches its climax in the elaborate portrait of Christ as priest according to the order of Melchizedek in chapter 7.

There are echoes of 3:1 in 4:14 ("Jesus"; "high priest"; "heavens/heavenly"; "our confession"), yet 4:14-16 has its formal counterpart in 10:19-23 (see below). Thus, 4:14–7:28 is the first stanza in the elaborate treatment of Christ's high-priestly person and work in 4:14–10:31, the heart piece of Hebrews.

An opening exhortation (4:14-16) precedes an exposition of Christ's qualifications as compassionate High Priest (5:1-10 corresponds to 3:1-6). As in the previous discourse, the writer reverts to exhortation in order to summon the readers to spiritual maturity (5:11–6:3), and to issue a third warning against the spurning of what God offers (6:4-8). This appeal is grounded on a reminder of the certainty of God's promises (6:9-20). Exposition of Christ's Melchizedekian priesthood (7:1-28) brings the argument back to the proof of his qualifications that began in 5:1-10.

Major Appeal: Hold Your Confession and Draw Near to God (4:14-16)

This brief exhortation contains the key elements of the parenesis and characteristic vocabulary of Hebrews. The plea for immovable firmness in confessing Christ (v. 14*b*) is complemented by another that suggests movement to God's throne (v. 16*a*). The basis for each action is stated (vv. 14*a*, 15), and the second appeal concludes by stating the purpose of bold access into God's presence: the reception of mercy that is ensured through the offices of the merciful High Priest (2:17).

George H. Guthrie has pointed to the parallels between 4:14-16 and 10:19-23, which "represent the most striking use of *inclusio* in the book of Hebrews" (1994, 79). The parallels are as follows:

4:14-16	*10:19-23*
Since we have	Since we have
a great high priest	a great priest
through the heavens	through the curtain
Jesus	Jesus
(the Son) of God	(the house) of God
let us hold fast to our con-fession	let us hold fast to the con-fession
let us approach with boldness	let us approach with boldness

The *inclusio* serves as an indicator of the extent of the Letter's central statement.

First Proposition (v. 14*a*): Christ's priesthood has been alluded to in 2:17 and 3:1, but now becomes the writer's main theme. Yet Christ's sonship remains clearly in focus in 4:14 (see also 5:5, 8; 6:6; 7:3, 28; 10:29). The author can closely associate the titles Son and High Priest because he sees both as designating the status of Jesus in his exaltation, a truth stated in Scripture (5:5-6). While "Son" remains the prime confessional title, the writer now focuses on Jesus' role as High Priest, since it is open to treatment in terms of both his past and present saving activity.

Christ is "great high priest" (the phrase occurs also in 1 Macc 13:42) in an absolute sense, since he is above Aaron and his heirs in the old covenant (see chaps. 7–10). That he is the ultimate "great priest" (10:21) is due to his present status: He has "passed through the heavens." The traditional, cosmic-spatial description of Christ's glorification in terms of an ascent (cf. 7:26; Eph 4:10) equates with what Hebrews elsewhere expresses in cultic imagery: entry into the heavenly sanctuary (6:19; 9:24). Passage "through the heavens" is the presupposition of priestly intercession (v. 16).

First Appeal (v. 14b): The phrase "since we have" (v. 14a) denotes apprehension of a faith reality (see 7:26; 8:1; 10:19), one that is formally confessed in a credal statement (3:1; 10:23). To "hold fast" to the confession means to cling to him who is its content. Such faithfulness is the proper response to his own faithfulness (2:17; 3:2, 6).

Second Proposition (v. 15): The exaltation of Jesus as Son and High Priest does not mean his removal from those whose human nature he shares (2:14). Like any other human being, Jesus was subject to human weakness (see 5:2; 7:28; 11:34). He experienced the agony of suffering and the fear of death (2:15; 5:7). He was also susceptible to temptation.

The sympathy of the heavenly High Priest does not denote a psychological process that begins with the recollection of what he once endured. As one who *still* shares humanity, Jesus "suffers with" those who are weak and open to temptation. That is why he can give help (v. 16). The great difference between him and his siblings is that he was and remains "without sin." Within the context of his appeal for fidelity on the basis of Christ's own faithfulness, the author is again asserting that Jesus never broke faith with God, even in the face of suffering and death (2:13; 5:7). That is the great temptation facing the readers: failure to trust God's promises.

Second Appeal (v. 16): Since believers have a compassionate High Priest in God's presence, one who still fully identifies with them in their weakness, they can approach God with confidence.

It was the special right and duty of the priesthood in the old covenant to "draw near" to God to offer sacrifices and to make intercession for the people, though only the High Priest had access to the inner sanctuary (9:6-7). The repeated assertion that all believers in the new covenant can "approach" God (7:19, 25; 10:1, 22; 11:6; 12:22) implies that they have a priestly role. They can approach with boldness since the sin that separated them from God has been removed through Christ's atoning death. They can thus address God freely in prayer (cf. 3:6) and confidently make their own sacrifice of praise (12:28; 13:15-16).

Through Christ's high-priestly work, the throne of God—symbol of divine majesty and power—has become the "throne of grace." On the Day of Atonement, only the high priest could approach the throne of God's mercy seat in the Holy of Holies (Lev 16). The throne Christ once approached is now the throne he shares (8:1; 9:11-14). His finished work of purifying sinners (1:3) and his ongoing intercession (7:25) ensure that those who are in need will "receive mercy and find grace" at the right time.

◊ ◊ ◊ ◊

Those who are enduring a trial of faith do not have the threat of judgment on unfaithfulness as God's final word (4:12-13). All that is needed to endure the trial is given in him who is the content of the confession that the author shares with the readers (note the use of the first person in 4:14-16). The faithful High Priest has blazed the trail, so that these people can "pass through the heavens" with him into the very presence of God. Bold access and freedom of speech in God's presence presuppose that the God to whom pleas for help are addressed still shares in humanity. Divine mercy and grace are mediated through the perpetual intercession of the faithful High Priest.

Though Christ's *past* atoning work has been mentioned to this point (1:3; 2:11, 14-17), appeals have climaxed in 2:18 and 4:16 with reminders of his *present* role as source of help. It remains for the writer to develop more fully the qualifications of the exalted Son for his present office as "priest forever" (Ps 110:4).

Parenesis expressed in cultic terms suggests a cultic problem in the community. It is not the threat of outright denial, but failure to live faith boldly and to express it in worship where every need, whether personal or communal, can be placed in the hands of a God who still shares humanness.

Christ Qualified to Be Compassionate High Priest (5:1-10)

A shift in genre from exhortation to exposition moves the focus from the Christian community to its High Priest. The Letter now establishes Christ's priesthood on the background of the Old Testament priesthood. The two prime qualifications for his office are indicated: divine appointment and solidarity with those he serves.

The argument is presented with "concentric symmetry" (see Lane 1991, 111, though he is hardly right in suggesting that humility is the central thought):

A: The ministry of the old priesthood and its function (v. 1)
  B: The solidarity of the High Priest with his people
    (vv. 2-3)
    C: The necessity of appointment to this office (v. 4)
    C': The divine appointment of the Son and High Priest
      (vv. 5-6)
  B': The solidarity of the High Priest with his people
    (vv. 7-8)
A': The ministry of the new High Priest and its function
  (vv. 9-10)

There are significant parallels in the description of priestly functions in 5:1-3 and the function of Christ in 7:26-28:

5:1-3	*7:26-28*
every high priest	such a high priest
chosen from among mortals	separated from sinners
is put in charge	the word of the oath appoints
must offer sacrifice for his	no need to offer sacrifices
owns sins	. . . for his own sins and . . .
as well as those of the people.	those of the people.

Also common to both texts is the note that priests in the old order are subject to weakness (5:2; 7:28). Christ's ability to suffer with those who are beset by weakness (4:15; 5:7-8) is not repeated in 7:26-28 but presupposed in the reference to his high-priestly intercession in 7:25. In short, 5:1-3 and 7:(25)26-28 complement each other to form an *inclusio* that brackets the first detailed description of Christ's priesthood in 5:1–7:28.

Scholars have debated whether credal or hymnic sources underlie 5:7-10 (for surveys of the discussion see Attridge 1989, 147-48; Ellingworth 1993, 284-86; Lane 1991, 112-13). Attempts to reconstruct an original Christ-hymn remain unconvincing since verse 7 reflects the language of the psalms, and verses 8-10 contain much that is characteristic of the language of Hebrews. We may call 5:8-10 (like 1:3-4) hymnic in a broad sense insofar as it contains the progression preexistence-humiliation-exaltation that is characteristic of a Christ-hymn, but the final product is the author's own creation.

The Old Priesthood (vv. 1-4): Present tenses describe in general terms the legal basis of the high-priestly office. The high priest functioned as an intermediary, representing God to humanity and humanity to God (v. 1). He had to be "chosen from among mortals" in order to act "on their behalf," and he had to be "put in charge" of his office by God (the circumlocutory passive implies this) to act on God's behalf. It is in this capacity that he offers "gifts and sacrifices"—the latter is a comprehensive phrase for priestly duty also in 8:3 and 9:9, and is not meant to distinguish between various kinds of offerings, though the author is primarily concerned with the sacrifices of Yom Kippur (v. 3; Lev 16).

Divine appointment did not remove the high priest from the common lot. Identification with those he served was the second requirement for office (v. 2). Whereas the Son had to be made like his siblings to endure testing and to suffer with them in their weakness (4:15; 2:14-18), every high priest was naturally one with his fellows in being "subject to weakness," that is, susceptible to temptation *and* to sin (see 7:28). He had to "deal gently" with the sins of the "ignorant and wayward" since harsh judgment on others would mean self-condemnation. Yet as God's representative, he could in no way condone willful sin (The Old Testament distinction between unintentional and deliberate sin, where only the former could be atoned for by sacrifice [Lev 4:2; 5:15; Num 15:22-31], will later become important in the author's argument concerning the unforgivable sin [see 6:4-8; 10:26-31].).

Leviticus 16:6, 11, 15-17 pictures the high priest on the Day of Atonement first making sacrifice for himself and his household, then for the people. This is recalled in Heb 5:3 (cf. 9:7) not to provide a contrast with Christ (see 7:27), but to underscore the high priest's solidarity with sinners. Reverting to the theme of divine appointment in verse 4 ("called by God" = "put in charge" in v. 1), the author indicates his chief concern: the question of legitimacy. He seems to assume a knowledge of illegitimate claimants to the office in the intertestamental period, people who "presumed to take this honor." The Hasmonean priest-kings did not belong to the line of Aaron!

The New High Priest (vv. 5-10): While 5:1-4 uses the present tense to depict the conditions under which the old priesthood was in force, verses 5-10 use the past tense to describe what has happened to replace it. Continuity between the old and the new order ("so also Christ . . .") demands that the new High Priest be appointed by God, and that he carry out his office in solidarity with humanity. Divine appointment is asserted by means of the Letter's key christological texts (Pss 2:7 and 110:4), here quoted together (Heb 5:5-6). The statement that Christ "did not glorify himself" echoes the note in the previous verse that the old office could not simply be claimed by anyone.

Psalm 2:7 is not quoted as a word spoken to the preexistent Son, nor does it recall a moment in Jesus' earthly ministry, such as his baptism (Matt 3:17). The "today" of the psalm is seen as fulfilled in the moment of his accession in glory; divine appointment is suggested already by the use of the royal title Christ, that is, "anointed one." Psalm 2:7 was cited in Heb 1:5 to show the transcendent dignity of the *exalted* Son, and alluded to again in 7:28 in the same context. The structure of 5:1-10 leads to the same conclusion; verses 5-6 and 10 complement each other in the same way as do verses 1 and 4. The issue is Christ's installation into an office, his authority to function as the royal Son.

His acclamation as Son also means his installation as the heavenly High Priest (v. 6). Psalm 110:4 is quoted for the first time as the key to understanding the uniqueness of the Son's high-priestly office (see Heb 5:10; 6:20; 7:3, 11, 15, 17, 21). This priesthood lasts "forever," continuing to be held and exercised by one person who requires no heirs and successors (7:23-24). It belongs to a different order, a new arrangement or dispensation (7:11-23).

Psalm 110 first speaks of the accession of the royal Son to his throne; so verse 1 has been alluded to in Heb 1:3, 13 (see also 8:1; 10:12)—priestly and royal actions are linked already in 1:3. Second, Melchizedek is both king and high priest (Gen 14:18), so Christ who resembles him (7:15) must hold both offices.

Verses 7-8 return to the theme of verses 2-3. Christ's identification with mortals in their weakness included suffering and death. Having stood the test of obedience as Son, he has demonstrated his ability and right to function as the compassionate High Priest (4:15-16). The "days of his flesh" when he faced death (v. 7) include his entire earthly life in which shared humanity's "flesh and blood" (2:14), and its fear of death (2:15).

References to fervent pleas, suffering, and death, but also obedient submission (vv. 7-8) may seem to recall the passion story. In Gethsemane Jesus pleads for the removal of suffering, yet submits (Matt 26:36-39 and par.). That he was "heard because of his reverent submission" could recall either the sending of an angel to comfort and strengthen him (Luke 22:43-44), or the divine voice from heaven when he was troubled by the prospect of death (John 12:27-28).

References to the gospel tradition become unnecessary when the special accents of verse 7 are viewed in context. First, the picture of Christ in suffering borrows from the language of the psalms. In particular, there are strong parallels with Ps 116:1-8 where the psalmist cries to God for help in distress and is heard (see also Pss 22:24; 31:22; 39:12). Second, verse 7 pictures Jesus' humanity in two ways. Like his siblings, he was put to the test (Heb 2:14-15;

4:15). Yet even in suffering he did not cease trusting in God (see 2:13) as "the one who was able to save him from death." The latter phrase describes God as the rescuer of the righteous (Ps 33:19; Hos 13:14; Jas 4:12). How God heard Jesus' cries and saved him (see Heb 13:20) is not the issue. Third, that Jesus "offered up" fervent pleas to God parallels the statement about the high priest's offerings in verse 3. That he was heard simply indicates the acceptability of his offering.

Obedient submission in suffering was the necessary prelude to the High Priest's enthronement (v. 8). "Although he was a Son" is a concessive clause that hints at a paradox: Jesus died as one who was already the eternal Son of God (1:1-3)—not merely one who was destined to be acclaimed as Son (5:5). The Son's solidarity with humanity required his entry into the school of suffering (the language of pedagogy will be continued in 5:11–6:3). His obedience had to be put to the test (see Heb 4:15) to equip him for his office as merciful High Priest (5:9-10).

The participles that introduce verses 9-10 mark two parallel statements. Both refer to the Son's accession as heavenly High Priest, but the "perfection" of the Son links his final office with the prior experience of suffering and death (as in 2:10). Suffering was the path that led to glory (12:2), the means by which the Son was brought to his appointed goal: the role of compassionate High Priest. As in 1:4 (also Phil 2:9), the giving of a name designates installation into an office, and divine acknowledgment of authority to function in that office (v. 10 corresponds to v. 1). It is in his office as Melchizedekian Priest (see v. 6) that the active obedience of the Son produces an "eternal salvation" (v. 9; the phrase is possibly borrowed from Isa 45:17). Like the eternal inheritance (9:15) that is part of the eternal covenant (13:20), ongoing rescue from every need (4:16) as well as final salvation are offered by one who is "priest forever" (v. 6).

◊ ◊ ◊ ◊

The beginning of the Letter depicted the status of the Son in terms of his relationship to God (1:1-14), then to humanity (2:5-18). The summary statement of Christ's high-priestly status and role in

5:5-10 follows a similar pattern: first his divine appointment is asserted (vv. 5-6), then his solidarity with humanity (vv. 7-8). By again focusing on the present status of the heavenly High Priest at the end (vv. 9-10), the author indicates that his prime concern is with Christ as now confessed: He is "the source of eternal salvation." But as yet there is no developed statement about Christ's sacrifice to match the statement about the sacrifices offered by the old priesthood (vv. 1-3).

Christ's Sonship was illustrated by means of contrast with the angels (1:4-14; 2:4-16) and with Moses (3:1-6). His priestly office is depicted on the background of the old priestly order. At first, the argument is one of analogy: Christ fulfills the prerequisites of any high priest. It remains to be shown how he supersedes all Levitical priests as the high priest after the order of Melchizedek (5:10 announces the theme of chap. 7).

Meanwhile the author pastorally reminds his readers that the pioneer and perfecter of faith knows their weaknesses, temptations, and trials. He is *for them* in their suffering because he was once *with them* in suffering.

A Call to Spiritual Maturity (5:11–6:12), Including *Third Warning:* Do Not Spurn the Heavenly Gifts (6:4-8)

In 5:11–6:20 the focus shifts from the High Priest to the community. The reference to Christ as High Priest according to the order of Melchizedek in 6:20 forms an *inclusio* with 5:10, as well as a link to 7:1. Thus, 5:11–6:20 forms a parenetic introduction to the Letter's centerpiece, the exposition of Christ's highpriesthood in 7:1–10:18, and finds its counterpart in the concluding exhortation of 10:19-39, though 10:19-23 also parallels 4:14-16.

Structural indicators suggest that 5:11–6:12 is a discrete unit within the exhortation of 5:11–6:20. There are framing references to being "dull/sluggish" (5:11 and 6:12; the Greek adjective, rendered differently in each case by the NRSV, appears only here in the NT). Second, the link-word "promise" in 6:12-13 serves to facilitate the transition from one section to the next. Finally, 5:11–6:12 has a balanced structure that is designed for rhetorical impact; it contains hyperbole (5:12), seeming contradiction (5:12 and 6:1; 5:11 and 6:12), and graphic imagery (5:13-14; 6:6-8).

The central statement is a description of apostasy that functions as a warning (6:4-8). This is prefaced by a description of the readers' present situation, characterized as immaturity (5:11–6:3; these verses are framed by references to future instruction). The implication that the present spiritual malaise of the community will have disastrous results, if left unaddressed, becomes explicit in 6:4-8. Positive words of commendation and encouragement (6:9-12) create a balanced assessment of the community's situation, and ensure that the opening words will have a positive effect. The pattern of warning followed by promise repeats the scheme found in 3:7–4:11.

A Call to Maturity (5:11–6:3): Using stock phrases and imagery, the writer adopts the stance of the teacher who expresses strong regret over lack of progress beyond "basic elements" (5:12)—"the basic teaching" that has provided the "foundation" for faith (6:1)—to deeper perceptions ("by this time" in 5:12 shows that the readers are not recent converts). The writer gives notice that he will develop the theme of Christ's priesthood further. His theme is "hard to explain" not because of his inability as teacher or the difficulty of the subject matter, but because his audience has "become dull in understanding." Mental dullness as failure to listen properly is a problem hinted at elsewhere (see 2:1; 3:7, 15; 4:1-2).

In what sense should the readers now be teachers, and in what sense should they still be taught? Since the "basic elements" of faith are listed in 6:1-2 but not retaught, the inference cannot be that the readers simply lack knowledge. The letter has presupposed a great deal of knowledge, whether in the form of a confession (3:1; 4:14), of the Scriptures as "the oracles of God" (for the phrase in this sense see Acts 7:38; Rom 3:2; 1 Pet 4:11), or of Christian teaching in general.

The imagery of verses 12c-13 suggests growth in experiential rather than cognitive terms. Metaphors of milk and solid food (1 Cor 3:1-2 and 1 Pet 2:2 show different applications) are common in hellenistic moral philosophy, especially in describing stages of instruction. Here they denote more than the natural diet of the infant and the adult; they stand for the difference in powers of discernment between the infant (v. 13) and the "mature," meaning adults (v. 14).

More difficult is the phrase in verse 13: "word of righteousness." One suggestion reads the phrase as a Semitism for "right speech"; the writer is speaking of being "unskilled" in talking clearly or in understanding correct speech. But the parallelism of verses 13 and 14 suggests that the "word of righteousness" equals "strong food" in the sense of instruction, whether doctrinal or ethical, that can be put to the test by experience. This interpretation makes better sense than others that find a reference to the teaching on Christ as God's gift of righteousness (P. Hughes 1987, 191), on Christology generally (Williamson 1970, 288-92), or readiness for martyrdom (Lane 1991).

Despite the assertion of their immaturity in verse 12, the author assumes that his readers can progress to "perfection" (6:1), to distinctions that mature adults can make (the Greek words for "made perfect" in 5:9, "mature" in 5:14, and "perfection" in 6:1 come from the same stem). The "teaching about" (not of) Christ must refer to the first instruction that brought the readers to their conversion (see vv. 4-5). This teaching is not to be left behind as irrelevant, let alone replaced by something else. It remains foundational for deeper insights into the faith and its practical consequences.

There is nothing distinctively Christian in the catechetical topics in verses 2-3 (the list is hardly exhaustive). This may reflect the fact that primary instruction in the faith was developed on the basis of the Old Testament (the "oracles of God"; 5:12). The Hebrew Bible often records the call to repentance and faith. Ritual washings and priestly laying on of hands belonged to the old cultus (Lev 16:21; Num 8:12; 19). Belief in a final resurrection and judgment, though rudimentary in the Old Testament (Dan 12:2-3), became firm elements in Pharisaic thought.

Specifically Christian instruction would have related all topics to Christ. Repentance and faith are fundamental elements in conversion. More specifically, repentance *from* "dead works" would mean a turning away from the old life that led to death, one that old cultic regulations were powerless to deal with, while faith in God represents the new confidence that the believer enjoys in worshiping the living God (see Heb 9:14). "Instruction about baptisms" (or "washings") would distinguish between old purificatory rites that could effect only an external cleansing (9:10), and the perfect washing in the blood of Christ and the water of baptism (9:22-27; 10:22). Instruction concerning "laying on of hands" probably refers to the confirmation of the gift of the Spirit (see Acts 8:17; 9:17; 19:6). Finally, Christian instruction in eschatology would concentrate on Christ's resurrection as the foundation for the general resurrection.

Whatever their precise meaning, these catechetical topics are foundational in the sense that they relate to the "knowledge of the truth" first received by Christians (see 10:26), and provide the basis for the deeper insights into which the author wants to lead his readers. "If God permits" (6:3) acknowledges that the attainment of such maturity (6:1) depends on God's blessing.

A Strong Warning (6:4-8): Failure to progress can result in regress. The event of conversion, previously alluded to in terms of primal catechesis (vv. 1-2), is now described as primal experience. Four participles ("enlightened"; "tasted"; "shared"; "tasted") underline the greatness of God's gifts (vv. 4-5). Enlightenment describes the first experience of the gospel that sets the convert's life in a new direction (see 10:32); the image of light suggests both new knowledge and a new way of life (see 2 Cor 4:6; Eph 1:18; 1 John 1:5-10). There are probably allusions to baptism in verses 4-5 ("once" suggests a unique experience), but "the enlightened" became a technical expression only later (see Attridge 1989, 169). The additional three clauses vividly express the experience of salvation as receiving a gift from God, as sharing in the Spirit's gifts (see 2:4), and as relishing the gospel of God's goodness (see Ps 34:8; 1 Pet 2:3). Believers experience now, in the working of the Spirit who produces miracles, the "powers" of "the coming world" (Heb 2:4-5).

In contrast to the reception of God's good gifts stands the dire possibility of absolute and final rejection (v. 6). The Letter has already warned against drifting away from or neglecting salvation (2:1-3), and of falling away from the living God and being hardened in sin (3:12-13). As the deliberate rejection of salvation, apostasy is not to be confused with sins of weakness (5:2; 10:26). Two phrases using present participles express the terrible significance of apostasy as a final stance. Apostates take their stand with those who first killed Jesus; in their contempt they join those who stood under the cross and mocked him (Matt 27:39-44).

Only of those who have finally rejected the Son does the writer say: "It is impossible to restore [them] . . . to repentance." The logic of this assertion, which has caused problems for both the early church and modern commentators, must be gained from the total argument of 6:1-6. "It is impossible" is an absolute, unqualified statement; it is not to be reduced to rhetorical hyperbole in order to rescue God's boundless grace from limitation. At issue is not what is possible for God. Nor is the writer concerned with the ancient question of whether postbaptismal sins can be forgiven.

Second, the particle "for" in verse 4a links verses 4-6 with the claim that only the teaching about Christ provides a foundation for repentance and faith (v. 1). The apostate rejects this foundation, making true repentance completely impossible. At issue is not whether a second repentance is possible, but on what basis any repentance is possible. By definition, apostasy means self-exclusion from renewal and faith.

Speaking again as a Wisdom teacher, the author uses an agricultural image with scriptural overtones to illustrate the difference between faith and apostasy, and between divine approval and final judgment (vv. 7-8). God originally blessed the land so that it would produce crops (Gen 1:11). After the Fall it was cursed to bear thorns and thistles (Gen 3:17-18). Israel was God's vineyard that he carefully cultivated, yet it was condemned to growing briars and thorns when it failed to produce fruit (Isa 5:1-7). A community of faith is like a field that soaks in the rain and produces good crops; it thrives on God's gifts and care (see Deut 11:11-12), and continues to be blessed. Conversely, a faithless community will produce the noxious growth that must be consigned to the fire (a symbol for eschatological judgment also in Heb 10:27 and 12:29), while the threat of God's curse hangs over the apostate community itself.

A Word of Encouragement (6:9-12): A *captatio benevolentiae* marks a change from warning to encouragement; the pastor takes over from the stern teacher. His "beloved" give him confidence, despite fears for their spiritual welfare (v. 9). They display the "crop" (see v. 7) that God's saving action and blessing have produced: love, hope, and faith (vv. 10-12; cf. 1 Cor 13:13; Col 4:1-5; 1 Thess 1:3). "Better things" (blessing, not curse; vv. 7-8) can be expected of them as heirs of God's better gifts (see 7:19, 22; 8:6; 9:23; 10:34; 11:16, 35, 40).

The community's past practice of love is on record (6:10). According to 10:32-34, it showed mutual care and support of the "saints," that is, fellow members of the church, in a period of extreme suffering that included ridicule, imprisonment, and loss of property. Those acts of love, done also for God's sake, continue into the present (6:10*b*), though the author implies elsewhere that the fires of love need to be fanned (10:24; 13:1-4). More pressing is the need for each member to show equal zeal in clinging to Christian hope "to the end" (see 3:14). "Full assurance of hope" (6:11) is simply the extension into the future of "full assurance of faith" (10:22).

Sluggishness, resulting from slowness to learn (see 5:11), is the chief threat to the community's welfare. By inviting the readers to be imitators (6:12), the author again adopts the stance of the teacher (see 1 Cor 4:16; 11:1; Phil 3:17; 4:9; 1 Thess 1:6; 2 Thess 3:7, 9). The model of faith and patience is not himself. Abraham and other past heroes, including the community's own leaders (6:13-15; 11:4–12:3; 13:7), model a tenacious faith that endures to receive what God has promised.

◊ ◊ ◊ ◊

In what is one of the most difficult passages in Hebrews, the author uses all of his persuasive powers—rhetorical, pedagogical, and pastoral—to lead his readers from immaturity to maturity, from basic knowledge to deeper perception, from flagging zeal to fervent hope. He has shown how Christ learned from his experience in the school of suffering (5:8). Now the question is whether his readers have progressed beyond the fundamentals of the faith to that Christian wisdom that marks them as adults in the faith.

The cause of the community's lethargy is failure to listen properly (5:11). This may be partly due to the passage of time (5:12), but allusions to earlier works of love, performed within a suffering community (6:10), suggest that external pressure is contributing to the present malaise. What the writer fears is a final failure of nerve as the community faces a continuing threat.

The reminder of their first instruction and of the nature of their conversion experience does not suggest that the readers are in danger of false teaching. They are immature in not making proper distinctions (5:14) between what is spiritually healthy and what is injurious. If the listing of catechetical topics in verses 2-3 is formulated in such a general way as to suggest themes that could belong to Jewish instruction, the question is whether the readers can recall what is distinctively *Christian* about faith's foundations.

Thus, 6:4-6 is not a general statement about the restoration of sinners (see Attridge 1989, 168-69, for a survey of this question in the early church), but a stern warning of the dire consequences of abandoning the only foundation there is for repentance and faith. Total commitment can be expected of those who have experienced the "heavenly gift" (6:4, 7). The fate of others who have not received the gift is not addressed.

The Certainty of God's Promises (6:13-20)

Exposition (last in 5:1-10) replaces exhortation as the author offers scriptural proof (Gen 22:16, 17) for the reliability of God's promises as the basis of hope. The focus shifts from the needs of the community to God's actions in the past. References to God's promise and to Abraham as a paradigm of faith (6:13) provide linguistic and thematic links with the preceding parenesis (6:12). The concluding reference to the Son as Melchizedekian High Priest (6:20) recalls the first announcement of a theme (5:10) that is about to be developed from 7:1 on.

Whereas the previous section was markedly pedagogical, 6:13-18 is full of legal terms: to "swear" an "oath" (vv. 13-17); "confirmation" and "dispute" (v. 16); to "show" in the sense of giving proof; to "guarantee" (v. 17); "unchangeable" in the sense of irrevocable; and to "prove false" in the sense of saying what is invalid (vv. 17-18). In verses 18 and 20 the writer moves to cultic terminology in anticipation of the full treatment of Christ's high-priestly person and work. Psalm 110:4 is God's legally binding oath that establishes a new priesthood.

◊ ◊ ◊ ◊

Abraham is an obvious prototype for those who call themselves his descendants (Heb 2:16). The prominence given to the patriarch in Hebrews (apart from 6:13-15, see 7:4-10; 11:8-19) reflects his standing in ancient Jewish and Christian thought. Hebrews cites Gen 22:16-17 to focus on the divine promise as the solid basis of patient endurance. Though Abraham remains an exemplary figure (the omission from the quotation of any reference to his "seed" in Heb 6:14 restricts attention to the patriarch himself), the stress lies on God's promise.

After showing unquestioning readiness to obey God's command to sacrifice Isaac, the son of promise (Gen 22:12), Abraham received a confirmation and extension of earlier promises of blessing (12:2-3; 15:5; 22:16-18; for the importance of the sacrifice of Isaac in the early synagogue and church, see Swetnam 1981, 23-75). That God "swore by himself" (see also Exod 32:13; Ps 89:35; Isa 45:23; Jer 22:5) is a feature of the Genesis narrative picked up also by Philo (*Leg. All.* 3.203). Whereas Philo goes on to interpret the oath as making Abraham's faith easier (see also *Abr.* 273), Hebrews sees it as underscoring the irrevocable validity of the promise. The two emphases are not far removed. Our writer sees another oath as both proving the reliability of a divine promise and as providing encouragement to believers to grasp what is promised (6:17-18).

The author is fully aware of the tension between promise and fulfillment in the Abraham story. Though Isaac was born as promised (Gen 12:2; 15:5), and though the promise of wider blessing was reiterated after Isaac's rescue from death (Gen 22:1-17), Abraham had to live without seeing fulfillment in the form of many descendants and possession of an earthly land (Heb 11:39). Isaac was restored to him "figuratively speaking" (11:19). So Abraham "obtained the promise" only *after* living his whole life as an example of patient endurance (6:15).

Verse 16 establishes two universal principles concerning the swearing of oaths. First, it means calling on a higher authority to attest the truth of what is said. Old Testament law required that oaths be sworn only "before the LORD" and by his name (Exod 22:11; Deut 6:13; 10:20); Abraham himself called on God in this way (Gen 14:22; 21:24). Second, an oath confirms the truth of a statement in any debate. "Matters in doubt are settled by an oath" (Philo *Somn.* 1.12).

God's oath to Abraham is cited in order to point to an even more important oath that is still valid. The "heirs of the promise" (v. 17) are not Abraham's immediate descendants, but "we" (vv. 18-20) who "inherit the promises" (v. 12). That God has no one greater than himself by whom to swear has been established (v. 13). Now the accent falls on God's absolute reliability.

It is not immediately clear what oath is referred to in verse 17, but the parallels between 6:13-20 and 7:17-21 suggest that the author is thinking of the declaration of the Son as High Priest (5:6; 7:17, 21). That oath is the guarantee that his will is constant and not fickle. So to confess Christ as the heavenly High Priest is to assert that "he who has promised is faithful" (10:23; see also 11:11).

That God does not change his mind or lie is asserted in the Old Testament (e.g., Num 23:19; 1 Sam 15:29; Ps 89:35) and by later Judaism (see Attridge 1989, 181). The "two unchangeable things" (6:18) that demonstrate the unchangeableness of God's purpose are hardly Ps 110:4 *and* Gen 22:17 (or Ps 2:7), but the first text as both promise and oath. God's word gives a secure refuge from all uncertainties. The objective character of hope is underscored: it lies before believers. All they need do is "cling" to it (not "seize" it as in the NRSV)—the verb is the same as in 4:14 where the readers are told to "hold fast" to their confession (cf. 10:23). Hope is objective because it is focused on a person (vv. 19-20).

The nautical metaphor of the anchor (v. 19a) serves the transition from a legal to a cultic frame of reference—the term "steadfast" (Gk. *bebaios*) also has legal connotations. Hope provides present stability and assurance in the storms of life in that it follows Jesus who has entered the "inner shrine behind the curtain," that is, into the heavenly sanctuary. Just as the high priest on Yom Kippur passed through the curtain that separated the Holy Place from the Holy of Holies (see Lev 16:2), so Christ has passed through the veil separating us from the innermost sanctuary of God's presence (v. 20: cf. 9:1-14; 10:19-21). He has blazed a trail as forerunner and pioneer of salvation that others can follow (2:10; cf. 12:1-4). The phrase "on our behalf" alludes to his perfect sacrifice for all sin (9:11-12; 10:12), as well as to his office of continual intercession (7:25). Christian hope is thus firmly anchored to God's own throne to which the Son has been exalted as Melchizedekian High Priest (see 5:6, 10). The word "forever" is now placed last since it will be the focus of special attention in chapter 7.

◊ ◊ ◊ ◊

This section again shows how Hebrews understands Scripture as past and present promise. The author placards Ps 110:4 as an oath that continues to confirm the Son's appointment as High Priest. It was spoken in the past, but remains as ratification of a present situation that is filled with promise for those coming into God's presence to seek help (Heb 2:18; 4:14-16; 7:25). Every promise already realized in Jesus, the forerunner, confirms a final promise that will become reality when Christians reach the end that he has reached (6:19-20). The doctrine of Christ as heavenly High Priest is promise for the present and the future.

Far from being a digression, 6:13-20 is a fitting introduction to the teaching for mature Christians (cf. 6:1) that now follows. The writer has shown that the confession to Christ as High Priest (4:14) is the confession of a hope by which the redeemed can now enter God's presence in priestly service (7:19; 10:23). The full implications of that confession must now be spelled out.

The Superiority of Melchizedek as High Priest (7:1-10)

Chapter 7 is exposition in the form of homiletical midrash. Specific details in biblical texts are interpreted and applied to show how they point to a greater reality. Following the principle of *gezerah shawah*, the writer links Gen 14:17-20 with Ps 110:4 by way of the common element of Melchizedek. His superiority over the Levitical priesthood must be demonstrated (7:1-10) before the theme announced in 5:5, 10 and 6:20 can be developed (7:11-28).

The logic of the argument in 7:1-10 presupposes other hermeneutical principles. First, the author works not with allegory but typology. Melchizedek becomes a type or model of Christ. Second, like the rabbis and Philo, the author assumes that the silence of Scripture has special meaning (see 7:3, 8). Third, the argument from the lesser to the greater is implied without being explicitly stated (cf. 2:2-3; 9:13-14; 10:28-29; 12:9, 25). Though great (vv. 4, 7), Melchizedek points to one even greater.

The mention of Melchizedek meeting Abraham in verses 1*a*, 10 (in Gen 14:17 it is actually the king of Sodom who meets the patriarch) forms an *inclusio*. There is a certain symmetry in the section (blessing in vv. 1*b* and 6-7; the tithe in vv. 2 and 4-5), but the statements about Melchizedek as priest forever (vv. 3, 8) and the final lesson drawn from the payment of tithes (vv. 9-10*a*) fall outside a neat chiastic structure.

The Meeting (vv. 1-2*a*): The writer cites what, for him, are key phrases of Gen 14:17-20, making small stylistic changes and highlighting the meeting of Melchizedek with Abraham. Abraham, returning home from pursuing and defeating the four foreign kings who had captured his nephew Lot, was blessed by the king of Salem who had come out of the city bearing gifts of bread and wine. In return, Abraham gave Melchizedek a tenth of the spoils of war.

Though the author of Hebrews probably assumes that Salem means Jerusalem (see Ps 76:2), he is interested only in the person, not the place. For him, the true and eternally important Jerusalem is the heavenly city (Heb 12:22). He is not interested in the question of how this priest-king could have known the true God whose self-revelation was as yet restricted to the patriarch. Only Melchizedek's mysterious person and the implications of giving a blessing and receiving a tithe are important.

The Meaning of Melchizedek's Person (vv. 2*b*, 3): According to Old Testament and Jewish thinking, a name is more than an identifying label; it may denote the origin, nature, function, or destiny of a person. So the name and title of Melchizedek must have special significance (v. 2*b*). "King of righteousness" and "king of peace"—Philo (*Leg. All.* 3.79) and Josephus (*Ant.* 1 §180) have similar popular etymologies—evoke messianic connotations; righteousness and peace are marks of the age of the Messiah (Ps 85:10; Isa 9:6-7; Jer 23:5; Dan 9:24; Zech 9:9-10). While the writer may be hinting that Melchizedek also prefigures the royal Messiah, he is finally interested only in his priestly office.

In Israel and early Judaism, the right to exercise priestly functions depended on an unbroken ancestral record. Legitimacy on the basis of Levitical lineage became a key issue after the Exile (see Ezra 2:61-63; Neh 7:63-65). The point of verse 3 is that Melchizedek stands outside the Levitical priesthood. That he is "without genealogy" means there is no record of his priestly descent. In that sense he is "without father, without mother." Because his birth and death are not recorded, he can be described as "having neither beginning of days nor end of life."

Suggestions that verse 3 is to be read on the background of hellenistic mythology run into a number of significant difficulties. "Without mother or father" could, in the hellenistic world, denote a person of divine or semidivine origin (see Neyrey 1991). But Philo (*Ebr.* 61; *Heres* 62) can speak of Sarah as "motherless" because the biblical text does not record her mother. The author of Hebrews, like Philo and the rabbis, is making a point based on the silence of the sacred text (Demarest 1976, 133-34; Horton 1976, 153). A reading of Heb 7:3, which turns Melchizedek into a suprahuman figure, runs counter to the Letter's stress on the uniqueness of Christ.

Melchizedek's lack of lineage marks him as belonging to a different order of priesthood. He remains a priest forever only as an antitype that foreshadows an eternal priesthood. While the psalm verse says that the anointed King is like Melchizedek, the situation is here reversed. Literally translated, "resembling the Son of God" means "having been made [sc. by God] to resemble the Son." Melchizedek "remains" only as a typological model, deliberately brought into the biblical narrative to point to the only one who truly remains a priest forever (7:24-25).

The confession of Christ is the basis of the author's portrait of Melchizedek. That is why the title "Son of God" frames the discussion of Christ's unique priesthood (7:3, 28). It is a reminder of the community's own formal confession (3:1; 4:14; 10:23) as the starting point for all christological reflection.

The Meaning of the Two Actions (vv. 4-10): Deductions are drawn from the actions of the two characters in the Genesis narrative. The aim is to prove how "great" Melchizedek is in terms of his absolute superiority over a later order of priests that was descended from Abraham—the title "patriarch" (v. 4) suggests that he is a representative figure and introduces the idea of ancestry that is prominent in what follows (vv. 5-6, 9-10).

Abraham's payment to Melchizedek of a tenth of his war booty is seen as having a significance beyond the surface meaning of the text (vv. 4b-6a). It is, literally, an anomalous act, one that deviates from the norm. A commandment or statute of the law (Num 18:21-24; "law" has negative connotations in Hebrews, suggesting superseded cultic regulations; see 7:12, 16-19, 28; 8:4; 9:22; 10:1, 8) specifies that Levites have the right to receive tithes in return for their service—the present tense states the general rule found in Scripture. For Hebrews, the "descendants of Levi" are those who hold the "priestly office" by human descent—ultimately, from the patriarch Abraham (see vv. 9-10). But (the contrast in v. 6a is emphatic) Melchizedek is outside the Law. He does not receive the tithe from Abraham as a representative of the Levitical priesthood; he does not even belong to the descendants of the patriarch: He is without their genealogy (see v. 3).

That Melchizedek's priesthood is therefore superior is argued on the basis of the blessing he gave to Abraham (vv. 6b-7, picking up v. 1b). To call down divine blessing is a priestly function (see the Aaronic benediction in Num 6:24-26), but not exclusively so.

Before he met Melchizedek, God had promised Abraham the special blessing of descendants (see Heb 6:14), so one could expect the patriarch, as the recipient of blessing, to bless the priest-king of Salem. In fact, the opposite is the case. The writer assumes that the act of blessing implies a greater status (the axiom of v. 7 is only a general truth and not to be pressed). Thus, the unassailable conclusion: Melchizedek is superior to Abraham and to Abraham's descendants, the Levitical priests.

Verse 8 draws a further contrast between the two orders of priesthood on the basis of the scriptural testimony cited in verse 3. At issue is the question of duration. Those who receive tithes according to the Law are marked by mortality; theirs is a priesthood by succession. Melchizedek's priesthood is free from temporal limitation because Gen 14 says that "he lives." No end to his life is mentioned, so he remains a "priest forever." He represents an abiding order now found in the eternal High Priest who has no successors (see 7:23-24), and whose office is based not on Law but on the "power of an indestructible life" (7:16).

The final statement (vv. 9-10) is more afterthought than climactic argument—"one might even say" shows readiness to admit that the logic is not compelling. Assuming the idea of corporate solidarity, the author suggests that the unborn Levi who later received tithes actually paid a tithe to Melchizedek through his ancestor Abraham. The inferior paid a tithe to the superior (see v. 7); Melchizedek's priesthood predates that of Levi. According to the principle that what is older or original is more authoritative and enduring, the conclusion must be that the priesthood of Melchizedek endures beyond that of Levi.

◊ ◊ ◊ ◊

This section is not the main argument, but an introduction to it. It seeks to establish the superiority of Melchizedek's priesthood over the Levitical priesthood before showing how Ps 110:4 must refer to Christ as eternal High Priest who is above the Levitical order. The writer is here backtracking to supply a foundational argument for two other arguments that he has already made. A new priesthood was first prefigured in the person of Melchizedek, then promised by God's solemn oath (6:17-20), and finally inaugurated with the enthronement of the Son as heavenly High Priest (5:5, 9-10; 6:20).

Given the hermeneutical principles with which he works, the author's typological interpretation and application of Gen 14:17-20 are consistent. Whether material from current Jewish traditions (surveyed by Demarest and Horton; see also Hurst 1990, 52-60; Attridge 1989, 192-95; Lane 1991, 160-63) has helped to elucidate his argument has been the subject of much debate. In the 11QMelch fragment from Qumran, Melchizedek is an angel who carries out judgment. While he may have royal features (lines 15-26), he has no specifically priestly functions, and there is no reference to the two texts important for Hebrews (Gen 14 and Ps 110). Philo's allegorizing of Gen 14 (he never refers to Ps 110 in the relevant passages; see *Leg. All.* 3.79, 82; *Congr.* 99; *Abr.* 235) is not interested in Melchizedek as a historical figure, nor in his priestly office. He is only a symbol of the divine revealing Word. For Josephus (*Ant.* 1 §180-191), Melchizedek is simply the first priest in the biblical record, one who built a temple in Jerusalem. The Targums and rabbinic literature reflect the view that his meeting with Abraham meant a transference of the priesthood to Abraham and his heirs—the very opposite of what Hebrews insists. Speculation on Melchizedek in later Gnostic (*Melchizedek* fragment, Nag Hammadi Codex 9.1) and patristic literature, depicting him as a heavenly figure, shows the further development of a tradition that is far removed from Heb 7:1-10.

Three factors render unlikely any direct dependence of Hebrews on a Melchizedek tradition. The author's theological method is to work with what is well known and accepted. He derives every lesson from Gen 14:17-20—even the "eternity" of Melchizedek is deduced by way of a typological reading of the text. Second, Melchizedek is made to conform not to a tradition about him, but to Christ. Finally, the situation of the audience demands more than speculations about Melchizedek as a mythical heavenly figure. He is a person of flesh and blood who points forward to a greater person who is likewise human, and who has become heavenly High

Priest only after suffering (Heb 5:8-10). The priestly order to which Melchizedek and Christ belong relates to earthly realities.

Christ as High Priest in the Order of Melchizedek (7:11-28)

The midrashic form of exposition continues, but the basic text is no longer Gen 14:17-20 but Ps 110:4: "You are a priest forever, according to the order of Melchizedek." The promissory oath referred to in Heb 6:17-18 is either alluded to (7:11, 15, 28) or expressly quoted (vv. 17, 21). Two elements within this prophetic oracle receive special attention: the concept "order" and the word "forever." These are examined in such a way as to show how the Son's (7:3, 28) eternal priesthood according to a prefigured order supersedes the old Levitical priesthood that was established under the Law (vv. 11-12, 16, 18-19, 28 recall v. 5).

Words denoting perfection form a bracketing *inclusio* in verses 11 and 28 and indicate the direction of the argument: what the Law could not "perfect" (priesthood) has been brought into being by the oath that appoints the Son who has been "perfected." The repetition of the first thought in verse 19 ("the law made nothing perfect") marks verses 11-19 as a subsection; the second subsection is bounded by the repetition of "oath" in verses 20, 28.

This section completes chapter 7 as a carefully structured and thematically unified discourse. That it is also transitional is clear from the way in which 7:26-28 echoes 5:1-3, and 7:22 announces the theme of the "better covenant" to be developed in chapter 8.

A New Priestly Order (vv. 11-14): The midrash on Ps 110:4 first focuses on the phrase "according to the order of Melchizedek," last cited in Heb 6:20. That this order exists has already been demonstrated (5:6, 10; 7:1-10). At issue is only its relationship to the order of Aaron to which the Levitical priesthood belongs (v. 11). A rhetorical question asserts that the appearance of "another [sc. kind of] priest" (Christ) exposes the essential weakness of the old priestly order.

The old system as a whole could not attain perfection—to this point the idea of perfection has been applied only to Christ (2:10; 5:9), though the words for Christian maturity in 5:14 and 6:1

belong to the same word group. It could not bring to completion God's plan of a perpetual priesthood offering a perfect sacrifice for sin and an eternal mediator (7:26-28). The NRSV makes little sense of the parenthesis in verse 11. Rather than suggesting that the Law was given while the old priesthood was in operation, it simply states that the people received regulations concerning this priesthood. What is implied is that the Law limited the exercise of priesthood to a certain physical lineage (see vv. 13-18).

The new order of priesthood represented by Christ has a different basis (v. 12); it is founded on the promise of Ps 110:4, not on the law. This point is first made with reference to Jesus' ancestry (vv. 13-14): he did not come from any hereditary priestly line. His ancestor was Judah, a tribe not associated with priesthood in the Mosaic Law. Thus, like Melchizedek, he is "without genealogy"; he lacks priestly ancestry (7:3, 6).

Hebrews assumes that the tradition of Jesus' Davidic ancestry (see Gen 49:10; Matt 1:1-3, 20; 2:6; 9:27; Luke 3:33; Acts 2:29-31; Rom 1:3; 2 Tim 2:8; Rev 5:5; 22:16) is "evident" to the readers. The title "our Lord" (v. 14) has a confessional ring (see Heb 13:20), and may be intended to recall the Davidic statement that comes at the beginning of the writer's key psalm (110:1: "The LORD says to my Lord . . . ," a verse alluded to in Heb 1:3, 13; 8:1; 10:12). A deliberate messianic allusion may be indicated by the Greek word for "descended" in verse 14; it suggests the "rising" of a star (see Num 24:17) or the "sprouting" of a branch (see Jer 23:5; see Buchanan 1972, 123-24). Since Hebrews is concerned with Christ's priesthood, hints at a royal, Davidic messianism remain undeveloped.

A Priest Forever (vv. 15-19): What makes Christ's priesthood radically new is not a new law (v. 12), but a new declaration from God—Ps 110:4 is again cited in full (v. 17; see 5:6). The point to be made "even more obvious" (v. 15) is still the annulment of the old priesthood by the new, but the operative phrase is "forever."

In 7:3 it is Melchizedek who resembles the Son of God. Now (v. 15) the writer wants to show how Christ ("another priest" as in v. 11) resembles Melchizedek—literally, "he arises according to the likeness of Melchizedek." As in his case, priesthood is not an inherited office, one based on "a legal requirement concerning physical descent" from the tribe of Levi (see vv. 13-14). Rather, he is priest "through the power of an indestructible life." Jesus' ministry as heavenly High Priest has no temporal limits; he cannot be touched by death (see 7:23-24) since his resurrection shows that he shares God's own life.

Though the resurrection of Christ is expressly referred to only in Heb 13:20, it is presupposed in his exaltation. That is the event in which the promise of Ps 110:4 becomes operative. In this oracle no one less than God ("it is attested" is a circumlocution) confirms that Christ's priestly office endures forever (v. 17).

The establishment of an eternal priesthood, unthreatened by mortality, has two results (vv. 18-19). The earlier law that regulated priesthood according to physical descent has been declared null and void (implied in v. 12). It was never intended to have more than temporary validity. It was weak because it dealt with men who were weak in their mortality (7:23, 28), and it was ineffectual because it could not bring God's plan for a perfect priesthood to its proper conclusion (v. 19a recalls v. 11a).

Second, Christ's accession as eternal High Priest is the basis of a hope that is better because it follows him into the innermost presence of God (6:19-20). In the old order it was consecrated priests who had the right and duty to "approach" God (Exod 19:22; Lev 21:21). While the idea is not developed at this point, access to God in Hebrews has cultic connotations. All who are sanctified by the High Priest's own blood (9:14) have priestly access to God. He has opened the way through his sacrifice (10:19-22), allowing believers to approach God with confidence as they plead for help (see 2:18; 4:14-16; 7:25) and offer their own sacrifice of praise (12:28; 13:15).

"The Lord Has Sworn" (vv. 20-22): Christ's resurrection-life is the power that undergirds his eternal priesthood, but it is God's oath that validates the office. The writer again cites Ps 110:4, leaving out the reference to Melchizedek but including the introduction: "The Lord has sworn and will not change his mind." It now becomes clear what oath he was referring to in 6:13-18, when speaking of the certainty of God's promises.

The significance of this oath is, typically, indicated by means of comparison. Priests in the old dispensation were not required to take an oath before assuming office, nor did God confirm their status with an oath (v. 20). By contrast, God speaks an oath directly to Christ (v. 21; see also 5:5) when he is installed as "priest forever." In this way God guarantees the "unchangeable character of his purpose" (6:17-18). An unchanging will establishes, validates, and guarantees a permanent office.

The eternal nature of his office ensures that Christ is the guarantee of a covenant that is better in the same sense that he introduces a better hope (v. 19). This covenant is a new dispensation that corresponds to a new order of priesthood. That this is the new covenant promised in Jer 31 and inaugurated by Christ through his death will be made clear later in the Letter (8:6-13; 9:15-20). The point here is that an eternal Priest stands as guarantor of an eternal covenant (see 13:20) that will never be annulled. He is not only the mediator of a new covenant (8:6; 9:15; 12:24), he is the pledge of its enduring character.

The use of the name Jesus—at the end of verse 22 in the Greek—is emphatic. It seems to belong to the formal confession of the community (3:1; 4:14), and is a reminder that the heavenly Priest can never be separated from a person in human history (see also 2:9; 6:20; 10:19; 12:2, 24; 13:12).

An Eternally Effective Priest (vv. 23-25): These verses again dwell on the phrase "forever" in Ps 110:4. Together with verses 15-19 they form a bracket around the discussion of the oath in verses 20-22. Special stress lies on the permanent effectiveness of Christ's priesthood. The sense of the comparison in verses 23-24 is enhanced by a neat chiasm:

A: the many have become *priests*
  B: through being prevented by death from *remaining* (in office)
  B': through his *remaining* forever
A': he holds the *priesthood* permanently

The enduring nature of Christ's office, attested by the divine oath, contrasts with the temporary tenure of office by priests in the old order, evidenced by their mortality. Though the heirs of Aaron were admitted to a "perpetual priesthood," it was only "throughout [their] generations" (see Exod 40:15). Multiple priests in a mortal lineage (see 7:8) signal the incompleteness, imperfection, and ineffectiveness of their office.

By contrast, the permanence of Christ (he "remains" and "always lives" in an absolute sense, since he participates in the life of God) means the permanence of his office, and thus its complete effectiveness (v. 25); he can offer perfect salvation by the power of an indestructible life (v. 16). As the NRSV footnote observes, the phrase rendered "for all time" can also mean "completely." Both meanings are possible, whether salvation is seen as eschatological inheritance in the future (1:14; 5:9; 9:28; 10:25), or as rescue from troubles in the present. Here the accent lies on the second thought. By his sacrifice, Christ has opened up access to God so that believers can "approach" with boldness and confidence (10:19-22) to present their pleas for help. Those who come *through* Christ can rely on his continual advocacy *for* them (2:18; 4:16; 9:24). The heavenly High Priest "always lives" to champion the cause of those who are still running the race of faith and endurance (12:1-2).

A Sinless Priest (vv. 26-28): In what has been called a "rhetorical flourish" (Attridge 1989, 207) or "concluding rhapsody" (Moffatt 1924, 101), the writer weaves a number of threads into a climactic statement on Christ's eternal priesthood. At the same time, verse 27 indicates the direction that the argument is about to take: a detailed analysis of the heavenly High Priest's sacrifice that preceded his installation.

To this point chapter 7 has spoken of Christ only as a *priest* like Melchizedek. Leaving Ps 110:4, and anticipating the analogy with the Old Testament high priests, the writer again speaks of him as *High Priest* (see 2:17; 3:1; 4:14-15; 5:5, 10). A fivefold description of his qualities (as with Melchizedek in 7:3, and with the word in 4:12) shows how he meets the needs of those whom he serves. Also the process by which he came to his office is "fitting" (see 2:10).

The first three terms, "holy, blameless, undefiled," recall the cultic purity required for entry into God's presence (see Ps 15), but especially the freedom from defilement that the law required of priests (Lev 21). As the sinless Son (4:15), Christ belongs in God's presence without prior cleansing (7:27).

Two participial phrases describe Christ's priestly qualifications in terms of his exaltation. The parallelism between 5:1-3 and 7:26-28 suggests that "separated from sinners" (7:26) stands in contrast to "chosen from among mortals" (5:1). High priests in the old order were set apart for service by fellow sinners. The Son has been exalted and proclaimed as High Priest by no one less than God (4:14; 5:5-6, 10).

Christ serves in God's presence by virtue of his personal attributes and appointment. His priestly service does involve a sacrifice, but it is unlike that of the old priesthood in two respects. Whereas the earthly high priests have to offer *continual* sacrifices, *also for themselves*, the heavenly High Priest has offered himself in one unique and unrepeatable sacrifice (7:27 picks up 5:3; see also 9:7, 25-26; 10:10-12).

The double offering alluded to is clearly that of the Day of Atonement (Lev 16:11, 16), but that occurred only once a year, not "day after day." This phrase could mean "on each Day of Atonement." More probably, the writer sees in the sacrifices of this one day a summary and climax of all the repeated offerings of high priests. In contrast to the frequency and plurality of other sacrifices, there is the unique (thus completely effective) sacrifice that matches the uniqueness of revelation through the Son (1:1-2), his unique entry into the heavenly sanctuary (9:12), and his unique act of sanctifying believers (10:10).

The final antithesis in 7:28 recalls key contrasts in the whole chapter. The cultic law that regulated priestly succession (vv. 5, 12-18) has been superseded by God's binding oath, which appoints one who does not belong to any earthly order (vv. 20-21). High priests who were weak in their mortality (vv. 8, 23) have been replaced by a "Son . . . made perfect forever." The Lord whom the readers confess as the eternal Son (1:2, 8; 5:8; 7:3) has, by his exaltation, been confirmed in an eternal, permanent office (7:24). His perfection (see 2:10; 5:9) means arrival at a goal that was set for him by God through a process also determined by God: suffering, self-sacrifice, session in glory.

◊ ◊ ◊ ◊

By linking Gen 14:17-20 with Ps 110:4, the author of Hebrews develops a priestly Christology that shows the significance of the Son's exaltation as a soteriological event. While his use of the texts, especially his concentration on the key phrase "priest forever," is highly original, he is actually undergirding an early christological tradition: the ascended Christ continues to serve as heavenly intercessor (see Rom 8:34; 1 John 2:1).

The statements in 7:19b, 25 are not incidental conclusions, but indicate the pastoral goal of the writer's Christology. He seeks to ground an uncertain community on an ultimate certainty. Its confession of the Son who has passed "through the heavens" (4:14) to be exalted "above the heavens" (7:26) does not imply his removal from all their troubles. On the contrary, the exalted Son is always with them and for them.

Hebrews sees Christ as both officiating High Priest and victim. Yet the author never expressly says that it was *as* High Priest that Christ offered himself. The analogy between Christ and the action of the high priest on the Day of Atonement allows such a conclusion, but it is more correct to say that the writer first concentrates on the *present* salvific status of the heavenly High Priest before speaking of his *past* unique sacrifice that qualifies him to serve as "priest forever." Pastoral concerns require that his Christology be developed in reverse: from an ongoing eternal function back to a unique event.

Early Judaism laid stress on the authentic claims of the Levitical priesthood, but the (high-)priestly office was brought into disrepute in intertestamental times through rivalry between priestly families and through the adoption of hellenistic culture by temple priests. The covenanters of Qumran set up their own rival priesthood, and looked forward to a priestly messiah of Aaron, as well as a royal messiah (1QS 9.11; for similar expectations in *T. 12 Patr.*, see Attridge 1989, 98).

It may be that Hebrews reflects a longing for ideal priesthood. It is also possible that its high-priestly Christology provides an answer to outsiders, both Gentile and Jewish, who question the readers' religious identity on the grounds that they lack both priesthood and sacrifice. Its insistence on Christ's unique priesthood may also be aimed at some who, because of extreme social pressure, are tempted to look to the old order as a valid expression of God's will. Certainly the writer's priestly Christology is designed to meet a practical need rather than a doctrinal error. The stress on the certainty of God's promise and on the present intercession of Christ suggests that the readers doubt the finality of Christ and his ability to help them in their present need.

Thus, the writer insists that the difference between the two orders of priesthood (of Melchizedek and of Levi) is not one of degree; it is fundamental. The old order with its supporting law is revealed by the new to be a temporary arrangement that actually points beyond itself to something better. The writer places both orders within the continuum of salvation history. Yet by relating Christ to Melchizedek, he is implying that the new priesthood is actually a return to an original order. What comes later actually precedes!

The theology of the law versus promise in Hebrews runs somewhat parallel to Pauline thought; the one is superseded, the other is eternally valid. Both the writer of Hebrews and Paul see Abraham as the bearer of promise (v. 7:6; Rom 4; Gal 3), but the precise meaning of "law" and "promise" is different. Paul sees law as moral requirement. Hebrews, rather, speaks of law as cultic regulations. And whereas Paul sees God's promise to Abraham as fulfilled in the righteousness that comes by faith in Christ (see Rom 4:20-21), Hebrews sees the promise of Ps 110:4 as fulfilled in Christ's eternal priesthood.

THE PERFECT SACRIFICE OF THE HEAVENLY HIGH PRIEST (8:1–10:31)

The author has demonstrated the qualifications that Christ met in order to be installed as eternal High Priest (4:14–7:28). He now analyzes Christ's sacrifice as the prior condition of installation into his office. Christ is minister of a heavenly, not earthly, sanctuary (8:1-5). He mediates a new covenant, better than the old (8:6-13). He has offered a final and eternally effective sacrifice in contrast to the repeated and ineffective sacrifices of the old cult (9:1-28), a perfecting offering that makes all others obsolete (10:1-18). Exposition is followed by exhortation in the form of encouragement (10:19-25) and warning (10:26-31).

Linguistic markers establish 8:1–10:31 as a unified discourse that is closely linked with 4:14–7:27. Both sections begin with a reference to Christ as exalted High Priest (4:14; 8:1). The exhortation, which in one case opens the discourse (4:14-16) and in the other brings the exposition to a parenetic climax (10:19-25), expresses its basic assumption in a parallel formulation: "Since we have a great high priest . . ." (see 4:14; 10:21). The statements of 5:1 and 8:3 ("every high priest is appointed to offer gifts and sacrifices") are parallel introductions that link the two parts of the letter's argument on Christ's priestly person and work. Hebrews 8:3 forms a literary bracket with both 9:28 and 10:18.

Christ as Minister of a Heavenly Sanctuary (8:1-6)

A change in topic is signaled by the summary statement in verse 1a; the writer moves from Christ's present position as High Priest to the sacrifice he offered prior to his installation. Since this is dealt with fully only from 9:1 on, chapter 8 forms a transition. It explains how one who is a *heavenly* High Priest can have offered a sacrifice. This leads to the question of covenant, since covenant, cult, and blood are closely connected.

A division between verses 6 and 7 is suggested by the *inclusio* formed by "minister" and "ministry" in verses 2 and 6, while the next section is bracketed by references to the two covenants (vv. 7, 13). The argument concerning the heavenly High Priest's sanctuary and sacrifice is structured in such a way that statements about the true sanctuary (vv. 2, 5) frame statements about priestly offerings (vv. 3-4). This sets the stage for chapter 9 where the "geography" of the cult is the context for understanding high-priestly offerings.

◊ ◊ ◊ ◊

The crowning conclusion of all that has been said, especially in chapter 7, is that Christ is now installed as heavenly High Priest at God's "right hand"—clearly a reference to Ps 110:1 (as in 1:3, 13; 10:12; 12:2), though the writer may also have in mind Zech 6:13 LXX: "the priest shall be at his [God's] right hand" (see Synge 1959, 25). "Throne," "majesty," and "heavens" are common circumlocutions for God, and underscore the fact that the High Priest is now permanently in God's presence. Formulated as a confession ("we have"), this truth recalls the present intercessory office of Christ (see 4:14-16; 7:26).

Two aspects of the (high-)priestly office, sanctuary and sacrifice, reveal the special nature of Christ's office as "minister" (v. 2). As leader of the heavenly cult, Christ functions in a sanctuary that is the true tabernacle, "set up" (literally, "pitched") by God, not by human hands (see also 9:11, 24). "True" denotes what is eternally valid in contrast to what is temporary. God is unchanging (6:18), so the heavenly sanctuary constituted by the divine presence must also be eternal, not temporary like the tabernacle in the wilderness (Exod 33:7).

The thought of Heb 5:1 is repeated in 8:3, though the different word order in the Greek of 8:3 serves to stress not the high priest's appointment, but his duty to make offerings. Instead of asserting that Christ offered himself (7:27; 9:14), the writer returns to his argument that the old regulations governing priesthood do not apply in the case of the heavenly High Priest. He could not possibly function on earth as a priest since he does not belong to the Aaronic or Levitical line (7:5-19, 27-28). By definition, a heavenly High Priest serves in a heavenly sanctuary.

Since the old cultic regulations are "only a shadow of the good things to come" (10:1), the earthly sanctuary in which priests function can be only "a sketch and shadow of the heavenly one" (8:5; cf. 9:23). The heavenly sanctuary is not an extension of an earthly model; it is the original archetype.

The contrast between shadow and final reality recalls Platonic distinctions, but the "similarity is word deep only" (Williamson 1970, 566). As always, the argument is scriptural. Hebrews recalls how God gave Moses specific instructions to build the tabernacle according to the pattern revealed to him on Mount Sinai (Exod 25:40; the passage is recalled also in Acts 7:44). Moses received a plan that reflected the form of the original, heavenly sanctuary. The addition of "everything" to the quotation from Exod 25:40 may well suggest that the author wants to include all the instructions concerning the cult in Exod 25–31, thus allowing features of the earthly cult to become clues to the meaning of the heavenly liturgies over which Christ presides (D'Angelo 1979, 205-22).

The difference between the two sanctuaries underscores the superiority of Christ's ministry (v. 6 recalls v. 2). Moses was mediator of the old covenant at Sinai, a covenant that was sealed with the giving of cultic regulations. But Christ is mediator of a "better covenant" (see 7:22; 9:15; 12:24), based not on legal requirements, but on "better promises." The old cult, with its sacred space, priesthood, and sacrifices was not a human creation. God set up the tabernacle worship, and gave Israel certain promises (see Exod 19:5-6). But all this is shown to be superseded by the heavenly High Priest's ministry in the heavenly sanctuary.

◊ ◊ ◊ ◊

A circuitous argument adds evidence to show that the Son's highpriestly ministry supersedes and transcends the cult established by law. He carries out his office in a transcendent realm, even though he was qualified for this office on earth (see 2:10-18; 4:15; 5:7-10). The close connection between sanctuary and sacrifice (8:2-5) suggests that the offering that Christ makes must also relate to the heavenly realm. Still to be demonstrated is the relationship between Christ's sacrifice on earth, and the offering of his blood in the heavenly sanctuary (9:1–10:18).

The notion that earthly sanctuaries are reflections of a heavenly archetype has a long history, being found in the Old Testament as well as early Judaism (see Cody 1960, 9-46; Attridge 1989, 222-24). Israel's worship stressed the close relationship between the earthly and heavenly temple (or palace) of God, so that some texts (Pss 11:4; 18:6; 29:9; Isa 6:1-5; Mic 1:2; Hab 2:20) can be read as referring to either, or both.

The tradition that pictures heaven as the place of perfect worship, with earthly worship as its counterpart, is continued in Jewish apocalyptic and Wisdom literature (e.g., *T. Levi* 3:4-8; 5:1; *2 Apoc. Bar.* 4:5; Wis 9:8), and in the *Songs of Sabbath Sacrifice* of Qumran (4QShirShabb). Its prominence in Judaism and in the Apocalypse of John explains the ease with which the author of Hebrews can link worship on the heavenly and earthly plane.

We can see the author's indebtedness to hellenistic-Jewish thought in the contrast between the earthly as the ephemeral, and the heavenly as the eternal (see Cody 1960, 36). Yet the author still presents his theology of worship within a salvation-historical, rather than metaphysical framework. The old cult was an imperfect order of worship, yet it points to the new worship inaugurated by the great High Priest's entry into the heavenly sanctuary after suffering on earth.

The Inauguration of a New Covenant (8:7-13)

Christ's eternal priesthood was established on God's promise (Ps 110:4). The better promises upon which the covenant he mediates is based are now spelled out in the longest scriptural quotation in the New Testament (vv. 8-12; see Jer 31:31-34). The quotation is enclosed within an *inclusio* formed by references to the second and first covenants (vv. 7, 13). Part of the quotation is repeated in 10:16-17, so that the entire discussion of Christ's high-priestly sacrifice in 9:1–10:14 is framed by references to the promise of the new covenant in Jer 31.

◊ ◊ ◊ ◊

Chapter 7 argued that the promise of a new priesthood and its fulfillment in the Son shows the old cultic regulations governing an earthly priesthood to be superseded. Similarly, the prophetic announcement of a second covenant shows the first to be obsolete (v. 7). The Sinai covenant was not faulty because of any deficiency on God's part; blame lay with disobedient Israel (v. 8). Like the Law that could not bring anything to perfection (7:11, 19), the first covenant was ineffective, and was shown to be so by the announcement of another to take its place.

Apart from a brief introductory comment (v. 8*a*) and a short conclusion (v. 13), the divine oracle ("says the Lord" is repeated in vv. 9-10) is quoted without midrashic comment. There is no reference to the human author since this oracle is the living voice of the Holy Spirit (10:15). Nor is the original setting of Jer 31:31-34 of interest. What is essentially a word of promise is here also seen as a word of reproach. Israel's breaking of the Sinai covenant (Heb 8:9*b*) requires a new initiative by God. In the phrase "*I* will establish" (emphasis added) there is a reminder that every covenant (with Noah, Gen 9:9; with Abraham, Gen 15:18 and 17:7; with Israel, Exod 19:5 and 24:8; with David, 2 Sam 7:12-16) is based on divine initiative and grace. Now that the promised covenant has been established, the "coming days" have become the "last days" (1:2).

The first covenant was a sign of God's continuing care of a people rescued from slavery in Egypt and guided in its desert pilgrimage (v. 9). Only later does the writer recall how that covenant was sealed in blood (Exod 24:1-8; Heb 9:18-20). Here he simply lets the text speak for itself: The forefathers did not keep the conditions of the covenant (see Exod 19:5, emphasis added: "*If* you obey my voice and keep my covenant . . ."). Disobedience meant the loss of God's special care (see Jer 7:23-26; 11:6-8). The last line of Heb 8:9 follows the reading of the LXX; the Hebrew Bible has: "though I was their husband. . . ."

The sins of Israel (see also 3:6-19; 4:11) show the weakness of the first covenant and the need for one that is entirely new. The Jeremiah oracle indicates a different mode of operation on God's part, resulting in a new people (vv. 10*b*-12). They will obey an inner direction that has become part of their thinking and being through the gift of an inner transformation (see Jer 24:7; Ezek 11:19-20; 36:26-27).

As a result of God's new intervention, the goal of the first covenant will be realized; a faithful God will again have a faithful people (8:10*c*; see Exod 6:7; Lev 26:12; Jer 7:23). Second, where the prophets once had to complain that there was "no knowledge of God in the land" (Hos 4:1, 6), all people will know God (in terms of relationship rather than mere cognition), obviating the need for special instruction (8:11).

The essential mark of the new covenant will be the totally effective removal of sin; in mercy God will both forgive and forget (v. 12). God forgave also under the old covenant (Exod 34:6, 7). New is that forgiveness is written into the terms of the covenant, not as possibility but as an accomplished fact. This verse is so important for the writer that it is cited as a separate word of the Spirit at the conclusion of his discourse on Christ's high-priestly work (10:17).

By mentioning a new covenant, God declares the first one obsolete (v. 13). In fact, the Sinai covenant was antiquated ("growing old") from the moment that the promise of Jer 31 was uttered.

◊ ◊ ◊ ◊

The argument concerning the necessity of a new covenant runs parallel with that concerning the need for a new priesthood (7:11-12). Human imperfections (the mortality of priests and the failure of Israel to keep the Sinai covenant) are not the full story. Rather, the old cultic order and first covenant did not represent the *final* will of God. That they were provisional pointers to a final goal in the divine plan has become clear in the light of the arrival of final realities (10:1).

The lack of commentary on the Jeremiah oracle indicates that the author's chief point is the replacement of the old covenant by the new (v. 13). Yet the use of the prophecy to frame 9:1–10:14 suggests connections yet to be drawn. One of these connections will be explained in 9:15-22 and 10:11-18: Both covenants are inaugurated in blood. Though Jer 31:31-34 contains no reference to priesthood or sacrifice, it is reasonable to suggest that, for both writer and audience of Hebrews, the phrase "new covenant" had sacrificial connotations by means of the eucharistic words, embedded in early Christian worship (Luke 22:20; 1 Cor 11:25). The double reminder that the new covenant will offer perfect forgiveness (Jer 31:34 in Heb 8:12 and 10:17) recalls that the new covenant in Christ's blood is "for the forgiveness of sins" (Matt 26:28).

The internalization of the covenant (8:10), with the implied contrast between what is internal and what is external, corresponds to the transcendence of the heavenly High Priest in contrast to earthly priests (8:1-6). Thus, the entrance of Christ into the *heavenly* sanctuary has lasting effects on the *inner* being of Christians: The conscience is cleansed (9:11-14; 10:1-10). This comes about because the Son perfectly embodies an essential element of the new covenant: He himself knows and does the will of God (cf. 8:10 with 10:7).

The Temporary Nature of the Earthly Sanctuary (9:1-10)

This section provides a further transition from the proof of the Son's heavenly priesthood in a heavenly sanctuary (8:1-6) to the proof of his superior sacrifice that inaugurates a new covenant ("first covenant" in 9:1 recalls 8:7).

An *inclusio* is formed by references to "regulations" (vv. 1, 10)—the word is used nowhere else in Hebrews. These regulations "for worship and an earthly sanctuary" are treated in reverse order. First, the writer describes the sanctuary (the tabernacle) and its appointments, laying stress on the distinction between the outer and inner court (vv. 1-5). He then outlines the rites that are proper to each sacred space, and draws a conclusion from the limited access of high priests to the Holy of Holies (vv. 6-10). These regulations point to the provisional nature of the Old Testament cult.

The Earthly Sanctuary's Appointments (vv. 1-5): The writer's description of the earthly sanctuary (in contrast to the heavenly; 8:2, 5) focuses on the tabernacle of the exodus wandering, not on the later temples of Solomon or Herod. The chief regulations of the old cultic order (vv. 1, 10) serve as a framework within which to depict the new.

The tabernacle was a double tent set within a court. The outer compartment, entered through a first curtain, was called the Holy Place (9:2). On its south side (Exod 26:35) stood the lampstand or *menorah*, made of pure gold, with three branches rising on each side of the main stem, forming seven candleholders (Exod 25:31-

39). On the north side stood a table made of acacia wood and overlaid with gold. On it was kept the "bread of the Presence," that is, "bread set before the presence" of God, as well as certain sacrificial utensils (Exod 25:23-30). Each sabbath, twelve freshly baked cakes were placed on the table to serve as a standing cereal offering. Only the priests were permitted to eat this holy bread (Lev 24:5-9; but see 1 Sam 21:1-6 and Mark 2:25-26).

A second curtain (Exod 26:31-33; cf. Matt 27:51) led to the inner sanctum, the Holy of Holies. The description of its contents (Heb 9:4) is problematic since the "golden altar of incense" was originally located in the first tent, not the second (Exod 30:6; 40:26).

In the LXX the word *thymiatērion* means "censer" rather than "incense altar," but this is hardly what is meant since the object in question is never described as golden (see 2 Chr 26:19; Ezek 8:11; also 4 Macc 7:11). Such an implement is not mentioned in the building of the tabernacle in Exod 25–31 and 35–40, and where it is mentioned in connection with the Day of Atonement (Lev 16:12-13; Num 16:46), a different term is used. Yet the same word is used with the meaning of "incense altar" by other ancient Jewish writers using Greek (see Attridge 1989, 234).

The simplest explanation is that the author is referring to a later positioning of the altar of incense in the Holy of Holies (1 Kgs 6:20, 22; implied also in 2 *Apoc. Bar.* 6:7; Rev 8:3; 9:13; on the anomalies of Heb 9:2-4 see Attridge, 236-38). In any case, the inner sanctuary could never be entered without incense from this altar. In addition, the author seems concerned to link this altar with the ark of the covenant; blood was sprinkled on both on the Day of Atonement (Exod 30:10; Lev 16:15, 18).

The principal object in the inner shrine was the ark of the covenant, a box of acacia wood overlaid with gold. Also called the "ark of the testimony," it contained the two tablets of stone as a lasting witness to God's covenant will (Exod 25:10-16; 37:1-5). Instructions that the urn containing manna and Aaron's rod were to be kept "before the testimony" (Exod 16:33-34; Num 17:10) led our author to infer that the ark also contained these objects.

Although the lampstand and table in the Holy Place were golden, Hebrews uses this term in referring only to the altar, ark, and urn (see Exod 16:33 LXX) in the Holy of Holies. Perhaps the author views gold as a fitting symbol of God's presence, though he does not, surprisingly, recall that the mercy seat (Heb 9:5) was a slab of pure gold (Exod 25:17). For him the mercy seat or "place of atonement" has special significance in that it was sprinkled with blood by the high priest on the Day of Atonement (Lev 16:13-16; Heb 9:7). He sees it as the earthly counterpart of God's heavenly throne; it represents the earthly presence of God who is elsewhere described as the one "enthroned on the cherubim" (1 Sam 4:4). For Hebrews, Christ—enthroned in glory—now occupies the mercy seat (4:16).

The Priestly Ritual (vv. 6-10): The focus shifts from furnishings to rituals—the present tense is again timeless. Ordinary priests had the outer tabernacle as their domain. Only the high priest was allowed to enter the inner sanctuary, and he but once a year on Yom Kippur; unlawful entry carried the death penalty (Num 18:3). Further, he could enter only if bearing blood to remove the defilement of sin (Lev 16:16). Clothed in special vestments, he entered the Holy of Holies twice: once to sprinkle the mercy seat with the blood of a bull sacrificed for himself and his household, a second time to sprinkle the blood of a goat sacrificed for the people (see 5:3; 7:27). There followed the ritual of the scapegoat, driven into the wilderness bearing the sins of the people (Lev 16:1-22). The description of the latter as "sins of ignorance" (NRSV: "committed unintentionally") is pointed; the author later argues that deliberate sin negates the forgiveness gained by Christ (10:26).

Reading Scripture as the living voice of the Spirit (3:7; 10:15), the writer sees a deeper meaning in these regulations; they point to their own inadequacy (9:8-10). The annual entry of the high priest into the inner sanctum is an exception to the general rule: "the way into the sanctuary has not yet been disclosed" in the sense that there is no open access for *all* into the heavenly sanctuary of which the earthly Holy of Holies is merely a symbolic pattern (8:2). Only Christ has opened up access into the true sanctuary of God's eternal presence (10:19-20). The "first tent" (9:8) is not the tabernacle as a whole, but its front compartment (as in vv. 2, 6). As long as it is standing (in the sense of having cultic status) it blocks the path to the inner shrine, and represents limited access to God.

The old system could not breach the gap between sinful humanity and God since it offered no more than an outward ceremonial purification (9:9-10). Since the Law made nothing perfect (7:18), the rites it provided could not perfectly cleanse the conscience. Their constant repetition could not remove the inner awareness that sin separating mortals from a holy God reaches into the heart and mind (see 10:1-4). "Food and drink" recalls the dietary laws of Lev 11 and Deut 14 and other regulations dealing with libations or drink offerings to be made by priests (Num 6:15, 17; 28:7-8). Various ritual ablutions (better than "baptisms" in the NRSV; see 6:2) were required for sins and ceremonial defilement (Num 19:13). In particular, it was the duty of the high priest to bathe himself after the ritual of Yom Kippur (Lev 16:24). But all this is seen as temporary, imposed by God until the establishment of a new and perfect order of worship in which consciences are perfectly cleansed (cf 9:14; 10:2, 22).

◊ ◊ ◊ ◊

The writer's choice of tabernacle rather than temple is theologically motivated. First, the architecture and plan of this building provide the archetypal setting for the ritual of Yom Kippur, which prefigures the sacrifice of Christ (9:11–10:18). Every point in the argument is established from Scripture, not from contemporary practice in Jerusalem. Second, it has been stressed that the old priestly order and its duties were established by law (7:5, 12, 16, 28; 8:4). Also the earthly sanctuary's plan was subject to divine regulations (vv. 1, 10). Yet these scriptural regulations, like the whole cultic law, point to something greater (10:1). Third, the building of the tabernacle at God's direction (Exod 25–27) immediately followed the establishment of the covenant at Sinai (Exod 24). But this covenant, like the Law, has become obsolete (Heb 8:13). Thus, the description of the tabernacle, taken from Scripture, serves as backdrop for a new cultic order under the new covenant, also announced in Scripture (8:8-13).

The distinction between two spaces in the tabernacle is developed in temporal terms. Limited access to God's presence in the old cult points forward to the unlimited access that has been opened up by the offering of Christ's blood (Cody 1960, 146-60). The writer does not dwell on the high priest's act of sacrificing the bull and the goat. What he does with the *blood* is the vital point; he enters the inner shrine, but "not without blood" (see 9:7). Here the writer hints at his future focus on the blood of Christ (see 9:12-14, 18, 20-22; 10:4, 19, 29). His choice of the term "offer" in 9:7 also shows that he is preparing for a broad typological connection between the events of Yom Kippur and Christ's self-sacrifice. While Lev 16 speaks of the application of blood in the form of sprinkling, our writer speaks of Christ's blood in terms of his self-*offering* (9:14, 25; see also 9:28; 10:12).

This brief description of the Old Testament cult is clearly intended to provide a framework within which to understand Christ's superior sacrifice. Imperfection foreshadows perfection. Yet the stress on the limited validity and efficacy of the old may contain a silent warning to the readers, if they are being tempted to readopt Jewish rules about what is clean and unclean. Later the letter stresses that the heart is "strengthened by grace, not by regulations about food" (13:9). With Christ's entry into the heavenly sanctuary, the old law, covenant, and ritual have been "reformed" (9:10). Christians live outside the camp of the old wilderness-people of God (13:12-13) and outside the old cultic law.

The Perfect Efficacy of Christ's Blood (9:11-28)

An emphatic "but" introduces an elaborate treatment of the antithetical correspondence between the ritual of the Day of Atonement and Christ's past high-priestly work. The contrast is relatively complete in 9:11-14: Christ has entered the *perfect* sanctuary with his *own* blood to provide *effective* cleansing from sin. A further point is made (vv. 15-22): The blood of Christ inaugurates the new covenant previously spoken of (7:22; 8:6-13). A third argument draws a connection between Christ's past and present work and his future appearing (vv. 23-28), recapitulating elements of the first paragraph: Christ approached God in the heavenly sanctuary (vv.

11-12, 24), not with animal blood but with his own (vv. 12, 14, 25-26), to effect complete purging of sins (vv. 14, 28).

There is good reason to treat this long expository section as a self-contained discourse (see G. Guthrie 1994, 86-87). It is marked by three references to Christ: he appeared to obtain redemption in the *past* (v. 11); he *now* appears in God's presence on our behalf (v. 24); he will again appear in the *future* to ensure final rescue (v. 28). The movement is thus from a past unique event of cleansing, to an ongoing process of mediation, to a final act of deliverance—all perfectly effective.

Eternal Redemption Secured by Blood (vv. 11-14): The better things to which the law pointed (6:9; 10:1) have arrived with the appearance of Christ. Scholars have debated whether he "came as a high priest" at his death or at his glorification in heaven. His entry into the heavenly sanctuary is clearly viewed as part of his exaltation. But this event presupposes his sacrificial death. Thus, as in 7:26-28, two themes are combined: The exalted Christ was recognized as heavenly High Priest on the basis of his death as a unique and effective sacrifice (9:26-28; 10:10).

On the analogy of the earthly high priest (9:7), Christ passed "through the greater and perfect tent" before entering the heavenly Holy of Holies (vv. 11-12). In 8:2 the "true tent" was the inner shrine of God's presence in which Christ now ministers. Here the writer views the heavens through which Christ has passed (4:14) as the equivalent of the tabernacle's first chamber, the Holy Place. He distinguishes between the created heavens that will pass away (1:10-12; 12:26-27) and the heavens that represent the transcendent realm of God. Unlike its earthly counterpart, this Holy Place, like the entire heavenly sanctuary, is "not made with [human] hands" (see 8:2; 9:24; cf. Acts 7:48; 17:24). Since it does not belong to any created order, it is eternal.

Verse 12 extends in chiastic form the antithetical parallelism begun in verse 11*b*: Christ entered the heavenly sanctuary (**A**) through the greater and perfect tent (**B**) not made with hands . . . ; he did so (**B'**) not with the blood of goats and calves, (**A'**) but with his own blood. The parallelism assumes that access to God is possible only through the medium of blood; the contrast concerns the nature of the blood involved. Christ's entry into the heavenly sanctuary "through/by means of blood" denotes more than the completion of a perfect sacrifice, and more than the ratification of his death as a saving event. Hebrews properly distinguishes between the death of a sacrificial victim and the application of blood. It is the blood of Christ, shed in his voluntary self-sacrifice (9:26; 10:5-10) and carried into God's presence (9:23-24), that continues to cleanse (9:14, 22) and to provide access to God's presence (10:19), ensuring a redemption that is eternally valid. That point is underscored by another essential difference between the actions of the old high priests and Christ. They entered the earthly inner sanctuary once a year; he entered the heavenly sanctuary "once for all" (7:27; 9:26-28; 10:12, 14). The uniqueness of the event ensures its eternal efficacy.

An *a fortiori* argument (for the same logic see 2:2-3; 10:28-29; 12:9, 25) shows the superior efficacy of Christ's blood (9:13-14). In the old cult, animal blood was sprinkled on people to remove ceremonial defilement. "The blood of goats and bulls" probably refers beyond the ritual of Yom Kippur to all animal sacrifices. The sacrifice of the red heifer (Num 19) is mentioned because it involved sprinkling. The heifer was killed "outside the camp" (see 13:11), and its blood sprinkled seven times in front of the tabernacle. Its body was then burned and the ashes stored, to be sprinkled with water on any who became unclean through contact with a corpse.

The author grants that such sprinkling has power to "sanctify" or make holy, but only in the sense that the "flesh," meaning external defilement (9:10; 10:4), is purified. Here he reflects the Old Testament distinction between purification from cultic uncleanness, as the necessary presupposition for entry into God's presence, and sanctification as being made holy in God's presence. True sanctification comes only from the sacrifice of Christ (2:11; 10:10, 14, 29; 13:12).

The blood of Christ is more potent than that of animals; it purifies the conscience by removing the guilt of sin (v. 14; cf. 1:3). It does not merely remove defilement from contact with the dead, but the defilement of all "dead works," that is, a life that leads to death (see 6:1; the opposite are "good deeds," 10:24). Only those who are so cleansed can offer priestly worship to the living God without fear (13:15).

Two reasons are given for the absolute effectiveness of Christ's self-sacrifice: He was without the blemish of sin (4:15; 7:26), and his self-sacrifice was made "through [an] eternal Spirit." Some (e.g., Bruce 1990, 217; Peterson 1982, 138) have seen here a reference to the guiltless Suffering Servant who, endowed with the Spirit, made an offering for sin (Isa 42:1; 53:9-10). Harold W. Attridge (1989, 251) suggests that the phrase alludes to the spiritual locale and inner quality of Christ's sacrifice. Probably, the life-giving "Spirit" stands in contrast to "flesh" as mortal (v. 13). "Through the eternal Spirit" may be an early Christian formula that recalls Christ's resurrection by the power of the Spirit (cf. Rom 1:4). Alternatively, the phrase may mean "through *his* eternal spirit." The blood of the heavenly High Priest continues to atone because his office rests on the power of an indestructible life (7:16).

A New Covenant Inaugurated in Blood (vv. 15-22): The promise of a new covenant (8:8-12) did not state how it was to be established. That Christ's death makes him the mediator of a new and better covenant (9:15 recalls 8:6) is first thetically stated, then supported by two arguments. A legal argument recalls that the validity of a human will rests with the person making the testament, but it comes into force only at death (vv. 16-17). A scriptural argument then shows how the establishment of the Mosaic covenant also involved death and the shedding of blood (vv. 18-21). A concluding thesis points to the connection between blood and forgiveness (v. 22).

That Christ *is* (not was) the mediator of a new covenant (v. 15) presupposes his continuing status as High Priest, subsequent to his entry into the heavenly sanctuary (vv. 11-12). But the focus now moves to his death as one that establishes a covenant that is qualitatively different. Under the old covenant there was temporary and external cleansing through repeated sacrifices; in the new there is permanent redemption from sin. A sacrifice with eternal power (cf. "eternal Spirit" in v. 14) gives an eternal inheritance, fulfilling

God's promise of complete forgiveness from all past sins (see 8:12). This is due to the initiative of divine grace. The "inheritance" is a gift to those who, like Israel in the wilderness, have been called to follow a path leading to a promise (see 1:14; 3:1; 4:1; 6:17). It is guaranteed to the siblings of the Son who is the "heir of all things" (1:2; 2:11*b*).

The Greek word *diathēke* can mean both covenant and will. This allows the author to illustrate a feature of the covenant from the general practice of validating human testaments, an illustration suggested by the word *inheritance* (v. 15).

The essential parallel between covenant and will lies in the fact that both presuppose a death. A testament comes into legal force only on the death of the testator (vv. 16-17). The parallel must not be pressed. In the case of a human testament, the testator cannot also be the executor; in the new covenant Christ is executor of God's will through his death, and guarantees the permanence of the covenant by remaining "priest forever" (see 7:21-22).

The exegetical argument no longer speaks of a necessary death (vv. 15-17), but of necessary blood (vv. 18-21), since it is blood that atones. Our author ignores the covenant with Abraham (Gen 15:9-11). His interest is in the inauguration of the first covenant (8:13) when the cultic law, with its commandments regulating worship, was read out by Moses, who then sprinkled blood on an altar and on the people (Exod 24:3-8).

Elements of Heb 9:19, not taken from the Exodus account, draw attention to the action of sprinkling. Scarlet wool, hyssop, and water were used in rites for the purification of lepers (Lev 14:4-9) and of priests officiating at the sacrifice of the red heifer (Num 19:6-8; see v. 13 above). The hyssop was also used to sprinkle the blood of the Passover lamb in Egypt (Exod 12:22). Goat blood is mentioned since it belongs to the ritual of Yom Kippur (Heb 9:12-13; 10:4). No special point is made of another new feature: the sprinkling of the scroll itself. Additional elements simply add to the idea that the Mosaic covenant was inaugurated with comprehensive sprinkling.

The words of Moses in Exod 24:8 ("See the blood of the covenant that the LORD has made with you.") are reformulated to read, "This is the blood of the covenant that God has ordained for you" (9:20). Though the substitution of "God" for "Lord" disassociates Jesus from the first covenant, the opening phrase ("This is . . .") suggests a veiled reference to the words of Jesus at the Last Supper—all the more likely since verse 22 contains two more terms ("shed"; "forgiveness") that appear in the eucharistic tradition (Matt 26:28 [NRSV has "poured out" rather than "shed"]).

Blood was not sprinkled on the tent and its sacred vessels neither at the inauguration of the covenant nor during the ritual of the Day of Atonement. Once more the author assimilates several rites (v. 21). Moses smeared and sprinkled blood on and around the altar at the consecration of Aaron and his sons to the priesthood (Lev 8:15, 19, 23-24, 30; see Exod 29:12). Further, he dedicated the tent and vessels by anointing them with oil (Exod 40:9, 16; Lev 8:11), but Josephus speaks of an anointing with oil and blood (*Ant.* 3.206). Important for the writer is that "*all* the people" (v. 19, emphasis added) and "*all* the vessels" (v. 21, emphasis added) were consecrated by sprinkling.

The thesis is thus established: under the provisions of the Mosaic Law "almost everything is purified with blood" (v. 22). Prime examples of sprinkling have demonstrated that there is no purgation of sins without blood. The writer must be thinking primarily of the power of Christ's blood in verse 22*b* since he stresses that the blood of animals was able to effect only an outer cleansing (9:9, 13; 10:4). Perfect redemption is given only through Christ's blood (cf. Eph 1:7; 1 John 1:7).

The writer's statement in verse 22*b* is usually understood to mean no more than that forgiveness of sin requires the substitutionary death of a sacrificial victim, but this is improbable. Every other mention of blood in this chapter (vv. 7, 12-14, 18-22*a*, 25—the phrase "not without blood" in v. 7 is echoed in vv. 18, 22) concerns what is done with the blood of sacrificial victims. "Shedding of blood" (*haimatekchusia* was probably coined by the writer) refers not only to the flowing of blood in the act of sacrifice, but to the application of blood thereafter (correctly seen by Lane 1991, 246), that is, to the "pouring out of blood" that is still available since Christ entered the heavenly sanctuary. This stress on the present power of Christ's blood is not negated by the uniqueness of Christ's death (see 9:26*b*-28*a*). How such application of "blood for sprinkling" (see 12:24) takes place now is not stated, but there is a hint at one eucharistic tradition (as in v. 20) that speaks of the cup as the "blood of the covenant *poured out* for the *forgiveness of sins*" (see Matt 26:28, emphasis added).

A Completely Effective Sacrifice (vv. 23-28): The author returns to the typology of Yom Kippur and to the analogy between the actions of the high priests and Christ's actions (see 9:11-14). For the reason stated in 9:22*a*, the high priests had to take blood into the sanctuary to purify it from defilement. The purification of what were only "sketches of the heavenly things" and a "mere copy" (vv. 23-24; cf. 8:5) suggests, by analogy, the purification of the heavenly sanctuary that is eternal and not of human making (8:2; 9:11-12). That new worship must be established by "better sacrifices" (the plural is used to state a general principle) is clear. But why should heaven need cleansing?

In Hebrew thought it is not strange to picture the taint of sin reaching into heaven itself (see Gen 6:1-4). The inseparable link between earthly and heavenly cultus (8:5; 12:18-24) requires that there be a cleansing that reaches into heaven (Cody 1960, 81-91). The tabernacle required purification to hallow it for sacred use, but the vital cleansing was that of the people themselves (9:19, 22). By analogy, the purified consciences of God's people now allow them to enter into God's presence for worship.

Christ, who entered the heavenly sanctuary at his exaltation, now continues to appear before God to advocate "on our behalf" (v. 24; see 7:25). Through him others can now "appear before God" (the phrase has obvious cultic connotations; see Exod 23:17; Deut 16:16). Thus, there is no need for an earthly temple, for a mediating priesthood, or for continuing sacrifices. All these have been superseded by Christ in a double sense: in his self-sacrificial death and in the offering of his blood in the heavenly sanctuary (vv. 25-26). The annual rite of carrying animal blood into the Holy of Holies (9:7) signifies its ineffectiveness. Christ's sacrifice is "once for all" (7:27; 9:12; 10:10) and therefore eternally effective. Though he appeared in history only at the "end of the age," his self-sacrifice is universally effective in removing sin's defilement (v. 26). Animals can be repeatedly sacrificed, but a person can die only once (v. 27). The absurd idea of Christ dying repeatedly signals the complete efficacy of his one death.

Christ's death confirms his humanity (see 2:17), for death is the universal fate of mortals, as is the final judgment (v. 27 sounds like a proverbial saying). But Christ's similarity with humanity ends there. First, the *one* person was offered (the passive suggests God is the subject, in contrast to the writer's normal stress on Christ's self sacrifice; see 7:27; 9:14, 25; 10:12) "to bear the sins of *many*" (emphasis added). The latter phrase recalls the role of the scapegoat on the Day of Atonement (Lev 16:22) and that of the Suffering Servant (Isa 53:10-12; 1 Pet 2:24). Second, Christ's death is not the end. He will appear again, not to be judged but to judge, and not to deal with sin (the motif of retribution occurs later in 10:27-31 and 12:23) but to save. Christ will make a second and final appearance to vindicate the faith of believers, and to call to their eternal rest those who are eagerly waiting for him. This consummation will be the final proof of his effective sacrifice.

◊ ◊ ◊ ◊

Hebrews has earlier linked Christ's high-priestly accession to his role as intercessor (2:18; 4:15-16; 7:25; 8:1-2), with only hints at a cultic interpretation of his death (see 1:3; 2:11; 5:1-3; 7:27; 8:3). The writer now clarifies, in consistently cultic terms, how Christ's death is the fundamental presupposition for all that is embraced by the term "salvation": cleansing from sin, present mediation, and final deliverance.

The writer interprets the Scriptures on the basis of Christian faith. An array of ritual data is collated to show how the Christ Cultus, which establishes both New Covenant Cultus and Heavenly Cultus, illuminates the typological function of the Old Covenant Cultus (on the terms see Pursiful 1993, 27-28). Priestly movements and actions in the Mosaic Law foreshadow Christ's eternally effective sacrifice, his entry into the heavenly sanctuary, as well as his final appearance from it.

There is essential discontinuity between old and new cult. Repeated animal sacrifices had limited efficacy; Christ's once-for-all self-sacrifice has complete power to atone for sin and to provide entry into God's presence. Yet the argument still assumes a conceptual continuity. It is blood, shed by the sacrificial victim and applied by the priest, that works forgiveness. Christ's blood has this power (9:22).

The Finality of Christ's Sacrifice (10:1-18)

These verses form the climax of the author's exposition of Christ's finished high-priestly work in 8:1–10:18. Thus, the opening statement of the heavenly High Priest's exaltation in 8:1 is recalled in 9:12-13, and the quotation of the Jeremiah prophecy in 8:8-12 is recalled at 10:16-17. Scripture quotations provide an interpretive framework for understanding Christ's sacrifice.

Less clear is the structure of the section. Verses 1 and 14 form contrasting statements with respect to "those who approach" God in the old order and "those who are sanctified" in the new (sacrifices/single offering; continually/for all time; can never make perfect/has perfected), but this proposed inclusion (see G. Guthrie 1994, 87) does not account for 9:15-18 and the continuity of the argument in 9:1–10:18. The section as a whole offers four paragraphs that form a double antithetical statement:

A: Repeated sacrifices under the law were *ineffective* (vv. 1-4).
  B: They are superseded by *one sacrifice* according to God's will (vv. 5-10).
  B': Many priests have been replaced by *one Priest* (vv. 11-14)
A': of the new covenant with its *effective* forgiveness (vv. 15-18).

In 10:1-18 there is a marked concentration of sacrificial language (the verb "to offer" and the nouns "offering" [only here in the Letter] and "sacrifice" appear repeatedly). There is also a shift in focus from blood (only in 10:4) to the body of Jesus (10:5, 10). At issue are two questions: Which sacrifice is totally *effective?* and

Which sacrifice reflects *God's will?* Thus, the section is framed by a contrast between what was ineffective under the Law (vv. 1-4), and the totally effective forgiveness offered under the new covenant (vv. 15-18). Christ's affirmation of God's will (vv. 7, 9) frames a statement about what is *not* God's will.

The Sacrifices Under the Law Were Ineffective (10:1-4): Revelation in Christ shows that the Law was never intended to be anything but a pale reflection of God's final will (just as the earthly sanctuary was only a "sketch and shadow of the heavenly one"; 8:5). The "good things" to which the Law pointed, like the cult upon which it was based, have become a reality (9:11). They are the "better things . . . that belong to salvation" (6:9): a better covenant based on better promises and sacrifices (8:6; 9:23). They are the true "form" (literally, "image") in which God's will finds expression.

Repetition again signals ineffectiveness (vv. 1*b*-2; cf. 9:25; 10:11). For reasons already stated (7:11, 19; 9:9-10), the annual ritual of Yom Kippur could not "perfect" worshipers; it could not remove the guilt that stains the conscience and bars sinners from God's holy presence. Yet the old sacrificial system served a purpose in the divine plan precisely in its inability to offer more than external cleansing (vv. 3-4). Annual sacrifices and application of animal blood served as a reminder that sin had not yet been permanently dealt with. These actions prophetically pointed to the perfect cleansing effected by the blood of Christ (9:12-14).

Christ Has Effectively Obeyed God's Will (10:5-10): Christ is not mentioned by name in the Greek text until verse 10, but he is clearly the speaker of Ps 40:6-8, and seen as appropriating the text (for other examples see Heb 2:12-13) when he "came into the world." "I have come" (10:7) is understood incarnationally, so the "world" is not the eschatological realm of 1:6 and 2:5.

Though the whole of Scripture points to Christ and is, for our writer, word of Christ, there may be another reason for placing this text in the mouth of Jesus. In the gospel tradition, Jesus cites Hos 6:6, "I desire mercy, not sacrifice" (Matt 9:13; 12:7), in calling for true inner obedience in contrast to performance of external ceremonies. A similar call is sounded in Ps 40:6-8. As in other Old

Testament texts (e.g., 1 Sam 15:22; Ps 51:16-19; Isa 66:2, 3; Jer 7:21-24; Amos 5:21-27), material sacrifices are not rejected but are seen as inadequate substitutes for repentance and obedience that comes from the heart. For Hebrews, all past sacrifices are superseded by Christ's obedient offering of his own body.

The text of Ps 40:6 in 10:5c varies from the Hebrew original that reads, "ears you have dug [or pierced] for me"—that is, the psalmist's ears have been opened to obey God's will. The LXX text suits the purposes of the writer; God has given the Son a *body* to be given to God in total obedience and self-surrender. It is in this body of flesh and blood (2:14) that the Son learned obedience in suffering in order to sanctify sinners (5:8; 10:10).

Verse 7 drops the reference to the Law found in the Hebrew text, and joins two statements to form one: "I have come to do your will, O God." The "scroll of the book" is no longer the Law, but the prophetic word that points to Christ as obedient Son. The brief midrashic treatment (10:8-10) focuses on Christ's body as the means by which God's final will has been effected. By recasting the Old Testament text, the author creates two statements in temporal sequence. A later word brings out the full meaning of a prior word (see 4:7-8; 7:12; 8:13). Psalm 40:5a and 6a are read together as a programmatic declaration of God's lack of pleasure in the sacrifices under the Law. That they are superseded becomes clear in Christ's second declaration: He has come to do God's will, that is, by offering himself as a sacrifice. Choosing verbs with legal connotations, placed in chiastic order (abolish/first/second/establish; v. 9b), the writer declares a final judgment on the Law's temporary provisions for multiple and repeated sacrifices (10:1), and on the finality of Christ's self-sacrifice.

A final exegetical statement (v. 10) picks up two key words from the psalm quotation: Jesus affirms and does God's *will* in offering his own *body* as a sacrifice. The final significance of this event for the community is expressed as a confession: "*We* have been sanctified." The shift in vocabulary from "purify" (9:13-14, 22-23; 10:2) to "sanctify" (10:10; used also in 2:11; 9:14; 10:29) is significant. The latter denotes that radical cleansing from sin which, after providing access to God (10:22), is the basis for a continual doing of God's will (see 10:36; 13:21) in a life of worship, including spoken praise and acted obedience (12:28–13:5; 13:15-16).

The uniqueness of Christ's self-sacrifice is emphatically asserted. It is an event in history, involving the body of a human being called Jesus (see 2:9; 5:7; 7:22; 10:19), that happened "once for all"—this key phrase (7:27; 9:26-28) comes last for emphasis. This is one of only two places in Hebrews where the full name "Jesus Christ" is used (see also 13:8). The sanctifying will of God was effected by a human being who is now the heavenly King.

His Exaltation Shows the Finality of His Sacrifice (10:11-14): Psalm 110:1 has been cited to prove that Christ, enthroned at God's right hand, now functions as the eternal High Priest (5:6; 7:17, 21; 8:1). Concentrating on the phrase, "*sit* at my right hand," the writer now uses the text to make a different point: the finality of Christ's sacrifice in the past.

Verse 11 recalls two features of the Old Testament sacrificial system that have already been highlighted. First, it involved repeated, multiple sacrifices, whether made annually by the high priest on the Day of Atonement (9:7, 25; 10:1), or daily by ordinary priests in the performance of their duties. Second, this ceaseless ritual could not remove the guilt of sin (9:9-10; 10:4). That priests *stand* to carry out their repeated tasks is seen as indicating their incompleteness.

In contrast to repeated, multiple, but ineffective sacrifices, Christ has offered "for all time" a "single sacrifice" that is effective "for [removing] sins" (v. 12). That he "*sat down*" at the right hand of God (see also 1:3, 13 and 12:2 for the progression from the act of atonement to exaltation) signifies that his sacrifice was complete, final, and totally effective.

At other places in Hebrews, Christ's session in glory prefaces a statement about his continuing intercessory ministry (4:14-16; 7:20-25; 9:24). Psalm 110:1*b* is cited in 10:13 to show that Christ is no longer a sacrificing priest but a reigning king. The priestly act of atonement is complete; incomplete is only the removal of everything that detracts from his reign—the motif of future eschatology is picked up from 9:28 and will surface again in 10:25, 30-31, 37-38 and 12:27.

Verse 14 repeats phrases from verse 12 ("single offering"/sacrifice; "for all time"), but the accent now falls on two verbs describing the effects of Christ's completed work. He himself has been *perfected* in his elevation to God's right hand. That is, God has brought him to his final goal (see 2:10; 5:9). But he who was perfected now perfects sinners; he brings them to their heavenly goal (11:40; 12:2). He who sanctifies and those who are *sanctified* have one goal, as well as one origin (see 2:11). The one complete, objective act ("we have been sanctified"; 10:10) is an ongoing subjective reality in the lives of those who now "are [being] sanctified" (v. 14; see Peterson 1982, 150-51).

The New Covenant Brings Effective Forgiveness (10:15-18): Final proof of the efficacy of Christ's sacrifice is given by the living witness of the Spirit (see 3:7; 9:8). Two verses from the Jeremiah prophecy cited in 8:8-12 (Jer 8:10, 12) are repeated to show how Christ's finished work has brought to fulfillment key features of the new covenant.

As often, the writer tailors the text to his purposes. "With them" (v. 16) replaces the more general phrase "with the house of Israel." "Hearts" and "minds" appear in reverse order, probably to prepare for the prominence of the heart in 10:22. The abridged quotation places the writing of God's will in the hearts and minds of people in close proximity to the forgetting of their sins.

The new covenant has come about through the obedience of the Son (10:7, 9). Those who are sanctified (v. 14) do the will of God not by external compulsion, but from a willingness that arises from the heart. Interiority is the mark of the covenant. But such obedience is possible because God no longer remembers their sins. Sacrifices in the old covenant provided a continual reminder of sin (10:3); the one effective sacrifice of Christ blots them out of God's memory forever.

The climactic conclusion of the argument (v. 18) is expressed in terms similar to those used in 9:22, but in reverse order. Total removal of sin through Christ's sacrifice means that there is "no longer" the necessity of any further "offering for sin."

◊ ◊ ◊ ◊

This section could be read as an argument meant to counter the assertion (whether of Jews or Jewish Christians) that, since the Law was the revelation of God's will, the sacrifices it prescribed could never be invalidated. Whether the author had this goal in mind cannot be proven—it would hardly be necessary if the temple were already destroyed. These verses do bring to a fitting conclusion the argument on the all-sufficiency of Christ's sacrifice. There are repeated echoes of the argument since 8:1.

The writer dwells on the unity of divine will between Jesus and God. Psalm 40:6-8 and Jer 31:33-34 are linked because Jesus, who mediates the new covenant, embodies one of its essential features: inner obedience. That he has done God's will in offering himself makes it possible for the people of the new covenant to do God's will (10:7, 9, 16). The stress on Christ's body (10:5a, 7a) has an obvious purpose. Though the efficacy of Christ's sacrifice is confirmed by Christ's entry into heaven (v. 12), history is the arena of its accomplishment (v. 10).

Hints at the subjective appropriation of Christ's atoning work are sparing, but the presentation of the efficacy and final validity of Christ's sacrifice provides a basis for the climactic appeals that now follow.

Second Major Appeal: Hold Your Confession and Draw Near to God (10:19-25)

Within 8:1–10:18 there were references to the readers only at the beginning and end (see 8:1; 10:10, 15). Exposition now gives way to personal exhortation as key arguments of 5:1–10:18—the absolute superiority of Christ as Son and High Priest, his perfect sacrifice, and the certainty of salvation in him—are applied to the readers in the form of appeal (10:19-25), warning (vv. 26-31), and encouragement (vv. 32-39).

In the opening exhortation (vv. 19-25 form a single, finely crafted period in the Greek) key terms with cultic associations reappear: sanctuary; blood; priest; approach; sprinkle; conscience (vv. 19-22). Other terms like "confession" and "promise" (vv. 23-25) recall earlier appeals in chapters 1–4. In form and content, 10:19-25 most closely parallels the first major appeal in 4:14-16; an opening affirmation in the indicative provides the basis for following exhortations. Here the foundational statement is more elaborate (vv. 19-21) and is followed by a fuller series of three appeals that center on faith, hope, and love (vv. 22-25; cf. 6:10-12)—qualities that will be developed later in the Letter (faith: 11:1-40; hope: 12:1-13; love: 13:1-5).

Two Affirmations (vv. 19-21): Direct address and appeals in the inclusive first-person plural are features of the author's parenetic style. They add a more personal tone to the exhortation. "We have confidence" echoes 4:14, 16 (see also 3:6; 10:35), and points to Christ's atoning work as the objective basis of Christian certainty in terms of freedom of movement, rather than freedom of speech (the original meaning of *parrēsia*). The cultic imagery of 10:19-21 also provides echoes of 6:19-20; present action by Christians is predicated on Christ's actions in the past.

Interpretation of verses 19-20 is aided by noting the parallel formulation: believers have (a) confidence for a *way into* the *sanctuary* by means of the *blood* of Jesus (v. 19), because (b) he has opened up the *way through* the *curtain*, that is, through his *flesh* (v. 20). The two clauses provide a complementary description of Christ's completed work: He has provided unhindered access into God's holy presence (the "sanctuary" of 8:2). His blood has made entry possible in a double sense. He first opened up the way with the offering of his own blood (see 9:12), and now makes it possible for others to enter by the application of that cleansing, life-giving blood (see the comments on 9:14, 22-23). The name "Jesus" in verse 19 (cf. 2:9; 5:7; 7:22; 10:10; 12:2; 13:12, 20) is another reminder that all this is anchored in history.

The first part of the parallel statement in verse 20 is clear. As long as the old sacrificial system was in place, the "way" into God's presence was closed (cf. 9:8). Now the path to God has been "opened"—the Greek verb is the same as in 9:18 where the writer speaks of the first covenant being "inaugurated" with blood. By going ahead as forerunner, as pioneer, and perfecter of salvation (2:10; 6:20; 12:2), Christ has blazed a trail for all to follow. It is "new" in that it replaces old, ineffective ways of approaching God;

"living" because it is the pathway to life opened up by one who himself lives forever (cf. 7:16, 24).

Less clear is the second half of verse 20. The "curtain" recalls earlier divisions of cultic space. As exalted High Priest, Christ passed through the second curtain of the heavenly sanctuary into the Holy of Holies, the inner sanctuary of God's presence (6:19, 20; 9:3, 11-14). According to 4:14, he has passed through the heavens, which represent the great gap between humanity and God. Here the focus is probably not on the curtain as barrier but as connecting point, explained by the statement, "that is, through his flesh." Since flesh in Hebrews refers to Christ's Incarnation (cf. 2:14; 5:7), the writer is saying that his full humanity is the means (understanding "through" in an instrumental rather than locative sense) by which he has united people with God. Through the sacrifice of his body, of his flesh and blood (9:12; 10:5, 10, 19), the way to God has been opened. Alternatively, the last clause may be seen as explicating the preceding sentence as a whole: through his earthly sacrifice, Christ has opened a way through (understood locally) the curtain of separation. Though this involves some grammatical clumsiness on the part of the writer, it is more in keeping with 6:19-20 (see Lane 1991, 275).

The second foundational statement in verse 21 moves from Christ's past incarnational act to his present function in glory. Having opened the way to heaven, he now serves as "great priest" (cf. 4:14), continually interceding for and helping those who are tempted (2:18; 7:25). That he is "over the house of God" emphasizes his exalted status (see 3:5-6). The house is not the heavenly sanctuary, but the priestly community of believers that is being called to act as such.

Three Appeals (vv. 22-25): The first appeal, "let us approach," echoes 4:16 and invites the readers to avail themselves of priestly access to God's presence on the basis of the past actions and present function of the heavenly High Priest. Coming into God's presence (see also 7:25; 10:1; 11:16; 12:18, 22) embraces the total experience of worship (cf. v. 25) as the reception of divine blessings and the response of adoration, thanksgiving, and prayer. It also means constantly living as in God's presence, since the writer sees the Christian life as a form of "acceptable worship" (see how 12:28 is followed by 13:1-6).

Approaching God in worship requires a "true heart," one that is genuine and sincere; only the pure in heart can stand in God's holy presence (cf. Ps 24:3-4; Matt 5:8). It also requires the "full assurance of faith" that clings to the certainty that what God has promised is true. Since Hebrews closely links faith and hope (see chap. 11), the "full assurance of hope" (6:11) and of faith belong together as the firm foundation of Christian existence. Worship is the core expression of trust in God.

What is required of worshipers is itself given in worship as the experience of God's saving presence. The double mention of the "heart" in 10:22 recalls the promise of Jer 31:33-34 (see 8:10, 12; 10:16, 17): The new covenant will be signaled by changed hearts and total removal of sin. These marks of the new worship are expressed in the writer's characteristic cultic terminology. Access to God is possible because of total inner (heart and conscience) and outer (body) cleansing from sin (v. 22b). That hearts are "sprinkled clean from an evil conscience" recalls the Letter's contrast between the constant but ineffective application of animal blood in the old order (9:13, 19, 21; 10:2) and the perfect cleansing effected by Christ's blood in the new (9:14 also links the purified conscience with true worship). Blood in Hebrews is not merely a cipher for Christ's past sacrifice, but signifies a present, atoning power (see the comments on 9:22 and 12:24), so an allusion to the application of Christ's blood in the Eucharist is possible, also in view of the following baptismal allusion.

"Bodies washed with pure water" is a parallel expression for the present effects of Christ's saving death. The application of water and blood marked the inauguration of the old covenant (9:19-20); the new cleansing by blood and water in 10:22b confirms the reality of the new covenant. Further, since Aaron and his sons were consecrated for priestly office by washing with water and sprinkling with blood (Exod 29:4, 21; Lev 8:6, 30; Lev 16:4 also required the high priest to wash his body before conducting the ritual of Yom

Kippur), the writer may be inferring that all Christians can now approach God as consecrated priests.

The language of cultic washing almost certainly refers to Christian baptism (cf. Titus 3:5). Consequently, the appeal to "hold fast to the confession" can be understood as alluding to an original baptismal confession (for objections, see Lane 1991, 288), one that is echoed in the worship life of the community (13:15). Earlier allusions to a confession (3:1; 4:14) suggest that it is directed to Christ as Son, though the Letter expands it to include Christ as High Priest. Confession of Christ is a confession of hope (suggested also by combining 3:1 and 3:6) since it is directed to one in whom God's past promises have been fulfilled, and who remains the basis for the realization of promises in the future (see 6:18-19; 9:28). In 3:6 the certainty of hope was grounded on the faithfulness of the Son (see also 2:17); here it is grounded on God's faithfulness. A faithful clinging to the certainty of God's promises will ensure that present or future trials can be endured "without wavering."

A call to communal expressions of love completes the series of appeals (vv. 24-25). "Good deeds" belong to a life of worship; the readers have been cleansed from "dead works" (9:14; for examples of love in action see 13:1-6). They have been told to "consider" Jesus, to keep their eyes fixed on him as their hope (3:1; 10:23; cf. 12:2); now they are told to "consider one another" (in the Greek text) so that the house of God (10:21) remains a family of love. The readers have a good record in this area (cf. 6:10; 10:32-34), but need to stimulate one another to ensure that it continues (cf. 13:16). A community under trial can disintegrate as much through absence of love as through loss of hope.

Despite appearing in two subordinate participial clauses, the call to worship in verse 25 expresses a major concern of the writer to be read in conjunction with previous calls not to neglect God's word (2:1-4; 3:7–4:13; 5:11–6:8). Slackness in corporately expressing faith, hope, and love, is evidenced in some members of the community "neglecting to meet together" for communal worship. Recollections of past sufferings (10:32-34) suggest that social pressure, rather than the delay of the parousia (see 10:25, 37), is the main reason for absenteeism.

Mutual encouragement (v. 25b) is necessary not merely *for* worship; it takes place *in* worship as believers are served by their ministering High Priest (8:1). Without him, wavering Christians are cut off from the source of faith, hope, love, and holiness. That "the Day" of his return is drawing near is a reminder of final rescue (9:28), but also of judgment against those who have spurned him (10:26-31).

The earlier appeal for mutual encouragement "every day" (3:13) may suggest that the community met daily—the phrase "house of God" (10:21) would have special meaning for a house-church. Essential elements of its worship are alluded to in verses 22-23: the confession of Christ, baptism, and, possibly, the Eucharist. Two observations support an allusion to the latter. First, the appeal for mutual love in the context of worship would recall the concrete expression of love in connection with the Eucharist (v. 24). Second, verse 25 links worship and eschatology. Early Christian celebration of the Lord's Supper included an eschatological motif: the Lord who came in this meal was coming again in the future (see Luke 22:16; 1 Cor 11:26; 16:22; Rev 22:20. The cry *Maranatha*, best understood as "Our Lord, come!" seems to have been a eucharistic formula).

◊ ◊ ◊ ◊

The exposition of Christ's high-priestly office and work has not been a theoretical exercise. The core of the Letter (7:1–10:18) now reaches its practical climax as the writer exhorts, warns, and encourages the readers to draw the necessary conclusions from their own confession. The opening appeal of this section continues to use a cultic frame of reference in challenging the audience to act as God's sanctified people. The heavenly High Priest has opened access to God's presence. He has provided a cleansing from sin that allows all believers to function as priests as they boldly approach God in worship (10:19-22). Such access is based on a tenacious clinging to the confession of Christ as the confession of an objective hope. Present appropriation of salvation always points to its consummation in the future (vv. 23-24b). But reaching that eschatological goal does not finally rest on believers' faithfulness, but on the faithfulness of God (v. 23b). Meanwhile, the priestly sacrifice of praise in worship is to be matched by the praise of a life of "good deeds," born of love (vv. 24-25a).

The parenesis of this section has a double focal point. It is based on present and future realities made sure by Christ's obedience in history and his entry into God's heavenly presence (see 10:12-13). Thus, the exhortation to enter boldly into God's presence is to be understood within the context of a realized and future eschatology. The sanctified can now enter God's presence with confidence (10:19-23), without waiting for the parousia. But living in the shadow of the end time (10:25) also means a life of obedience expressed in love (10:24, 32-34; 13:1-5).

We can only guess at the causes for the writer's pastoral concern. The first and last appeals (vv. 22, 25) are explicit calls to worship, but we are not told why some are "neglecting to meet together." There are hints at a crisis situation in the appeals for confidence and faithfulness (vv. 19, 22-23). It is reasonable to suggest that the community's good record in enduring earlier trials is recalled because a parallel threat to the community has arisen (see 10:32-36). Reminders of what the readers "have" and are to "hold fast to" (vv. 19, 23) would have more force for people whose property and earthly security are under threat.

Fourth Warning: Do Not Spurn Christ's Sacrifice (10:26-31)

The movement from appeal to warning follows the pattern employed in 5:11–6:8 (in both cases encouragement based on past performance follows; cf. 6:9-12 with 10:32-39). The appeals of 10:19-25 were based on the thesis that "there is no longer any offering for sin" (10:18) in view of Christ's sacrifice. In parallel formulation, verse 26 states that "there no longer remains a sacrifice for sins" where Christ is rejected. The words "fearful" and "judgment/judge" in verses 27 and 30-31 frame the powerful warning that the approaching "Day" (v. 25) is one of judgment.

As in 6:4-8, the warning against apostasy is couched in vivid language. Biblical references underline the solemn lesson that curse, not blessing, must fall on those who reject God's covenant. An opening statement points to the terrible consequences of a final rejection of Christ (10:26-27). The lesson is underlined with an *a fortiori* argument that, like 2:1-5, argues that rejection of a greater gift implies greater punishment (vv. 28-29). Allusions to the biblical text are followed by a quotation from Scripture and a final warning (vv. 30-31). Though legal language is prominent (judgment; law; adversaries), the ultimate sin is described in cultic terms (v. 29).

◊ ◊ ◊ ◊

Those who neglect worship gatherings run a terrible risk. Neglect can become contempt, leading to a final stance in which they "willfully persist in sin." The writer can mean nothing other than deliberate rejection of the gospel *after* conversion. The reception of the "knowledge of the truth" (a phrase found also in 1 Tim 2:4; 2 Tim 3:7; Titus 1:1) refers to the primal catechesis and first experience of the faith, described as "enlightenment" (cf. 6:4-5; 10:32). Everyday sins of ignorance and human weakness are covered by the compassionate High Priest (2:18; 4:15-16; 5:2). But those who "[turn] away from the living God" (3:12) in apostasy reject the sacrifice for sins provided by Christ, and so negate its saving power (cf. 6:6; 10:29). His sacrifice "no longer remains" valid for them; they are the people who cannot be restored to repentance (6:4), since they have contemptuously rejected its basis.

Those who consciously distance themselves from the source of holiness become contaminated with unholiness. God's sanctified people await final rescue (9:28; 10:25); apostates have nothing less than a "fearful prospect of judgment." Its description as a "fury [literally, zeal] of fire that will consume the adversaries" comes from Isa 26:11, though Zeph 1:18 LXX speaks of God's judgment as "zealous fire" (cf. Heb 12:29).

As in 2:2-3, an *a fortiori* argument illustrates the justness of God's judgment on those who reject Christ's sacrifice. Deuteronomy 17:2-7 stipulated the death penalty for any person guilty of transgressing God's covenant by idolatry. Those who sinned knowingly and high-handedly by reviling the Lord were to be cut off from God's people (Num 15:29-31). They were to die without mercy (Deut 13:8).

The readers are asked to draw the obvious conclusion. If God's covenant will was "violated" through the rejection of its basic tenet (Exod 20:3: "You shall have no other gods before me."), the rejection of God's new covenantal will must require a "worse punishment" (10:29). Three vivid expressions underline the terrible nature of apostasy as rejection of the new covenant (cf. 6:6). First, instead of confessing him in faith (3:1; 4:14; 10:23), apostates "spurn" the Son of God—the verb suggests a trampling underfoot in utter contempt. Second, apostates "profane" what is most holy (only the most holy things, such as God's name and the sanctuary, could be profaned in the old covenant; cf. Lev 18–22). The "blood of the covenant" (see Heb 9:20, citing Exod 24:8) is deemed by apostates to be no more than common blood. Thereby the efficacy of Christ's atoning death in the past, and the power of his cleansing blood in the present, is negated—a shocking situation considering that it was this holy blood that once sanctified those who now reject it (see 10:10, 14; 13:12). Third, such rejection is an insult against the Spirit who mediates God's gifts (cf. 2:4; 6:4). Grace is met with insolence (Gk. *hybris*). To reject Christ's sacrifice is to reject the Spirit who guarantees the reality and efficacy of that sacrifice (see Attridge 1989, 295; cf. the sayings on the sin against the Holy Spirit in Mark 3:29 and par.).

The author underscores his warning by recalling the scriptural lesson that God's grace is not to be taken for granted (10:30-31; cf. 1 Cor 10:1-12). Christians know God as one who saves, but who cannot be expected to wink benignly at willful disobedience. Two verses from the Song of Moses (Deut 32:35-36 is cited as two separate oracles for extra weight) show that God's own people are not exempt from punishment. The first text is cited in the same form by Paul in Rom 12:19, but with a different purpose; the second appears also in Ps 134:14. They originally spoke of God's promise to rescue his people by taking vengeance on their enemies. The author of Hebrews changes the focus: God who vindicates will also be the judge of a sinful people! The fearful reality of judgment (v. 31 picks up v. 27) is directly related to the reality of the "living God" (cf. 3:12; 9:14; 12:22) who is no dumb idol that one might mock with impunity (see Ps 134:14-18). Sinners have to reckon with God as "consuming fire" (12:29).

◊ ◊ ◊ ◊

In the writer's view, apostasy is no better than idolatry (see vv. 28-29). This does not imply that the readers are looking for security in other gods. The grim warning against apostasy suggests that the author sees a *potentially* disastrous situation in the community. His pastoral insight sees past the present to final eventualities, so his rhetoric is designed to shock the audience out of its present complacency. Neglect of the word can become hardened revolt against it.

The motif of judgment in Hebrews is not merely a hangover from Jewish apocalyptic. For the author, judgment on willful sin is no less real than the living God, the Spirit of grace, the sacrifice of Christ, and the certainty of God's promises. To negate all the latter is to invite the former. Yet, apart from the imagery of fire that suggests destruction (10:27, 39; 12:29), there is no description of the final judgment, only the implication of final loss—loss of salvation (2:2-3); failure to reach the promised rest (4:1), the homeland (11:14-16), or the lasting city (13:14).

A CALL TO PERSEVERING FAITH (10:32–12:17)

Words of praise and encouragement (10:32-39) follow appeals and warning (10:19-31; see 5:11–6:12 for the same pattern). Yet there is good reason to see 10:32 as beginning a new discourse. Cultic and covenantal language is no longer prominent. The focus shifts from the sacrifice of Christ to the life of faith that he has set for his followers (cf. 12:1).

Faith is still viewed as confidence in God's promises (10:35), but the accent now falls on the call to perseverance. All occurrences of the noun "endurance" (10:36; 12:1; NRSV: "perseverance") and the verb "to endure" (10:32; 12:2-3; 12:7) occur in 10:32–12:17, that is, in sections that frame the *encomium* of the faithful in chapter 11. The challenge to endure in the face of temptations, to "shrink back" (10:38-39), is developed with the help of athletic metaphors (see 10:32; 11:33; 12:1, 4, 12-14).

Endurance Will Gain the Promised Reward (10:32-39)

Structural elements of an early "persecution-form," first identified in 1 Pet 4:13-17 by E. G. Selwyn (1947, 439-58), appear in 10:32-35: a persecution setting (vv. 32-33); joy in suffering (v. 34); the reason for suffering (vv. 34-35). The form is used to recall the community's past, but also to imply the ever-present reality of suffering for the faith.

More striking is the parallelism between 10:32-35 and 6:9-12; both follow dire warnings. In each case the author recalls past services to fellow Christians (10:32-34; 6:9-10) to encourage continued commitment and endurance, with the reminder of a final reward (10:35-36; 6:11-12). Whereas 6:13-20 gave scriptural argument for *God's* enduring faithfulness, 10:37-39 cites Scripture to call for enduring faith on the part of the *readers*. Thus, 10:32-39 is an overture to the examples of enduring faith in chapter 11.

The exhortation well illustrates the author's characteristic blending of traditional elements, such as the call to remember the past, suffering as a "contest" (v. 32), and his own literary skill. The latter is evident in the chiastic formulation of verses 33-34 (statements on suffering frame expressions of compassion), in the wordplay of verse 34, and in the combination of scriptural quotations in the service of his appeal (vv. 37-39).

◊ ◊ ◊ ◊

An appeal to "remember" the past is a regular element in early Christian exhortation (cf. 1 Cor 4:17; 2 Tim 1:6, 8, 14; 2 Pet 3:2). Whether the "earlier days" (10:32) belong to the remote or recent past is unclear. Presumably, the crisis of suffering took place soon after the readers were "enlightened" in the process of conversion (cf. 6:4).

In calling the past experience of persecution a "hard struggle," literally, a "great contest" (Gk. *athlēsis*), the author uses an athletic metaphor popularized by the Cynic-Stoic diatribe and adopted by hellenistic Judaism (see Pfitzner 1967, 16-72). Paul dips into this tradition in describing his own struggles to preach the gospel (1 Cor 9:24-27; Phil 1:27-30; cf. Col. 1:29–2:1; 1 Tim 1:18; 2 Tim 2:5). While Paul can link the Christian contest with suffering (Phil

1:29-30), this aspect is dominant in the use of the athletic metaphor in Hebrews (see also 11:33; 12:1-4; cf. Pfitzner 1967, 196). Use of the metaphor as a standard picture for Christian martyrdom begins with the portrayal of Peter and Paul as athletes for Christ in *1 Clem.* 5 (197-202). There are no martyrs in this community (see 12:4).

Four statements in verses 33-34 recall that the persecution involved verbal and physical attacks. To be "publicly exposed" means, literally, to be placed on public show as in a theater. Like the athletic image, this expression was at home in the Cynic-Stoic diatribe: the "athlete" pursuing virtue was an object of admiration (Epictetus *Diss.* 2.19,25; 3.22,59; Seneca *De Prov.* 2,9; [see Pfitzner 1967, 33 for other references]). Here, as in 1 Cor 4:9 (see also 4 Macc 17:11-16), the figurative meaning is entirely negative, suggesting public exposure to humiliating abuse (cf. 11:26; 13:13).

The response to this crisis was communal solidarity. Those not made the butt of public humiliation or subjected to violence clearly identified themselves with those who were—the language of partnership in verse 33b recalls both Christ's own solidarity with humanity (2:14-18; 4:15) and the picture of Christians as holy partners (3:1, 14) or sharers in heavenly things (6:4; 12:8). A practical expression of solidarity was compassion for those in prison (v. 34a; see the appeal in 13:3). More than feelings of pity are meant, since prisoners normally had to look to visitors for the provision of proper food and clothing. Such help naturally incurred suspicion, thereby also placing the help givers in danger of personal loss and further ridicule over their defenselessness. (Lane [1991, 299] argues that the chiastic structure of vv. 33-34 suggests that ridicule was related to defenselessness against seizure of property.)

The writer is more concerned with the motivation for bold confession and group solidarity than with details of the community's sufferings. Members could cheerfully accept loss of earthly possessions, knowing that they owned something that could not be taken from them (v. 34c; cf. the synoptic sayings about heavenly treasures; Matt 6:19-20; Luke 12:33). There is a subtle play on words in verse 34; the second reference to "possessions" employs a noun suggesting that which has "substance" (Thompson 1982, 65). The addressees could, like Christ (12:2), joyfully accept their trials in view of a reward that has substance. The reminder of what they "have" (in the Greek text) recalls expressions of what Christians, as potential have-nots in this world, do possess: an eternal High Priest (4:14-15; 8:1; 10:21); a sure hope (6:18-19); confidence to approach God (10:19); a "better" country that is a "lasting" home (11:16; 13:14).

The use of traditional images for suffering does not mean that 10:33-34 should be viewed as a summary of typical early Christian experience, without specific reference to the audience. The crisis in the past was real. Yet details are too sparse to allow us to suggest a precise setting. Christians were "theatrically" exposed (see v. 33) during the Neronian persecution (cf. Attridge 1989, 298), but the Letter, if written to a Roman (or Italian) community, cannot refer to this event because of the comment in 12:4. For the same reason, Jerusalem cannot be the Letter's destination; there were martyrs very early in the history of the mother church (Acts 7:59; 12:2; 26:10).

Recollection gives way to direct exhortation in verses 35-39. Confidence is the mark of those who belong to God's household and can boldly approach the divine throne (3:6; 4:16; 10:19). To jettison the boldness demonstrated in the past would amount to a tragic forfeiture of a "great reward" (cf. 11:6, 26).

Endurance is required to gain the reward, just as stamina is required of the athlete (v. 36 recalls the readers' endurance in the past). Abraham and others in Israel's history are outstanding examples of faith that endures to receive God's promises (6:15; 11:4-40), but the final paragon of endurance is Christ (12:2-3). To do the will of God means to follow Christ in affirming God's will, though it means suffering (cf. 10:7, 9; 13:21).

The writer cites Scripture in 10:27-28 as word of warning (Do not shrink back.) and promise (Christ is coming soon.). A phrase from the "Song of Isaiah" (26:20) lies behind the introductory phrase in verse 37a. It is part of a call to retreat to safety for "a very little while" until God's judgment on Israel's enemies is over. The call for concealment is completely dropped, perhaps to negate the position of some "who sought to justify . . . withdrawal and concealment on the basis of this text" (Lane 1991, 304).

The main part of the quotation (vv. 37*b*-38) cites Hab 2:3*a*-4 in a version that is close to the LXX. That which is coming in the Hebrew text is divine judgment; in the Greek version it is *someone* "who is coming" and "will not delay," allowing a messianic interpretation. Our author makes this explicit by adding the definite article so that the text speaks of "*the* coming one," a title for the Messiah in Judaism as reflected in New Testament diction (see, e.g., Matt 3:11; 11:3; John 1:15, 27; 3:31; 6:14). He gives the text a new slant by reversing the order of the quotation in verse 38. The one "who shrinks back" is no longer the Coming One, but the person who does not eagerly wait for the Lord's parousia and so meets with God's disapproval.

Placed early, "my righteous one will live by faith" now defines those who affirm God's call to patience in suffering, in the light of the parousia. The righteous faithfully cling to God's promises and so inherit life as eschatological salvation (2:3; 11:35; 12:9). Verse 39 states, in reverse order, the alternatives suggested by the quotation in verse 38: "shrinking back" or faithful endurance; being lost or saved (literally: "gaining life"; the sentence in Greek is alliterative). Instead of timidly retreating into safe anonymity, with neglect of worship an immediate result (10:25) and apostasy as a possible final outcome (10:26-31), the readers are to align themselves with the examples of faithful endurance about to be listed in chapter 11.

◊ ◊ ◊ ◊

Though the author of Hebrews uses a common image for endurance in suffering, there is no trace of the heroics associated with the picture of the moral athlete in the Cynic-Stoic diatribe. There the struggle for self-control against fate and one's passions makes the philosopher an object of admiration. Also, the Maccabean martyrs, athletes of godliness in their "contest" of endurance against the persecuting tyrant, are lauded as heroes (see especially 4 Macc 17:11-16). In recalling past endurance, Hebrews does not laud the readers, but calls for renewed faithfulness in the light of God's promises and the certainty of the parousia.

Enduring faith is not a virtue of the individual; it is the communal experience of clinging to God's promises. Suffering for the faith—

also a communal experience—has meaning and purpose in the context of the letter's eschatology (cf. 10:34-37; also 10:25, 27). In recalling Isa 26:20 and Hab 2:3-4, the author is working with texts with messianic and eschatological significance for his audience. The expectation of the Lord's return gives meaning to suffering: it is the sign of sharing in Christ who was perfected in both his passion and exaltation to glory.

Follow the Examples of Persevering Faith (11:1-40)

This example list is linked to the previous call for endurance by the word "faith" (10:38-39; 11:1). An *inclusio* marks the beginning and end of the chapter (vv. 1-3 and 39-40): the "faith" of people in the past has been "attested" (the NRSV has "received approval" [v. 2]) and the people "were commended" (v. 39), but the author uses the same verb in each case; "what is seen" (v. 3) is echoed by what "God has foreseen" (v. 40; NRSV: "provided").

The form of this chapter is integral to its argument. It is the outstanding New Testament example of exposition with exhortatory intent. Its rhetorical power, aimed at aural impact (see Cosby 1988, 4-6), is enhanced by repetition (Gk. *anaphora*) of the phrase "by/in faith" as the writer provides past examples of enduring faith. His literary skill becomes even more apparent when we note that "the term *pistis* [faith] was the technical term for a rhetorical proof. . . . Thus, Hebrews 11 presents a series of examples . . . of confidence *(pistis)* as proofs *(pisteis)*" (Mack 1990, 73).

Example lists occur in different types of ancient literature (see Lane 1991, 316-20). A variety of techniques could be employed to make "the examples cited appear to represent a great many other exemplary people who could also be used as evidence" (Cosby 1988, 19). In addition to the repetition of "by faith" (eighteen times in Heb 11:3-31), the author uses antithesis (vv. 3, 9-10, 24-26), hyperbole (v. 12*a*, *b*), descriptive circumlocution (vv. 8*a*, 11*b*, 17*b*), and wordplays (Gk. *paronomasia*) for aural effect (see Cosby 1988, 75-84).

Formal parallels to Heb 11 are found in hellenistic-Jewish adaptations of the example list. Philo lists Old Testament figures as moral *exempla* (e.g., *Praem.* 11-15 gives examples of those who maintained hope), and Wisdom literature sings the praises of famous people in sacred history (Sir 44–49) or extols the power of Wisdom from Adam to the Exodus (Wis 10:1–11:4). We come closer to the actual theme of Heb 11 in the homiletical citing of biblical examples to motivate an audience to emulate the faithfulness of past heroes (see, e.g., 1 Macc 2:51-61; 4 Macc 16:16-23).

The distinctive form of Heb 11 as a list of *attested examples* finds its best parallel in *1 Clem.* 17:1–19:3 (see D'Angelo 1979, 18-26; Lane 1991, 317-19). After a thematic introduction (Heb 11:1-3), those in the antediluvian age who have been attested by God (NRSV: "received approval") as persevering in faith are listed (vv. 4-7). Following the chronology of salvation history, the author then lists the examples of the patriarchs (vv. 8-22), of Moses and the Exodus people (vv. 23-31), and of later generations (vv. 32-38; here the list drops the anaphoric "by faith"), ending with a summarizing statement concerning divine attestation of all who lived "by faith" (vv. 39-40). By framing his examples of faithful endurance with references to divine attestation (vv. 2-6, 39), and by highlighting the promises of God that sustained the faithful in salvation history, the author has turned an *encomium* on the faithful into a song of praise to a faithful God.

Faith's Essence and First Attestation (vv. 1-7): Distinctive subject matter and linguistic features mark these verses as an opening subsection. Each main statement begins with the word "faith"; divine attestation is mentioned three times (vv. 2, 4, 5; again only in v. 39); an *inclusio* is formed by "not seen" and "unseen" in verses 1 and 7.

Hebrews 11:1 functions as a programmatic statement, not as a complete definition. Faith is defined by its object, not by the act of believing. The Greek word for "assurance" *(hypostasis)* suggests that which is substantial—in 1:3 it means God's own being or essence; in 3:14 it denotes solid confidence. The word suggests the certainty that comes from the perception of realities that are no less substantial because they are "things hoped for," meaning the total content of God's promises referred to in this chapter (11:9, 11, 13, 17, 33, 39), and elsewhere (4:1; 6:13-17; 7:6; 8:6; 9:15; 10:23, 36).

The second half of the definition speaks of faith as "conviction," using the language of the law-court where facts are attested, proved, or disproved. Faith attests the existence of final realities that are true, not despite being unseen, but precisely because they are "things not seen." The author is not echoing distinctions in hellenistic metaphysics (see Thompson 1982, 73-75, 79). Like Paul (cf. Rom 8:24-25; 2 Cor 4:18), he relates the unseen to God's promises that await future fulfillment (11:7).

Faith arises from, is sustained by, and is directed to God's word as promise. The word as Scripture illustrates the power of faith in the lives of the "ancestors" (literally, "elders"; the Greek of 1:1 speaks of them as the "fathers"). They not only "received approval" from God because of their faith (11:2, 39), but Scripture, as God's own enduring witness (7:8, 17; 10:15), continues to attest their faith to later generations (11:4; 12:1).

What "we" believe concerning creation (v. 3) seems out of place in a catalogue of believers within salvation history, but creation is recalled in other historical catalogues (e.g., God's creative power is portrayed in Sir 43 before the historical survey in chaps. 44–50; see also Ps 136:4-9 as part of a recitation of God's enduring love) and in appeals for faithful endurance (see 2 Macc 7:28). "We understand" may be an allusion to those who do not understand that the unseen God stands behind all that can be seen (see Wis 13:1). More probably, creation is recalled since it illustrates how faith is directed to unseen realities (cf. v. 1), and because it shows the power of the performative "word of God" (see Gen 1:3; Ps 33:6, 9). The contrast between "what is seen" and "things not visible" does not imply the doctrine of *creatio ex nihilo* (creation from nothing). It affirms that the sensate world has an invisible, divine source (see 11:27).

Examples of past faith begin with three antediluvian figures who attracted special interest in early Jewish and Christian circles. The Hebrew Bible does not explain why Abel's sacrifice was more acceptable than Cain's (11:4; see Gen 4:4-5). Speculation provided a variety of answers: Cain's offering was at fault ritually (this is suggested by Gen 4:7 LXX); it was qualitatively inferior; it was offered with impure motives (see Lane 1991, 333-34). The writer possibly knows such traditions, for example, Abel's confession of faith in God in the targumic treatment of Gen 4:8. Yet his thesis in 11:6 is sufficient basis for the conclusion that faith made Abel's sacrifice acceptable and showed that he was righteous (cf. Matt 23:35; 1 John 3:12). Even in death, Abel witnesses to the power of faith in the unseen God: "he still speaks," exemplifying the truth of Hab 2:4 quoted in 10:38 (a different point is made with reference to Abel's death in 12:24).

In its brief note on Enoch, the Hebrew Bible twice states that "Enoch walked with God," and ends with the cryptic note, "then he was no more, because God took him" (Gen 5:22-24). The statement in Heb 11:5 that Enoch "did not experience death" but was "taken away" reflects the LXX version according to which he was translated directly to heaven because "he had pleased God" (cf. *1 Clem.* 9:3). In the intertestamental period, Enoch came to be viewed as the father of all learning. As the companion of God and a type of the righteous who please God (Wis 4:10-14; Sir 44:16), he was considered to have been given insight into all the mysteries of God, of the created world, and of history (*Jub.* 4:17-19).

Enoch's great faith is deduced from the scriptural statement that he pleased God. This, in turn, becomes the basis of a general principle (11:6*a*), followed by two explicating comments (v. 6*b-c*). The first, though probably reflecting a credal formula from the hellenistic synagogue, is not an anti-atheistic truism or polemic against polytheism. By placing the verb "to believe" first in the clause, the writer asserts that approaching God (in worship; see 4:16; 7:25; 10:1, 22; 12:22) requires faith in the existence of God *despite his invisibility* (11:1, 27). Second, faith looks to future rewards (see 2:2; 10:35; 11:26) without present proof. Faith is not merely credence; it is a relational trust in divine providence on the part of those who "seek" God (the verb reflects the language of the psalms; see, e.g., 14:2; 34:4, 10; 53:2; 119:2), who devote themselves to the service of God.

The faith of Noah (v. 7), the first to be called righteous in the biblical record (Gen 6:9; 7:1; cf. Heb 10:38), illustrates an aspect of faith that figures largely in the rest of the chapter: Faith is obedience to God. By building the ark, Noah showed respect for God's warning of impending destruction, and hope in the reality of

God's promise of rescue. The "things not seen" (v. 1) that faith grasps include "events as yet unseen."

Noah's obedience "condemned the world" in a twofold sense. By building the ark, he put his evil contemporaries to shame and prophetically announced God's impending judgment (a later tradition pictures Noah as a preacher of repentance; see 2 Pet 2:5; 1 Clem. 7:6; 9:4; Sib. Or. 1.125-136). As with Abel, Noah's faith still preaches a message; it is a reminder of divine judgment on all disobedience (see Matt 12:41, 42).

Noah is also an abiding witness to the rewards of faith (cf. 10:38; 11:6). Called righteous before the flood (see also Ezek 14:14, 20; Wis 10:4; Sir 44:17), he became an heir to righteousness as a gift commensurate with his faith. He thus belongs at the side of the patriarchs who were heirs of divine promises (vv. 8-9). Noah is a type of all those who are heirs of the salvation contained in the promises of God in Christ, himself the "heir of all things" (1:2, 14; 6:12; 9:15; 11:39-40).

The Faith of the Patriarchs (vv. 8-22): The last word of verse 7 in the Greek, "heir," provides the link to this subsection; it is echoed in verses 8-9 with "inheritance" and "co-heirs." Prominence is given to the concepts of promise (vv. 9, 11, 13, 17) and blessing (vv. 20-21). The listing of examples is interrupted briefly in verses 13-16 by an explanatory comment on the eschatological nature of patriarchal faith, but these verses still contribute to a parallel development of the twin themes of promised land (vv. 8-10, 13-16) and promised progeny (vv. 11-12, 17-19).

That Abel, Enoch, and Noah lived by faith was inferred from the biblical record with the help of later traditions. In the case of Abraham, the writer cites a figure long celebrated as the father of the faithful. Hebrews 6:13-15 recalled the patient endurance by which he obtained God's promise. His obedience in response to God's call, implicit in Gen 12:1, 4 (22:18 and 26:5 refer to his obedience in a different context), is highlighted also by Philo (*Abr.* 60, 62, 85, 88) and 1 Clem. 10:1-2. The repetition of the verb "to set out" in Heb 11:8 is deliberate; faith requires a "going out" from earthly securities (13:13) before it can lead into God's presence and the final rest (4:1-11; 6:19). The description of the patriarch's destination as an "inheritance" uses Old Testament land-terminology (cf. 1 Chr 16:18; Ps 105:11; Acts 7:5), but points to the eschatological focus of Abraham's faith (see 9:15; 11:13-16). That Abraham acted on trust, not knowing where he was going, is deduced from the phrase, "the land that I will show you" (Gen 12:1; Philo makes the same connection in *Migr. Abr.* 43-44).

Though the promise of land was repeated (Gen 15:18), Abraham never saw its fulfillment—just as Israel did not inherit the promised rest (4:8). It remained the promised land, not the possessed land (11:9). He lived as a resident alien in a foreign land (see v. 13 below). The nomadic existence of Abraham, Isaac, and Jacob, despite the repeated promise of land (see Gen 26:2-3; 35:12), highlights the tension between promise and earthly nonfulfillment.

Abraham could endure nonfulfillment, symbolized by the impermanence of "living in tents" (v. 9), because he looked forward to living in a permanent city. The author leaves the Genesis account, and builds on the apocalyptic expectation of a new Jerusalem (shown to Abraham, according to 2 *Apoc. Bar.* 4:4, though Hebrews is not referring to this tradition; see also 4 Ezra 10:27; 13:36), understood as a transcendent reality (an "eternal inheritance" in heaven according to 2 *Enoch* 55:2; see Gal 4:26; Phil 3:20; Rev 3:12; 21). The reality of this city, to which Christians have come (12:22), is assured since God is its "architect and builder."

Hebrews now moves to the promise of descendants (11:11-12; cf. Gen 12:2; 13:16). The textual problems associated with 11:11 are indicated by the change in translation from the RSV where Sarah is the subject, to the NRSV in which Abraham is the subject, with the phrase "and Sarah herself was barren" as a parenthesis (another Greek text has Abraham receiving power to procreate "with Sarah").

While the original text remains uncertain, the NRSV reading (adopted also by the NIV and TEV) is preferable for the following reasons: (1) Abraham is the natural subject of verses 11 and 12; "too old" and "as good as dead" are parallel descriptions for the same person. (2) The "power of procreation" refers to the function of the male in begetting, rather than to that of the woman in conceiving (but see van der Horst 1990). (3) Sarah laughed in unbelief at the thought of conceiving (Gen 18:9-15), though she later laughed with joy at Isaac's birth (Gen 21:6). Abraham also laughed at the idea of having a child at his age, but 15:6 specifically says that Abraham believed God's promise.

As in Heb 6:13, a circumlocutory participle, "he who promised," is used to describe God. Abraham's faith is exemplary in asserting that the God who promises is "faithful"—a credal expression for God's absolute reliability (cf. 1 Cor 10:13; 2 Cor 1:18; 1 Thess 5:24; 2 Thess 3:3; 2 Tim 2:13; 1 John 1:9; Rev 1:5). In the case of this second promise, Abraham's faith was partially rewarded: Isaac was born to a man "as good as dead" in terms of procreative power (cf. Rom 4:19 and Heb 11:17-19: God can create life from death).

Returning to the land theme (vv. 13-16 pick up vv. 9-10), the writer presents a typological, rather than allegorical (as in Philo *Migr. Abr.*) reinterpretation of land as final homeland. The repetition of "by faith" is momentarily dropped as he stresses the eschatological focus of faith—with an obvious message for his readers who live under the threat of continuing social alienation (cf. 10:32-34).

Even in death the patriarchs clung to the hope of a promised land—"promises" in verse 13 probably refers to the repeated promise of land rather than to the multiple promise of land, a great nation, and blessing. Nonfulfillment in this life meant not less faith, but properly directed faith, as the patriarchs looked to ultimate realities. They greeted their final homeland "from afar," like travelers in sight of their final destination, or like Moses who was permitted to catch a glimpse of the promised land from a mountain before his death (Deut 32:49; 34:4).

The author finds evidence for the eschatological nature of the patriarchs' faith in the "confession" of Abraham on purchasing the cave of Machpelah to bury Sarah: "I am a stranger and an alien residing among you" (Gen 23:4). This profession—providing a model for Christians called to confess Christ as their final hope (cf. 4:14; 10:23)—was repeated by Jacob and his sons (Gen 47:4, 9). Abraham and his heirs were resident aliens in the lands in which they lived. Hebrews sees this as typifying existence "on the earth" in contrast to existence in a final heavenly homeland.

The stance of the patriarchs is continuing witness ("they make . . . clear that they are seeking"; v. 14) to the existence of a final homeland to be equated neither with Canaan as their temporary home, nor with Mesopotamia as the original homeland (see Gen 24:6; 31:3; for a contra-factual argument see also 4:8; 7:11; 8:4, 7; 10:2). What they longed for was a better country (v. 16); as often in Hebrews, "better" refers to what is heavenly in origin and therefore lasting (7:19, 22; 8:6; 9:23; 10:34; 11:35). The better country corresponds to the city with foundations (v. 10).

Faith in the promises of God, expressed in the patriarchs' confession, met with God's confession of them (v. 16b). To be ashamed of someone means nonrecognition; the opposite means open acknowledgment (cf. 2:11; Mark 8:38; Rom 1:16; 2 Tim 1:8). By allowing himself to be called the God of Abraham, Isaac, and Jacob (Gen 28:13; Exod 3:6, 13-16; Matt 22:32), God acknowledged the faith of the fathers, a faith that is well founded: he "has prepared a city for them" (cf. v. 10; the preparation of "a place" for Israel, signaled in 1 Chr 17:9, became a theme in apocalyptic literature and early Christian eschatology; see 2 Apoc. Bar. 4:3; Rev 12:6; 21:2; cf. John 14:2).

Resumption of anaphora ("by faith") marks the writer's return to the story of Abraham and the promise of seed (vv. 17-19 resume vv. 11-12), and to a subtheme: faith trusts in God to create life out of death (vv. 12, 19). As with the first and last examples of persevering faith (11:4; 12:1-3), a sacrifice is involved. The story of Abraham's readiness to sacrifice his son (Gen 22:1-18) was widely commented on in haggadic tradition (see Swetnam 1981, 23-80). Our author is interested only in the testing of Abraham's faith (cf. Sir 44:20; 1 Macc 2:22). God's command to sacrifice an "only son" (Gen 22:2) was not merely a monstrous offense against paternal love, it attacked the very promise that Abraham would be the father of a great nation (Gen 12:2-3; 13:16). Isaac, not Ishmael, was to be the bearer of these promises (Heb 11:18 cites Gen 21:12).

Abraham trusted God despite God. Like other writers (see Jas 2:21-22; Sir 44:19-23), Hebrews sees in Abraham's submission a perfect demonstration of faith as trusting obedience. Genesis 22:1-10 does not state why Abraham acted without questioning God's will. Hebrews 11:19 infers what the patriarch was thinking (similarly, 11:11, 16, 26), probably on the basis of the promise itself (Gen 21:12) and Abraham's assurance to his servants that he and the boy would return to them (Gen 22:5). In addition, the writer draws a parallel to the way in which the original promise of a son was fulfilled: the God who could give a son to one as good as dead (v. 12) could also "raise someone from the dead." The latter phrase echoes early Christian credal formulations (see Rom 4:17; 2 Cor 1:19) that recall the Jewish confession of God as the one who gives life to the dead.

Christian readers would naturally recall another Father's readiness to surrender his "only" Son (see John 1:14, 18; 3:16, 18; Rom 3:32), and that Son's rescue from death (5:7). Yet Heb 11:19 shows no interest in a christological typology. Instead, it records how Abraham's faith was rewarded; the rescue of Isaac from virtual death was a symbolic foreshadowing of the future resurrection to which Abraham could look in hope (cf. 11:13).

The faith of Isaac, Jacob, and Joseph (vv. 20-22) illustrates the truth enunciated in verse 13: they "died in faith." By blessing their heirs and mentioning the future deliverance, they showed unwavering trust in God's promises, even in the face of death. Blessing comes from the God who makes promises (6:14). To bless means to share in God's activity as he puts his promises into effect (see 7:1-7), even if they run contrary to human expectation. Isaac thus exemplifies faith as "assurance of things hoped for" (11:1); he accepted God's choice of Jacob as the future bearer of the promise.

Jacob's blessing of Joseph's sons (v. 21; see Gen 48:1-22) includes them among his own sons as bearers of blessing, even though they had been born in Egypt, not in the promised land (48:5-6). There is again a preferential blessing of the younger son, but Hebrews recalls this event for another reason. The accent lies on "when dying" and on the posture of the patriarch. The Hebrew Bible records that Jacob, before pronouncing the blessing, "bowed himself on the head of his *bed*" (Gen 47:31, emphasis added). By reading the unvocalized Hebrew *mittah* as *matteh*, the LXX has

Jacob "bowing in worship over the top of his *staff.*" This has double significance for our author. In death (cf. Heb 11:13) Jacob adores God as the author of blessings and promises; the (walking) staff in his hands marks him as a pilgrim on the move to the heavenly homeland.

Approaching death, Joseph also looked to things still unseen (v. 22; cf. 11:1). He was so sure of Israel's future deliverance in the Exodus that he "gave instructions about his burial" (literally, "his bones"; Gen 50:24-25). In death, he became a member of the wandering people of God on their pilgrimage to the promised, heavenly homeland (Exod 13:19; Josh 24:32).

The Faith of Moses and the Exodus Generation (vv. 23-31): The mention of the Exodus in verse 22 paves the way for the story of Moses and the Exodus generation. Prominence is given to the motif of not fearing the king (pharaoh) in the context of "seeing" something (vv. 23, 27). Faith is now more clearly identified as perseverance in the face of opposition and suffering.

Three moments in the life of Moses illustrate how faith leads to deliberate choice and decisive actions (vv. 23-27; see D'Angelo 1979, 17-64). In each case the author offers an explanatory comment on the motivation provided by faith. Hebrews follows Exod 2:2 LXX in saying that both parents hid the infant Moses for three months (so also Philo *Vita Mos.* 1.7-10 and Josephus *Ant.* 2.218; the Hebrew text mentions only the mother). The biblical account suggests no motivation for this action. Hebrews follows a tradition in hellenistic Judaism (see Acts 7:20; Philo *Vita Mos.* 1.9; Josephus *Ant.* 2.225) in seeing a deeper significance to the child's beauty: he is marked by God for a role. Faith's insight allowed the parents to ignore Pharaoh's edict that all male infants be killed (Exod 1:22). They trusted God to preserve the child for his future task. The lesson is clear: Faith in divine providence removes fear (cf. Heb 11:27). The reference in some manuscripts to Moses' murder of an Egyptian (Exod 2:11-12; see NRSV, note to Heb 11:23) was probably inserted by a copyist with the next verse and Acts 7:23-25 in mind.

The first example of Moses' own faith "when he was grown up" (see Exod 2:11) makes him a companion of Abraham who also rejected earthly security (vv. 24-26). Hebrews alludes to Exod 2:10-11, but also reflects the later hellenistic-Jewish Moses traditions (see D'Angelo 1979, 36, 42-53). Instead of enjoying princely luxury and prestige, Moses chose to identify with his own people, though this meant sharing their ill-treatment rather than enjoying the "pleasures of sin" (v. 25). The latter phrase probably implies more than the rejection of a pagan lifestyle enjoyed at the expense of the Israelite slaves (Exod 1:11). Our author assumes that Moses was fully aware both of his call to lead Israel, and of his calling to a lasting reward in contrast to "fleeting" pleasures (cf. 13:14; for the contrast between temporal security and eternal salvation, see 4 Macc 15:2, 8, 23). Failure to obey both calls would have meant a sinful rejection of God.

Verse 26 confirms the eschatological orientation of Moses' faith, though in what sense he chose the "abuse suffered for the Christ" (literally, "the reproach of Christ") is not clear. "The Christ," that is, "the anointed," could be understood as a collective term for the people of God (v. 25; cf. Ps 105:15; 1 John 2:20, 27). The writer may have had in mind Ps 89(LXX 88):50-51: in the Greek version the psalmist calls on God to remember "the *reproach* of your servants" with which God's enemies "have reproached your *anointed one*" (for the theme of reproach suffered for God, see also Ps 69:6-12). But whether the LXX equates God's servants with the Anointed One is not certain; it may have understood verse 52 as referring to the king or to a future messiah. The use of "the Christ" for Jesus in Hebrews, in contrast to Moses in 3:6, makes unlikely a reference to Moses himself as God's anointed prophet.

With Ps 89:51 in mind, our author seems to be making a double point. First, the phrase "reproach of Christ" allows for allusion rather than specific statement—in identifying with the suffering Hebrews, Moses typifies the life of faith that involves suffering for Christ. Second, he prefigures Christ's own bearing of shame (cf. 12:2-3), though not vicariously—Moses is never a savior-figure in Hebrews. By choosing suffering over prestige, he serves as a model of faith for those who are called to leave earthly security and bear abuse for Christ (10:33; 13:13). He kept the vision of faith alive by "looking ahead to the reward" (11:26*b*; cf. 10:35). Moses is the antithesis of the apostate who denies membership in God's people by denying Christ and refusing to suffer for him.

Moses twice left Egypt (v. 27), once to escape punishment for murder (Exod 2:15), then to participate in the Exodus (Exod 12:51). The narrative sequence of verses 27-29 suggests that his escape to Midian is meant, since the Passover (v. 28) preceded the Exodus flight (v. 29). Though this first flight was motivated by fear for his own safety according to Exod 2:14, later tradition could see it as exemplifying confidence and endurance (see Lane 1991, 375). Hebrews affirms Moses' readiness to abandon an earthly homeland, and to do so without fear of the pharaoh like his parents (v. 23). His trust in God to rescue himself and his people makes Moses an exemplar of persevering faith (cf. 10:36), which looks to the future for divine intervention and reward.

The basis of Moses' faith was his vision of the "invisible" God. This traditional epithet (see John 1:18; Rom 1:20; Col 1:15; 1 Tim 1:17) here has special significance. Though the relevant Greek phrase could be translated "as one who saw . . . ," the writer means "as if he were one who saw." Moses heard God's voice from the burning bush and later spoke face-to-face with God (Exod 33:11; Num 12:8; Deut 34:10; Sir 45:6) without actually seeing God's face (Exod 33:20-23). The use of the present participle ("as seeing") characterizes Moses as one who lived continually by the vision of realities seen only with the eyes of faith (cf. 11:1). He trusted God to lead the people out of slavery and perceived the truth of an invisible but eternal world in contrast to the attractiveness of any temporary, earthly home.

Verse 28 marks the transition from Moses to the Exodus. By faith Moses "kept the Passover" (see Exod 12:11-28) so that the angel of death, the "destroyer" (Exod 12:23; cf. 1 Cor 10:10 and Wis 18:25) would "pass over" their households, sparing their firstborn. The writer shows special interest in the life-giving power of blood (9:7-25; 10:4, 19, 29; 12:24; 13:11-12, 20), so he focuses attention on the application of the blood (see Exod 12:7, 13, 22-23), not on the Passover meal.

Despite the Israelites' fear at the sight of the advancing Egyptian army and their murmuring against Moses (Exod 14:10-12), the author can see faith at work in the safe crossing of the Sea of Reeds (Heb 11:29 and Acts 7:36 follow the LXX in calling it the Red Sea) and in the destruction of the pursuers (Exod 14:21-29). He is probably recalling Exod 14:13-15: trust in God allowed the people to move forward without fear.

The faithless wilderness generation (3:7–4:2) is bypassed to recall the most spectacular event in the capture of Canaan (11:30). God worked the destruction of Jericho after the people obeyed instructions to carry out an improbable siege strategy (Josh 6:1-21). In response to God's promises (6:2, 16), faith accepted the destruction of the city as a fait accompli before the event.

Rahab the harlot (11:31; see Josh 2:1-21) is an unlikely candidate as an example of faith—she and Sarah (v. 11) are the only women in this catalogue—but she seems to have held special interest for early Christians (her faith is stressed also in Jas 2:25 and *1 Clem* 12:1-8). Attempts were made already in ancient times to give her a more respectable occupation—the New Testament text was amended to read "the so-called harlot," and Josephus calls her an innkeeper (*Ant.* 5.7-8)—but her morality is not the issue. In harboring the Israelites sent to spy out Jericho, she aligned herself with the wandering people of God and expressed her faith in God to give them the land (Josh 2:8-11). Her faith initially put her own life at risk; it finally meant rescue from the fate suffered by "unbelievers" (Josh 6:17, 22-25).

The Faith of Subsequent Generations (vv. 32-40): The repetition of "by faith" is dropped. Instead, this last section is framed by the Greek phrase "through faith" (vv. 33, 39). Examples of triumphant faith (vv. 32-35*a*) give way to examples of endurance in the face of persecution (vv. 35*b*-38). A summarizing statement brings this peroration to a conclusion (vv. 39-40).

Using standard rhetorical phrases in verse 32*a* (see Lane 1991, 382 for parallels), the audience is reminded that only a selection of examples is being offered. A sampling of six figures from the period of the Judges and the early monarchy is given without comment.

Why the writer does not list them in correct sequence (i.e., Barak, Gideon, Jephthah, Samson, Samuel, David) is not clear, but the first two judges are listed in reverse order also in 1 Sam 12:11 (see also *Apost. Const.* 7.37.1). Perhaps the writer was thinking of three pairs of examples, with the more important figure always placed first. Barak was called by God through the prophetess Deborah to defeat a league of Canaanites (Judg 4–5); Gideon rescued Israel from the Midianites with a small force of three hundred (Judg 6–7). Jephthah led the eastern tribes against the Ammonites (Judg 11–12); Samson's proverbial strength and cunning led to victories over the Philistines (Judg 13–16).

It is easier to see why David is cited as an example of faith, despite his great sins (see Sir 47:2-11). He received the promise of an eternal throne, fulfilled in Christ (1:5*b*; 2 Sam 7:11-16). His psalms bear testimony to his deep faith in God. Samuel, the last charismatic judge, is possibly listed after David in order to associate him also with the prophets (see Sir 48:1–49:10).

In finely honed formulation the writer offers three sets of three statements (vv. 33-34) that are designed for rhetorical effect rather than precise identification of faith's heroes. It was primarily Joshua, the judges, David, and Solomon who conquered kingdoms by capturing Canaan and extending Israel's borders. It was especially Samuel, David, and Solomon who administered justice (e.g., 1 Sam 12:3-5; 2 Sam 8:15; 1 Kgs 3:28; 10:9). The obtaining of promises seems to refer to military victories, such as those promised to Barak, Gideon, Samson, and David (Judg 4:14; 6:16; 7:7; 13:5; 2 Sam 5:19), possibly also to the gift of wealth and wisdom, promised to Solomon (1 Kgs 3:11-14).

The second triplet refers to deliverance from death. Samson and David killed lions (Judg 14:6; 1 Sam 17:34-37), but Daniel "shut the mouths of lions" (v. 33; Dan 6:22-23). His rescue and that of his three friends, who "quenched raging fire" to escape from the fiery furnace (v. 34; Dan 3:23-27), are usually associated in example lists (cf. 1 Macc 2:59-60; 3 Macc 6:6-7; 4 Macc 16:3, 21; 18:12-13; *1 Clem.* 45:6-7). Daniel, unlike Babylon's wise men, escaped the edge of the sword (v. 34; Dan 2:13), but the reference is broader; David escaped from Goliath, Saul, and Absalom (1 Sam 17:41-54;

19:10-18; 2 Sam 15:14), and prophets such as Elijah, Elisha, and Jeremiah escaped the murderous plots of rulers (1 Kgs 19:2-10; 2 Kgs 6:32; Jer 26:7-16).

The final triplet (v. 34*b*) recalls those who, though weak, were empowered by God. For example, Gideon gained victory with a small army (Judg 7), Samson's strength was restored for one last triumph (16:28), David defeated Goliath with only a sling and a stone (1 Sam 17:48-51), and Judith and Esther were women "empowered" to give victory to their people (see *1 Clem.* 55:3-6). The last two phrases are complementary; faced with overwhelming odds, Israel's leaders celebrated stunning military victories. The routing of large armies by small Jewish bands is well illustrated in the story of the Maccabean revolt (e.g., 1 Macc 3:10-19; 4:8-15, 26-35).

Verse 35*a* forms a transition from examples of triumphant faith to examples of enduring faith. The faith of weak and defenseless women like the widow at Zarephath and the Shunammite woman was vindicated in the raising of their sons from the dead by Elijah and Elisha (1 Kgs 17:17-24; 2 Kgs 4:25-37). Like Abraham, they trusted God to create life where there was death (cf. 11:19).

The reference to resurrection provides the link to the story of the martyrs' faith (vv. 35*b*-38). They endured appalling suffering, hoping in a "better resurrection" than restoration to normal life (cf. v. 35*a*). The author is probably recalling the story of the Maccabean martyrs in 2 Macc 6–7. An old priest, Eleazar, was stretched on the rack, refusing to be released from death (2 Macc 6:22, 30). A mother and her seven sons suffered excruciating agonies rather than renounce their faith, believing that "the King of the world will raise us up . . . to live again forever" (7:9 JB, see also vv. 11, 14, 20-36).

Before the Maccabean martyrs, others endured mockery, flogging, and imprisonment (v. 36; cf. 2 Chr 16:10; 36:16; 2 Macc 7:1, 7, 10). Jeremiah is the type of suffering prophet who endured insults, beatings, and confinement (Jer 20:2, 7; 37:15-16; 38:6); sufferings that the readers know about from experience (see 10:32-34).

Biblical and postbiblical traditions record the death of prophets by stoning (11:37*a;* Zechariah; 2 Chr 24:20-21; a later legend includes Jeremiah), by being sawn apart (Isaiah; *Mart. Isa.* 5), and by the sword (Uriah; Jer 26:23). Such traditions are reflected in Jesus' complaint against Jerusalem (Matt 23:37; Luke 13:34).

Even while escaping death (cf. v. 34), the prophets suffered extreme privation. Wearing only sheep and goat skins, Elijah and Elisha (see 1 Kgs 19:13; 2 Kgs 2:8; *1 Clem.* 17:1 adds Ezekiel) were marked as itinerant prophets, separate from city life and its comforts. Destitute and tormented (see 1 Kgs 19:14), the prophets were forerunners of later martyrs who fled to remote areas to escape persecution (v. 38; cf. Ps 107:4). One hundred prophets took refuge from Queen Jezebel in caves; Elijah had to flee to the desert (1 Kgs 18:4; 19:4). Judas Maccabeus and his companions lived like wild animals in the mountains (see 2 Macc 5:27; 10:6; *Mart. Isa.* 2:9-11 has Isaiah doing the same).

Rejected by society, such martyrs belonged to a better world (cf. v. 35). Like Abraham and Moses, they spurned the comforts of this life for something better and more enduring. That is why their faith is commended by God in the form of scriptural attestation (v. 39; cf. 11:2). Yet "all these" people who lived by faith are different from "us" (i.e., Christians; v. 40). These martyrs received various promises, but only partial fulfillment in their own lifetime (vv. 11, 33). They did not receive "the promise" (the singular noun recalls the promise of an eternal inheritance [9:15]), an eternal city in a permanent homeland (11:10, 15-16). This was not due to any fault on their part, but was ordained by divine providence. God's ultimate promise has been fulfilled in Christ through whom believers have now received something "better" (see 7:19, 22; 8:6; 9:23; 10:34; 11:35).

The author implies that past believers who once lived in hope of perfection, without receiving it, now experience it in glory. His argument in verse 40*b* aims at inclusion, not exclusion. Those who looked forward to the realization of God's promises and those who can now look back to their partial fulfillment are finally united in the one faith. In worship, Christians are already part of the heavenly city and united with the "spirits of the righteous made perfect"

(12:22-23). But until they are perfected with Christ in glory (see 2:10; 7:28), they must emulate the enduring faith of past witnesses (12:1) who kept their gaze fixed on future realities.

◊ ◊ ◊ ◊

Hebrews 11 does not offer a theoretical phenomenology of faith, but a celebration of faith with practical implications. The writer has already indicated the essential characteristics of faith in other exhortatory passages: it includes confidence (10:19, 35), obedience (10:26, 36), endurance (6:12, 10:36); it clings to God's promise of salvation (2:1-4; 4:1) and is thus the ground of hope (3:6; 6:11, 18-19; 7:19; 10:23). By illustrating faith from examples in history, the author avoids a heavy-handed castigation of a perceived lack of faith in the present (10:23, 39; 12:3, 12). His appeal to emulate past saints is set within the context of salvation history as the story of God's own faithfulness.

The characteristics of faith in Heb 11 are as follows:

(1) Faith is *knowledge of unseen realities.* It grasps truths that escape the physical eye but are more enduring than empirical realities, for example, the mystery of creation and the existence of the invisible God (11:3, 6, 27). It gives certainty and substance to what still lies in the future (11:1).

(2) Faith is *response to God's word,* especially the word of promise (11:8-12). That is why the whole letter, as an appeal for faith, is a scriptural argument.

(3) Faith is unquestioning *obedience* to the call of God (11:8, 17), and thus the opposite of apostasy and rebellion, the ultimate disobedience (2:1-3; 3:12; 4:11; 6:6-8; 10:26-31).

(4) Faith is *orientation to the future* in which God has something "better" in store for believers. Faith in action emulates the stance of those who looked beyond present earthly realities to what is final and eternal (11:10, 14-16, 25, 35).

(5) Faith is thus the *ground of hope* (11:1); the "full assurance of hope" is virtually synonymous with the "full assurance of faith" (6:11; 10:22). It is not a hoping against hope, but a confidence

grounded on God's own reliability (11:11; cf. 10:23; 6:13-18). By faith, objects of hope become present possessions.

(6) In particular, faith is *trust in the promises of God* (11:9, 11, 13, 17, 33, 39) even—and especially—when present reality seems to call them into question. Faith is the power to endure temporary nonfulfillment.

(7) That is why chapter 11 focuses on the *endurance of faith* (see 10:35). The patriarchs and Moses had to live by faith in the sense that present circumstances often belied the promise. The martyrs persevered in faith despite their trials (11:35-38).

(8) Faith in God involves *faithfulness* to God in the face of suffering—death, or the threat of death, is a subtheme in chapter 11 (vv. 4-5, 7, 11-13, 17-31, 35-38). A community that has experienced suffering, and faces trials in the future (10:32-34; 12:3-4), is reminded that fidelity to God can be sustained only where there is the certainty of something that outweighs present trials (see 11:26, 35).

In the main, the author allows the example list to speak for itself without applicatory comment. The audience is expected to connect with the exemplars of faith. For example, like Abraham they are called to leave earthly security behind them; like Moses they are to consider abuse suffered for Christ part of their calling (cf. 11:8, 26 with 13:13). The faith of the patriarchs, expressed in their confession (11:13), calls their heirs to equal faithfulness in clinging to the confession of Christ (4:14; 10:23). Not yet explicitly stated in Heb 11 is that Christ, the ultimate focus of faith, is also the greatest example of enduring faith (12:1-3).

Run with Discipline the Course Set by Jesus (12:1-11)

A change from historical recital to exhortation marks the beginning of a new section. Yet there are clear linguistic and conceptual links with the preceding argument. The word "witnesses" picks up the verb "attested" in 11:2, 39 (NRSV: "received approval" and "commended"), the distinction between past witnesses and "us" is carried over to 12:1 from 11:40, while the use of "perseverance" and "endured" in 12:1-3 recalls the appearance of the verb and the noun in 10:32, 36 (NRSV: "endurance"). The athletic image, introduced in 10:32, is again employed (12:1-4, 11). Finally, the example of Jesus who endured suffering in view of a final reward forms a fitting climax to the example list of chapter 11 (especially 11:35-38).

The limits of the section are open to dispute since the author does not employ the usual device of *inclusio*. Instead, he uses keywords ("endure" in vv. 1-3; "discipline" in vv. 5-11) and link words ("race" and "struggle" in vv. 1, 4; "lose heart" in vv. 3, 4). An appeal for endurance extends to 12:13, yet the imperative form of appeal suggests that verses 12-13 belong to the next section. Closing the section at verse 11 gives the following sequence: The writer presents the suffering and glorified Jesus as the supreme example of one who has "run" with endurance (vv. 1-3); he recalls the audience's past experience, still using the athletic metaphor (v. 4); he then interprets the experience of suffering under the rubric of discipline, using a Wisdom text as his basis (vv. 5-11). The section closes with an explicit reference to the athletic image ("trained" in v. 11).

◊ ◊ ◊ ◊

As in other appeals (see 4:14; 10:19), the author begins with a reminder of what the readers have—a literal translation of verse 1*a* would be: "*having* such a great cloud of witnesses surrounding us." The witnesses (the Greek word *martyres* is not yet used in the later sense of "martyrs") are those of chapter 11 who, in life and in death, testified to the power of faith (11:2, 4-5, 39). Deceased leaders of the community (see 13:7) are probably included. The use of the athletic image in verses 1-4 suggests that the "cloud of witnesses" surrounds Christian athletes like spectators in an arena, even if verse 2 accents what Christians look to as they "run" the race of faith.

Runners do not determine the course or the conditions of the race; the "race [literally, contest] . . . is set before" one—a fixed phrase in classical and hellenistic Greek, also in the athletic metaphor, to denote the concerted effort required in attaining a goal (see the comments on 10:32 above; for the Christian calling as a race in other NT passages, see Pfitzner 1967, 134-38). Our author keeps to his main theme: the need for stamina to endure the rigors of the contest (cf. 10:36; see 4 Macc 17:12-17 and *1 Clem.* 5:1-7 for the endurance of martyr-athletes). The "athlete" must strip off excess weight that would impede progress (the desire for earthly security and social acceptance may be implied). The one encumbrance that must be shed is the sin that "clings so closely," that is, any besetting sin that might cause the runner to fall (see 12:12-13). Another reading suggests something that "easily distracts" attention from the goal (see Lane 1991, 398). The writer does not identify "sin"; the readers can fill out the metaphor for themselves. Spiritual lethargy (see v. 3) rather than total loss of faith (the race would in that case be over) is the great retarding sin.

The Maccabean martyrs endured suffering by looking to God (4 Macc 17:10); Christians look to Jesus for their prime source of encouragement. Like other New Testament calls to imitate Christ (e.g., Phil 2:5-11; 1 Pet 2:21-24; 3:17-22), Heb 12:2 presents him as more than a model to be emulated; he is "pioneer and perfecter of the faith" (not just "our faith" NRSV) also in a salvific sense (see 2:10). The NEB paraphrase points in the right direction: Jesus is the one "on whom faith depends from start to finish."

The human name "Jesus" (cf. 2:9; 5:7; 7:22; 13:12, 20) directs attention to a person of flesh and blood, not to a mythical hero. From beginning to end, he remained the faithful and obedient Son (see 2:13; 5:7-8; 10:7, 9). The course that he completed is now the way along which he leads others (10:20). The "forerunner" (6:20) has become the source of salvation (5:9); the one perfected now perfects his siblings (5:7; 10:14). Thus, Jesus is initiator and completer of faith in a double sense. He is its source and prime exemplar.

Jesus endured suffering with the prospect of future joy (12:2*b*). The cross as symbol of shame contrasts with the honor represented by enthronement at God's right hand (the reference is again to Ps 110:1; see also 1:3, 13; 8:1; especially 10:12). It is linguistically possible to translate, "who instead of the joy set before him . . ." (see NRSV footnote). In this case Jesus would be like Moses who chose ill-treatment rather than avoidance of suffering (see 11:25; the Pauline parallels would be 2 Cor 8:9 and Phil 2:6-7). Whether "joy" can be reduced to avoidance of pain remains problematic. The more likely meaning is that Jesus endured "for the sake of the joy set before him," with 11:26 as the parallel: Moses endured abuse by looking forward to a reward. By inference, the suffering of Christians is made lighter by the joyful prospect of future glory (cf. Rom 8:18), guaranteed by the glorified Son himself.

Others suffered persecution (11:23, 27, 29, 33-38), but Christ is the prime example of enduring hostility in pursuit of a set goal (12:3). Those who attacked him during his public ministry and passion were "sinners" since unbelief is the great sin (see 3:13, 19; 6:6). A well-attested though more difficult reading says that their hostility was "against themselves" (see NRSV footnote), suggesting that sin leads to self-injury. The exact phrase has no biblical parallel, but the thought that opposition to God brings self-destruction is not uncommon (see Rom 2:5; Phil 1:28; Rev 19:19-21; 20:8-10). An allusion to proverbial wisdom (see Prov 8:36: "Those who miss me injure themselves.") is quite possible in the light of the quotation from Proverbs in verses 5-6.

Believers who "consider" Christ by fixing their attention on his example will not grow weary in running when they meet with opposition. The expression, "lose heart," foreshadows the quotation in 12:5, but also belongs to the athletic image that again becomes explicit in verse 4: the race (Gk. *agōn*) involves an*tagon*ists who stand in the runner's path, and with whom one must come to grips like a boxer or wrestler (for a similar mixture of athletic images see 1 Cor 9:24-27). The parallelism between verses 3 and 4 suggests that the struggle is to be understood in personal terms; "sin" means sinners. The parallel with Christ is incomplete in that none of the readers has yet shed blood in a martyr's death. That is recalled not to minimize past experiences of conflict (see 10:32-34), but to indicate where future opposition could lead.

Some commentators detect a chiding tone in verses 4-5: the phrase, "to the point of shedding blood," is meant to imply that the readers have not yet engaged in serious combat, the kind that produces blood in a wrestling or boxing match. Also the introduction to the quotation in verse 5 is read as rebuke. More probably, the latter is a rhetorical question, posed in the style of the wisdom teacher, inviting the readers to evaluate the meaning of suffering in the light of Scripture and experience. The scriptural "exhortation"—like the author's own "word of exhortation" (13:22)—is meant to encourage rather than reprove.

Proverbs 3:11-12 LXX is cited with the addition of "my" to "son" (NRSV: "child"). Little is to be made of the addition, since it is implied in the relationship between the learner of wisdom as son and the teacher as father. Reading this text as a word addressed by God to his children, the author reinterprets it in the light of his Christology in 2:10-17: the Father's children are such by virtue of the unique Son's solidarity with them. Echoing common Wisdom themes, the quotation offers two parallel statements (the second in v. 6 has a chiastic order in the Greek). Divine discipline, like normal parental discipline (see Prov 23:12-14—the Greek word *paideia* means instruction given to a child), must include reproof (see also Deut 8:5; 2 Sam 7:14). Such chastening is not to be despised (see also Job 5:17; Prov 5:12; 15:32), nor seen as cause to lose heart, that is, to doubt the parent's love. The second couplet asserts that discipline is proof that the child is acknowledged and affirmed as one who is loved (cf. Prov 13:24; Sir 30:1).

"Discipline" and "child" are the key words in the application of the text in verses 7-11. The opening sentence could be read as a statement or as a command, but the latter is more likely (see how the writer's homiletical midrash begins at 3:12). Not all human suffering is divine discipline; it is in trials endured as confessors of Christ that the readers are to recognize the parental love of God at work and a confirmation of their status as God's children (12:8). Greater attention is lavished on legitimate children, in contrast to illegitimate, in view of their status as heirs (see 1:14; 6:12; 9:15). Thus, suffering is a concomitant of being God's children, and not an extraordinary experience.

Earthly and divine discipline are paralleled and contrasted in verses 9-11 to show the gracious purpose of the latter. Collective wisdom teaches that discipline, administered appropriately by human parents (literally, "fathers [in the sphere] of the flesh"), leads to respect. The *a fortiori* argument suggests that even greater respect, in the form of submission, is owed to the "Father of spirits." This latter phrase contrasts with "fleshly fathers" in verse 9a. God is Lord over angelic beings and the spirits of the dead (see 12:22-23; 1 *Enoch* 37:2-4; 38:4; 2 Macc 3:24; 1QH 10.8). Less probably, "spirits" is to be understood in the anthropological sense; earthly fathers passed on physical life, but God is the creator of people as spirit-beings (see Num 16:22; 27:16) who will "live" even if suffering leads to physical death.

Like the sapiential tradition, the writer links discipline with life. (In Prov 6:23, "you shall live" is a promise attached to covenant fidelity, but Deut 30:11-20 lacks the key thought of discipline; *pace* Lane 1991, 424.) God's children live the better life (see 10:38; 11:35) now and in the future by virtue of Christ's victory over the power of death (2:14-15; 7:16), but the promise of life in 12:9 is not christologically based.

The difference between earthly and divine discipline is not seen in verse 10 in terms of duration (12:10). The brevity of earthly discipline (due either to the mortality of human parents or to the brevity of childhood itself; Wis 16:6 speaks of the brevity of divine chastening) is not the point. Divine discipline is always "good" since it is based on a true assessment of needs, and is salutary in an ultimate sense. It ensures a share in God's own holiness. What God has and demands (see Lev 19:2) is given in Christ: cleansing from sin (1:3; 9:14; 10:10, 14, 29). Suffering is a divine means of preserving Christians in their status as God's special children.

The benefit of discipline can be appreciated only in retrospect (v. 11). That "temporary suffering associated with discipline pro-duces a lasting good" is also Jewish and Greek proverbial wisdom (see Attridge 1989, 363-64). What at first seems only painful produces a lasting "fruit" (see also Matt 3:8; Gal 5:22; Eph 5:9; Phil 1:11; and Jas 3:18). The rather complicated formulation, "peaceful fruit of righteousness" (i.e., the harvest of peace that comes from doing what is right) calls to mind several ideas. Peace and righteousness are associated with the Messiah and the mes-sianic age (Ps 85:10; Isa 9:6-7; 11:4-9; 32:17), but this connection (despite Heb 7:2) is probably not intended at this point. Since Proverbs has been quoted in verses 5-6 above, the writer has Prov 11:30 in mind: the "fruit of the righteous" is "a tree of life" that produces peace. Our author soon speaks of peace as harmonious relationships with others (12:14), but this presupposes being at peace with God. Suffering can disrupt; God's tested children are to know peace as total wholeness (in the sense of the Hebrew *shalom*) even in suffering. A reference to peace as final "rest" and eschatological salvation (3:6–4:11) is not thereby excluded.

The testing that suffering provides is pictured as athletic training (cf. 1 Tim 4:7-8), so verse 11 rounds off the image begun in verses 1-4. Enduring discipline is like being subjected to strenuous exercises, but the final outcome makes all the pain worthwhile.

◊ ◊ ◊ ◊

When read with 10:32-35, 12:1-11 gives the clearest clues to the situation that the Letter addresses. The experience of suffering abuse has led to a loss of communal confidence and to doubt in the providential care of God. In summoning his audience to enduring faith, the author separates Christ from the example list in chapter 11. Jesus is not merely the prime model of endurance that leads to glory; he remains the source and object of faith, its origin and goal. He is the beginner and perfecter of faith. To suffer shame for him is to follow in his footsteps (see 13:12-13).

Christ's path from suffering to glory (12:1-2) was unique, yet it sets the pattern for those who are his "partners" (3:14). Here Christology is the basis for parenesis (see the same pattern in Rom 8:14-17, where sonship and suffering belong together; also 2 Tim 2:11-12; 1 Pet 3:17-22). By contrast, the exhortation in 12:4-11 is not explicitly based on the author's Christology, though he presupposes that God's children owe their new status to the unique Son. Here proverbial wisdom and common experience provide the basis for the assurance that those who suffer for Christ are being confirmed and affirmed as God's children, and are being refined for even greater endurance.

There is no suggestion that the readers' sufferings are to be interpreted as punishment for lack of faith. Nor does the writer treat suffering within a general discussion of theodicy. Those who suffer increasing hostility *as Christians* are called to see their lot through the lens of God's special care for them, and to submit to divine discipline in the certainty of his good purposes. Such suffering is to be seen as the assurance of the Father's love, and as a promise of participating in Christ's triumph.

Remove All That Hinders Your Progress (12:12-17)

Exhortation continues with the use of imperatives (indicative verbs appear again in vv. 18-24). The form and content of this section suggest that it serves as the conclusion to the call for enduring faith, rather than as the opening stanza of the letter's final major discourse—the repetition of "peace" in 12:14 and 13:20 hardly forms an *inclusio*.

Though it recalls the image of the runner in verse 1, the language of 12:12-13 contains no explicit athletic terminology. It rather recalls two Old Testament texts (Prov 4:26; Isa 35:3). A connection with the preceding verses is established linguistically by the repetition of "peace" and "holiness" (vv. 10-11 and v. 14). The motif of communal responsibility in verses 15-16 ("see to it that no one . . .") also recalls past appeals (see 3:12; 4:1, 11).

The stern warning of verses 15-17 (the negative example of Esau contrasts with the positive examples of 11:4–12:3) repeats past appeals to consider the dire results of faithlessness (2:1-4; 3:7-19; 4:11-13; 6:4-8; 10:26-31). Another warning follows in 12:25-29, but as the counterpart to 12:18-24, which begins a new discourse on the practical consequences of "drawing near to God" as people of the new covenant.

◊ ◊ ◊ ◊

Scripture provides the basis for this last appeal for endurance. Discouraged and despondent Israel was told to take heart, to "strengthen the weak hands, and make firm the feeble knees," since deliverance was on the way: "Your God . . . will come and save you" (Isa 35:3-4). The writer omits the reference to eschatological rescue in verse 4, though he has earlier linked the call for endurance with the parousia of the Lord by alluding to Isa 26:20 (see 10:37). He allows the reformulated text to stand on its own as summons to remove spiritual lethargy and slackness of resolve. Like long-distance runners suffering fatigue (the image is not specifically athletic; see also Job 4:3-4; Sir 2:12; 25:23), the readers have begun to drop their hands and buckle at the knees.

A second text, Prov 4:26, extends the image. The strong in faith are to make straight paths for the feet of those who are "lame." Those wavering through exhaustion are to be strengthened and redirected to the goal, so that they do not fall by the way. Most translations of 12:13b speak of limbs being "put out of joint" (GNB and NIV have "disabled," JB has "wrenched"), suggesting that failure to renew the strength of the weak can lead to a fall. Others (e.g., Spicq 1953, Buchanan 1972, P. Hughes 1987) take the relevant Greek verb to mean "turned away," that is, diverted from the "straight paths" (v. 13a), but this makes more difficult the following reference to being "healed." The general sense is that weaker members of the community are to be strengthened so that none fall by the way. Healing denotes the present renewal of spiritual energies, rather than the final outcome of reaching the goal—the eschatological perspective is reintroduced in verse 17.

The injunction to "pursue peace" (v. 14—the formulation recalls Ps 34:14, cited also in 1 Pet 3:11) is not an abrupt intrusion into the writer's thought. Peace is the fruit of divine discipline (12:11), and accompanies those who follow wisdom's paths. Proverbs 4:26 LXX (referred to in 12:13) is followed by the parallel line: "He [God] will make your *paths straight,* your ways he will lead forward *in peace*" (v. 27b). The pursuit of peace, in the present context, would mean preserving a gift that comes from the "God of peace" (13:20). Communal harmony and solidarity in the face of suffering can be ensured only as the church lives in the wholeness God has worked in Christ.

The linking of peace and holiness was possibly also suggested by Ps 34:14. Holiness, too, is both gift and goal (see vv. 10-11 above). The sanctity that flows from the sacrifice of Christ and his cleansing blood (see 10:10, 14; 13:12) is to be expressed in a life of corporate holiness (see 13:1-5). That holiness is necessary in order to "see the Lord" (meaning God, rather than Christ, as in 8:2) is a reminder of its cultic setting. Purification by Christ's blood (see also 1:3; 9:14, 22-26) creates the state of holiness that allows access into God's holy presence. To see God thus means as much as to "come to"

God in worship (12:18, 22). The author is not speaking of a mystical or apocalyptic vision of God, nor of a final seeing after death (cf. 1 Cor 13:12).

Communal responsibility is expressed in mutual oversight and concern (12:15-16; cf. 2:1; 3:12). Hebrews 4:1 speaks of "failing" in the sense of falling short of a goal, but the meaning here is more akin to the image of shrinking back found in 10:38-39: what has been obtained is not to be forfeited. God's grace is ground, goal, and gift in the salvation worked through Christ, from his sacrificial death to his enthronement (2:9; 4:16). But the free gift of divine favor (13:25) can be lost by despising the Word and by outraging the "Spirit of grace" who speaks through the word (10:29; 13:9).

Worse than the neglect of saving grace (see 2:3) is outright rebellion that works as an unholy contagion (12:15b). The writer recalls Deut 29:18 (Heb 12:15a alludes to the Greek version of this text) where "bitterness" is a stubborn turning from God to idolatry; it is a noxious "root" that will destroy others if allowed to grow. Apostasy must be nipped in the bud before it disrupts the whole community. Its effects are expressed in cultic terms. Christ removed the defilement of sin; the one has sanctified the many (2:10; 10:10). One person can reverse the process by defiling the many.

Defilement can spread from any "immoral and godless person" (12:16). The second adjective has cultic connotations, suggesting the distinction between the holy and the profane. Esau behaved in an irreligious manner in selling a birthright that included a divine blessing. He chose momentary gratification through something profane, despising a holy gift with long-term effects (see Gen 25:33-34). Why Esau should also be considered *sexually* immoral is less clear. Some commentators, noting the association of idolatry with sexual immorality in the Old Testament (Lane 1991, 455, cites Exod 34:15-17; Deut 31:16), argue that "immoral" here means no more than unfaithful in the religious sense (see also Manson 1951, 85; Williamson 1970, 265-66). Others draw attention to a Jewish tradition, occasionally based on Esau's marriage to two Hittite women (Gen 26:34-35), that Esau was a sensual person (see Attridge 1989, 369; Lane 1991, 454-55). Perhaps our writer simply thinks of Esau as "selling himself" cheaply, like a prostitute.

Verse 17 assumes an understanding of divine blessing and curse as performative words that, once spoken, cannot be revoked. When Esau wanted to reclaim the blessing (Gen 27:30-40) he was refused; it had already been pronounced. Esau could receive only a secondary word, one that 11:20 calls a blessing but was actually a prophecy of servitude. Esau was finally "rejected" by God—not by Isaac—and so inherited a curse rather than a blessing (see 6:7-8 for the contrast between divine blessing and the curse that falls on the "rejected" [NRSV: "worthless"]). That Esau "found no chance to repent" means that he could not reverse the effects of his first action. As in 6:4-8 and 10:26-29, the lesson is that those who reject the divine blessing must expect to be rejected. By using the verb "inherit" (it does not appear in Gen 27:30-40, although it belongs to the language of the patriarchal promises) the author refers to that greater gift that, once rejected, can be forfeited forever (for the greater inheritance of all God's children see 1:14; 6:12, 17; 9:15). The finality of apostasy makes repentance impossible.

◊ ◊ ◊ ◊

The writer again reveals deep pastoral concern. His call to vigilance seeks to arouse communal responsibility. Inherent in the athletic image is the idea of rivalry and individual achievement. Hebrews removes from the discussion of discipline and purposeful endeavor any individualistic, agonistic connotations. Attainment of faith's goal is a matter of both mutual responsibility and corporate action. Suffering can lead to self-preoccupation and isolation; the writer pleads for a broader vision and group solidarity, with special care for the weakest members, so that the whole faith community is marked by harmony and holiness.

In warning that the fruit of Christ is not to be endangered by the weed of rebellion, the writer reintroduces cultic concepts—holiness, defilement, the profane ("godless" in 12:16). Christ's sacrifice as a perfect peace offering is not to be negated by the ultimate uncleanness of apostasy as rebellious rejection of the ultimate blessing: inheritance in Christ. Esau is seen as the type of those who willfully and contemptuously reject the divine gift and suffer irretrievable loss as a consequence.

How much can be implied from 12:16 about the readers' present situation? Are the readers "selling" themselves and their heavenly inheritance for some specific present gain? They are certainly being tempted to forfeit the "lasting city" by seeking earthly security, instead of suffering abuse for Christ (13:12-14). The author expects his warning to hit the mark without spelling out details. His audience must make the right application or reach the point where repentance comes too late.

How members are to be reinvigorated for their faith-struggle can be inferred from the Letter's repeated appeals to listen to the word of God as warning and promise. The warning against neglect of worship in 10:25 is echoed in the call to worship in 12:22-24. It is in the fellowship of God's holy people that there is peace, holiness, and blessing.

THE CALL TO HEAVENLY WORSHIP (12:18–13:25)

The final discourse contains exposition (12:18-24), warning (12:25-29), exhortation (13:1-19), and a personal conclusion (13:20-25) with no immediately apparent connecting theme. Contrasts abound—between the experience of a pilgrim people under the old covenant and under the new (12:18-24), between that which is earthly and ephemeral, and that which is heavenly and eternal (12:25-28), between holy and unholy living (13:1-9), between external legalism and internal grace (13:9), between earthly security and eternal well-being (13:10-16).

Another thread runs through this section: the picture of Christians as a new worshiping community. They have "come to" the presence of God in the new cultus (12:22-24), to "offer to God an acceptable worship" (12:28), also in a life of holiness (13:1-6). The call to "remember" leaders summons the readers back to the word that produces and sustains faith (13:7), a faith that calls forth a "sacrifice of praise" in the form of confession, though it means following Christ "outside the camp" (13:8-16). The injunction to obey leaders and to pray for the writer, as well as his own benediction and "Amen" (13:17-21), bring to a fitting conclusion the whole Letter as a call to worship.

You Share in the New, Heavenly Worship (12:18-24)

The connective "for" in verse 18 (omitted in the NRSV) suggests that this section provides motivation for the preceding appeal. Like Israel in the wilderness, the new pilgrim people is summoned into God's presence. Previous contrasts are recalled: between the old and the new covenant (8:6-13), Moses and Jesus (3:2-6), the sensate world and unseen realities (11:1-3), past revelation and God's final word in the Son (1:1-2).

The depiction of two encounters with God, past and present, determines the structure of the section. Israel's terror when confronted with the awesome presence of God at Sinai extended to Moses, the mediator of the old covenant (vv. 18-21). Christians are now called into God's presence to be part of a festal gathering where heaven and earth meet, and where Jesus is mediator of the new covenant (vv. 22-24). Through him the unapproachable has become the accessible.

◊ ◊ ◊ ◊

Using his favored expression for drawing near to God in worship (see "come to" also in 4:16; 7:25; 10:1, 22; 11:6), the writer recalls Israel's experience of God's holy presence at Sinai (12:18-21). That which could be "touched" may mean the mountain itself (despite v. 20); its tangibility marked it as belonging to the sensate, earthly realm in contrast to the heavenly Mount Zion (v. 22). Yet the author may be describing the whole event as one that was overpoweringly perceptible to earthly senses (see Thompson 1982, 45-47, though he goes too far in reading a Platonic metaphysic into these verses). Mysterious and terrifying sights (fire, darkness, and gloom) and sounds (tempest, trumpet blast, and heavenly voice) marked the holy God as unapproachable (see Exod 19:16-19; 20:18; Deut 4:11-12; 5:22-23).

The writer closely associates the people's fear at this epiphany with the voice that uttered the interdict against touching the holy mountain (12:20 refers to Exod 19:12-13)—thus the plea that all further communications be directed through Moses (Exod 20:18-19; Deut 5:25-27). Moses, on the other hand, expresses extreme fear at the entire manifestation of divine majesty (12:21)—"I tremble with fear" is based on Deut 9:19 (in a different context) or on nonbiblical tradition.

Stress on the subjective experience of Israel is followed by a listing of the objective realities to which Christians have come under the new covenant, where fear is replaced with festivity (vv. 22-24). Apart from recalling Deut 4:11 and the thought of worship, "you have come" may be a reminder of the readers' conversion; the Greek verb used is related to "proselyte," meaning a person who "has come" to the faith.

The new realities are listed in four pairs, describing the place, people, presence, and power involved in access to God's throne in worship. Mount Zion was originally the citadel that David captured (2 Sam 5:6-9). The name was later used for the temple mount (Isa 8:18; Joel 3:17), then for the whole city of Jerusalem (2 Kgs 19:21; Ps 51:18). It was from Zion that salvation would come for all peoples (Ps 50:2; Isa 2:3; 28:16). Joel 3:16-17 looks to a theophany on Zion like that on Sinai, and Jewish apocalyptic could link the two mountains (see *Jub.* 1:28; 4:26; 8:19). The designation of Zion as the "city of the living God, the heavenly Jerusalem," recalls the apocalyptic hope of a transcendent city (see the comments on 11:10; cf. also 13:14; Rev 3:12; 14:1; 21:2, 10). The description of God as "living" usually belongs to warnings in Hebrews (see 3:12; 10:31); here it suggests assurance. This city exists as surely as God exists (11:6).

The transcendent city is also the heavenly sanctuary or temple. Its inhabitants (vv. 22b-23a) are the myriads of angels; they attended the theophany at Sinai (see 2:2; Deut 33:2; Ps 68:17) and now surround God's heavenly throne (see Isa 6:2-3; Dan 7:10; Rev 5:11). They form a "festal gathering" (the Greek word *panēgyris* occurs only here in the NT). In coming to the heavenly city/sanctuary in worship, Christians are united with angelic hosts.

Some commentators (e.g., Käsemann 1984, 50; Montefiore 1964, 231) take the "assembly of the firstborn" (v. 23a) to refer again to angels, citing Ps 89:5 LXX, which speaks of the "assembly of the angels" ("holy ones" in the Hebrew Bible). They are "sons of God" from creation (Gen 6:2; Job 38:7), whereas Hebrews sees human beings becoming God's children through the incarnate Son (2:10-18).

There are good reasons for taking "firstborn" to mean human beings. It is more natural to speak of believers as "enrolled in heaven." The image of a heavenly register refers to the enrollment of God's elect people, both in the Old Testament (see Exod 32:32; Ps 69:28; Dan 12:1) and the New Testament (Luke 10:20; Phil 4:4; Rev 3:5; 13:8; 17:8; 20:12, 15; 21:27). Second, Israel as God's people, also at Sinai, is called a "gathering" (*ekklēsia* in the LXX; see Deut 18:16). Though this term is not used in the sense of "church" in Hebrews (also in 2:12), the author suggests that Christians belong to the assembly of God's elect in which earthly praise is joined to heavenly. Third, it would be odd for Hebrews to give the epithet "firstborn" to angels, since this is the title of the Son who is superior to angels (1:6). It is entirely natural that those who are made God's children through the Son (2:11, 14) be seen as "firstborn," the counterpart to Israel as God's "firstborn son" (Exod 4:22-23). Finally, it would be strange if the writer twice mentioned angels but spoke of Christians only once (v. 23*b*), when his intention is to remind the readers of where *they* belong.

The third pairing—God as judge and the spirits of the perfected (v. 23*b*)—returns to the transcendent realm. The Holy One is surrounded by the holy ones. As Creator of all (2:10; 11:3), God punishes sin (10:30-31; 13:4). But here, as in the previous reference to the "living God" (12:22), the keynote is assurance (warning begins in v. 25). The divine judge is vindicator of the righteous who have lived by faith (cf. 10:38. All who have been cleansed by Christ's sacrifice have been perfected already in this life (see 10:14), but those who have died in the faith have been perfected in the same sense as Christ: they are now glorified with him (see 2:10; 11:40). Hebrews gives the Christian counterpart to the vision of Jewish apocalyptic: the spirits of the righteous who have died live with the "Lord of spirits" (see, e.g., *1 Enoch* 22:3-13; 39:7; 103:3-4).

This gathering of the saints on earth and in heaven in God's presence is founded on Jesus and his sacrifice (v. 24). The old covenant at Mount Sinai was mediated through a fear-filled Moses (v. 21), and inaugurated with animal sacrifice (9:18-21); the new covenant is mediated by Jesus through his self-sacrifice (see 8:6; 9:15).

Believers come to God *through* Jesus' atoning sacrifice in the past, but they also come *to* him as the living "guarantee" of a better covenant in the present (7:22) since he intercedes for the saints at God's right hand (cf. 2:18; 4:16; 7:27; 8:1). "Sprinkled blood" (v. 24*b*) recalls the means by which Jesus' sacrificial death remains effective. Blood is again more than a metaphor for death. Old Testament ritual required the application of blood, so Hebrews speaks of the better cleansing that is effected *by* Jesus' blood in contrast to animal blood (see 9:13, 19, 21; 10:22). The Greek phrase, "blood of sprinkling" is patterned on "water of sprinkling" that appears five times in Num 19:9-21 LXX. This phrase means water for the purpose of sprinkling, so we can translate "blood for sprinkling" in 12:24. That is, the blood of Christ continues to have cleansing power for those who enter the heavenly sanctuary (see the comments on 10:22).

The blood of Abel, one of those who lived by faith (11:4), once cried out for vengeance (Gen 4:10; *Jub.* 4:3). Jesus' blood continues to speak, but with a "better word," that is, with its message of effective cleansing from sin. This "word" is not addressed to God, but comes from God (see v. 25).

◊ ◊ ◊ ◊

In Hebrews, Israel's experience at Sinai typifies worship under the old covenant. No less a person than the mediator of the old covenant confirms the fear and foreboding that must attend standing in God's presence. Those at Sinai were anything but confident to approach God. But Christ has opened the new and living way by which people can now come into God's holy presence with joyful confidence to offer acceptable worship (10:19-22; 12:28).

To a community suffering a crisis of identity as a result of social pressure, to people no longer sure of their location in this world (whether in relation to the Jewish community or pagan society), Hebrews offers a vision that reaches far beyond time and space. Christians are citizens of another world. Faith looks to future realities—a final rest, an ultimate inheritance. Yet faith also gives the present experience of these realities. Past event and future hope are actualized as eternal realities as the pilgrim people come into God's presence and the presence of Christ in whom past, present, and future mean constant grace (see 13:8). The eschatology of Hebrews makes sense only when understood within the context of worship. Indeed, the stress here is not on pilgrimage to the future, but on present arrival. Faith grasps the future as though it were in the present (11:1). Earthly beings join heavenly beings in worship, so that angels and humans are no longer separated as at Sinai (Westcott 1903, 415).

Final Warning: Do Not Reject God's Warnings (12:25-29)

Following the author's usual pattern, words of assurance give way to a warning (see 1:14–2:3; 4:9-13; 10:19-31). Its structure and language indicate a close connection with 12:18-24. The Greek participle "speaking" links verses 24 and 25, while the mention of "fire" in verse 29 recalls verse 18. Other link words are "voice" (vv. 19 and 26) and "heaven" (vv. 22-23 and 25-26).

The warning begins with an *a fortiori* argument that runs parallel to that in 2:1-3*a*. God's way of speaking in the two covenants (see 12:18-24) is decisively different, so refusal to listen to God's final revelation will incur even greater displeasure (12:25). A reference to Hag 2:6, 21 establishes that God's final speaking is both warning and eschatological promise (vv. 26-27). Though finishing on the note of warning (v. 29), the writer sets the tone for what follows by calling the readers to a life of praise (v. 28).

◊ ◊ ◊ ◊

In 3:12 the readers were challenged to "see to it" that unbelief did not lead to a final rejection of God's word. That warning is repeated by again contrasting past and present revelation (12:18-24; 2:1-3*a*), and by recalling the disobedience of the Exodus generation (4:1-2). God is now speaking more clearly and more powerfully than at Sinai, so refusal to listen is even more reprehensible (12:25). The Israelites "begged" not to have to listen to God's voice as it thundered from the mountain (12:19). Using the same verb, the writer says that the people "begged off" listening to God. Such disobedience meant no escape from punishment (see 3:7-19).

The last *a fortiori* argument in the Letter draws a pointed conclusion. The voice that now comes from the heavenly Zion (12:22) speaks an eternal message ("heaven," contrasted with "earth," suggests that which is both superior and eternally valid). Escape from divine punishment for rejecting God's eschatological message in the new covenant is now even less possible (see 2:3 and 10:29 for the same logic).

That it was God, not Moses, who "warned on earth" is made clear (v. 26) as the writer refers to the apocalyptic notion of a final shaking of the universe. The shaking of the earth at Sinai (cf. Exod 19:18; Judg 5:4-5; Pss 68:8; 77:18) became a feature in prophetic visions of future theophanies (see Ps 18:7). There would be a shaking of the created universe, of earth and sky, on the day of judgment (see Isa 13:13; Joel 2:10). While recalling apocalyptic images of a universal convulsion that reaches to the heavens (see, e.g., *1 Enoch* 60:1, 4; *4 Ezra* 6:13-16; *2 Baruch* 32:1), the writer cites only Hag 2:6 (see also v. 21) since its warning to Israel's enemies is a promise of rescue. By transposing "heaven" and "earth" and adding "not only . . . but also" to the text, he sees the promised shaking of both earth *and* heaven as a final theophany that will outdo the revelation of glory at Sinai.

The brief midrashic comment on Hag 2:6 in 12:27 provides a parallel to 1:10-12 where Ps 102:25-27 was cited to contrast the eternal rule of the Son with the impermanence of earth and sky. "Yet once more" could be understood in the sense: "Yet again once and for all." Either way, the writer sees the text as referring not to some temporary disturbance as at Sinai. The final removal of the created order ("what is shaken") points to the permanent durability of the heavenly order ("what cannot be shaken"). The transitory must give way to the eternal. Creation is not shattered in order to build a new heaven and earth (see Isa 65:17; Rev 21:1), but to reveal what will "remain."

What cannot be shaken is the heavenly world of the "lasting city" with its inhabitants (11:10; 12:22-23; 13:14). The image of the "kingdom that cannot be shaken" (12:28) probably recalls the promise of Dan 7:18: God's saints will "possess the kingdom forever." But Hebrews sees this kingdom as now ensured by the eternality of the Son whose throne is forever (see 1:8, 13).

The idea that the readers "*are* receiving" this kingdom shows how Hebrews modifies traditional apocalyptic motifs. It implies that the shaking of Hag 2:6 has begun with the work of Christ, climaxing in his exaltation. The "removal" of what is shaken corresponds to the "change" (the Greek noun is the same) in the law and priesthood (7:12). The faithful are already becoming members of the heavenly kingdom (12:22-24). The future removal of all that is earthly will simply confirm their status as unshakable citizens in an unshakable kingdom.

How the readers respond to God's final revelation will indicate whether they are already part of that world. The wrong response is rejection (see v. 25); the only fitting response is to "give thanks" (v. 28*b*; for reasons why the phrase should not be translated "let us hold on to grace," with an allusion to 12:15, see Lane 1991, 443, note *fff*). Through their High Priest's sacrifice, and by the power of his cleansing blood, the faithful can "serve" the living God with their own sacrifice of praise (see 9:14; 10:21-22).

The sacrifice of praise and confession (see 13:15) is "acceptable worship" because it is offered in faith (cf. 11:5-6). It includes a life of good works that is pleasing to God, as the final chapter will show (13:16, 21). But bold and confident access to God in worship (see 10:19-22) does not mean presumption. "Reverence and awe" (a *hendiadys;* two words expressing one idea) is appropriate in the presence of the holy God who is a consuming fire (12:29). A fiery judgment will destroy anything impure and unholy (see 6:8; 10:27-31). The image recalls 12:18-22, but is based on Deut 4:24 (see also 9:3 and Isa 33:14), which is a warning against breaking the covenant through idolatry.

◊ ◊ ◊ ◊

Contrasting distinctions between "they" and "we" (12:25), "then" and "now" (v. 26), and "earth" and "heaven," serve as a framework within which the writer depicts God's final speaking in the Son (see 1:1-2) as eschatological warning and promise. Those who deliberately spurn God's final revelation cannot possibly escape judgment. Greater gifts mean greater responsibility in the reception of those gifts.

Though the section begins and ends with stern warnings (vv. 25, 29), the dominant message is comfort. Christians need not fear the end as cataclysmic disorder; it will confirm their place in an eternal order that already exists and one to which they already belong as they worship.

As in 12:22-24, the stress is on a realized eschatology, but without the surrender of future perspectives. The future will bring vindication for the faithful (see 9:28). But the author addresses a more urgent question: Where do his readers find themselves *now?* Suffering social dislocation and without the comfort of earthly securities, shaken by past suffering and now shaky in faith, they are assured of their place in an unshakable world. That world is theirs as long as they cling to the faith and hope they have in Christ.

An Expanded Note on Chapter 13: Without chapter 13, Hebrews could be read as a sermon. Personal touches in verses 18-24 suggest that it is a real letter intended to make up for the lack of the writer's presence (v. 19). Vocabulary, literary style, method of argumentation, and thematic development indicate that chapter 13 is of a piece with the whole Letter. There are echoes of earlier chapters in verses 3, 6, 8-17, and 20-21. Most important, the whole chapter (with the exception of the personal note in vv. 22-23) develops the theme of worship announced in 12:22-24 and 12:28. "Acceptable worship," in response to the blessings of the new covenant, includes the sanctified life (13:1-5, 21) and the confession of faith (v. 15). The basis of the community's sacrifice of praise in word and deed is Christ's own sacrifice (vv. 9-13, 20-21). Catechetical, credal, and liturgical material (for the latter see vv. 20-21, 24-25) are combined with personal appeals to form a fitting conclusion to the entire Letter. This combination of parenesis, praise, prayer, personal greetings, and final blessing conforms to a common epistolary pattern in the New Testament (see Filson 1967, 22-25).

The Offering of Brotherly Love (13:1-6)

The larger parenetic section of 13:1-19 is dominated by direct imperatives, with only two cohortatives ("let us . . ." in vv. 13, 15). The call to "remember" (vv. 3, 7; the motif of emulation occurs in vv. 12, 17-19) and "not neglect" (vv. 2, 16) is an appeal to a common memory that is also the source of the traditional catechetical teaching in verses 1-6.

The section contains four pairs of commands, each pair addressing a related issue: mutual love and hospitality (vv. 1-2); care for the imprisoned and tortured (v. 3); respect for marriage and avoidance of adultery (v. 4); and rejection of greed and pursuit of contentment (v. 5). Apart from verse 3, each pair is provided with a motivational statement. The final motivational comment is in the form of a scriptural quotation (v. 5c), which leads to a concluding confession, also taken from Scripture (v. 6).

Though the injunctions are traditional, the final formulation shows the writer's literary skill. His appeal to let love "remain" (13:1 [NRSV: "continue"]) provides a link with the promise of the unshakable kingdom that will "remain" (12:27-28). There is further play on words in verses 1-2: the Greek word for "hospitality" means "love" shown to "strangers"; the verbs translated with "neglect" and "without knowing it" are related in Greek. Chiasms appear in verses 2 and 4 (in the second instance the order is honored/marriage/marriage bed/undefiled), and the Greek of verses 5-6 is alliterative.

◊ ◊ ◊ ◊

Virtues like love, hospitality, compassion, chastity, and contentment could be expected of any Christian group. These verses echo early catechetical instruction (the first three virtues appear together in Rom 12:9-15), but the context suggests a pointed application. A life of holiness is part of "acceptable worship" (12:28). In addition, specific virtues are vital for a community under threat of persecution.

The use of *philadelphia* in verse 1 (the NRSV has "mutual love" for what is, literally, the love of brothers and sisters) rather than *agapē* may have been suggested by traditional parenetic formulations (see 1 Thess 4:9; Rom 12:10). Yet the term is especially apposite in Hebrews; it recalls the nature of the church as a community of siblings with whom the Son has fully identified (see 2:10-17; 3:1, 12; 10:19; 13:22-23). Where such love "remains" (NRSV: "continue") there is evidence that Christians belong to an unshakable world that remains (cf. 12:27-28). Love sets them apart from the world while giving group cohesion to stand united against its attacks. A good record in the past (see 6:10) is no guarantee that love, like faith and hope, will not grow cold (cf. 12:12-14). It may occasionally need rekindling (see 10:24).

Structural analysis has suggested that hospitality (v. 2) is seen as a concrete expression of love within the Christian family (see Elliott 1981, 145-50, 165-200 for the relationship between hospitality and the household of faith). Prized by the ancients in general, this virtue is often enjoined in the New Testament (see Matt 25:35; Rom 12:13; 1 Tim 3:2; Titus 1:8; 1 Pet 4:9). Times of persecution increased the need for homes in which to take temporary refuge. Like 3 John 5, Hebrews calls for readiness to welcome strangers. That these might turn out to be angels represents a "common folkloristic motif" in the Greco-Roman world (Attridge 1989, 386 with note 34). Our author is probably thinking of biblical examples of people who entertained angels unwittingly, for example, Abraham, Sarah, Lot, Gideon, Manoah, and Tobit (Gen 18:1-22; 19:1-4; Judg 6:11-21; 13:2-20; Tob 12:11-22).

In the second couplet (v. 3), remembering means as much as not neglecting (v. 2). Remembering those in prison would include a sympathetic identification that finds expression in communal prayer on their behalf (cf. 13:18 and the comments on 13:7). Group solidarity means that those who are free are "bound" to those in "bonds" (the Greek includes a play on words). Sympathy for prisoners, shown in the past (see 10:34), could include the provision of food and clothing—not necessarily supplied in ancient prisons— and even sharing the living conditions of a person in detention (see, e.g., Lane 1991, 515).

Solidarity also means identifying with those "being tortured"— the verb could mean physical abuse (as in 11:25, 37) or verbal maligning (see 10:33; 11:26; 13:13). The clauses beginning with "as" in 13:3 complement each other. Thus, the second (literally, "as being in the body yourselves") does not refer to the Pauline concept of the "body of Christ," but to the obvious fact that people share the same physicality. The readers can suffer with others by stepping, as it were, into their skin.

Sexual sins and greed (vv. 4-5) are linked by Greco-Roman, Jewish (see Attridge 1989, 387), and early Christian writers (see 1 Cor 5:10; Eph 5:3-5; Col 3:5; 1 Thess 4:4-6). The holiness code in Leviticus deals with use of property (19:9-14, 35-36), sexual matters (19:20, 29; 20:10-21), and hospitality as a sign of love (19:33-34). The "marriage bed" (a euphemism for sexual relations) is to be undefiled, since marriage is a sacrosanct ordering of life and a prime area in which cultic cleanness is to be maintained (cf. 12:14-15). Infidelity is an offense against the brother or sister (13:1; cf. 1 Thess 4:6). A clean record in the area of sexuality will help to blunt attacks against the community by outsiders, but the final motivation is expressed in traditional terms (see the end of 1 Thess 4:4-7): God's judgment falls on the sexually impure (cf. also Lev 20:10; 1 Cor 6:9-10; Eph 5:5-6; Col 3:5-6).

Also the final couplet (13:5) enforces a traditional theme: freedom from the "love of money" (see Luke 16:14; 1 Tim 3:3; 6:10) means contentment. The readers had not been dismayed by past loss (see 10:34), but threats of renewed social hostility could make them anxious about their homes and other property. So they are reminded that to value temporal things more than the coming kingdom is not worthy of those who are destined to inherit lasting possessions (cf. 10:34; 12:28; 13:14). God's promise never to desert his people is reenforced with an allusion to Deut 31:6, 8 (possibly also to Josh 1:5).

Trust that triumphs over care leads to the confession of Ps 118:6 (13:6; Paul refers to the same text in Rom 8:31). The sacrifice of praise (13:15) to God for his constant help (given through the heavenly High Priest; see 2:18; 4:16) will drown out querulous fears in the face of persecutors (see 11:23, 27).

◊ ◊ ◊ ◊

Attention to the literary and historical context—a holy life as worship (12:14-16, 28) and the past experience of suffering within the community (10:32-34; 12:4)—shows that the verses have special meaning for this community. General parenetic traditions become exhortations loaded with meaning. Practical expressions of love complement the confession of faith (13:15). They confirm the ultimate destiny of the family of faith (see 12:27).

What is not explicitly stated can be presupposed at this point. First, identification with sufferers recalls the Son's own identification with his flesh and blood siblings so that he can suffer with them (see 2:14, 18; 4:15). Second, the warnings against immorality and greed suggest the importance of Christians maintaining a good reputation so as to avert public attack in a time of persecution (cf. 1 Pet 3:16-17 and 4:12-19). Yet the final motivation for holy living is not the need for socially acceptable behavior, or even the threat of divine judgment, but trust in God.

Life Within the Worshiping Community (13:7-19)

Further imperatives (vv. 7, 9, 16-18), including the repetition of calls to "remember" and "not neglect" (vv. 3, 7; 2, 16), and the concept of acceptable worship (12:28; 13:16) provide links with the previous verses. Yet this section seems, at first sight, to contain a number of new and unrelated thoughts. Structural considerations help to show its inner coherence.

An opening paragraph (vv. 7-9) calls on the readers to remember past *leaders,* to consider the outcome of their *conduct* (NRSV: "way of life"), and to imitate their faith. The latter is expressed in terms of the constancy of Jesus Christ, a confession that stands in contrast to "strange teachings" (vv. 7-9). A framing *inclusio* is formed by verses 17-19 with the summons to obey present *leaders* and to pray for the writer who seeks to *conduct* himself (NRSV: "act") honorably.

The central section recalls the cultic imagery of earlier chapters (esp. 9–10; the connection between vv. 9 and 10 is provided by the reference to food and eating). An exposition (vv. 10-12) provides the foundational argument for concluding appeals (rather than imperatives; vv. 13-16). There is a chiastic order in the central section (see Lane 1991, 503):

A: We have an *altar* from which others cannot eat (v. 10);
   B: *for* animal victims were burned *outside* the camp (v. 11);
      C: so Christ suffered *outside* the city gate (v. 12).
      C': so let us go *outside* the camp, bearing abuse for him (v. 13);
   B': *for* here we have no lasting city (v. 14);
A': let us continually offer a *sacrifice* of praise (vv. 15-16).

Even the climactic statement forms a chiasm; references to *sacrifices* offered to *God* (vv. 15*a*, 16*b*) frame statements that identify them as praise and good conduct (vv. 15*b*, 16*a*).

7-9: Remembering past leaders who spoke God's word (v. 7— original apostolic witnesses are not meant; see 2:3)' means more than recalling the community's founders. When God remembers his covenant or his people, he reenacts his promises and saving works (see, e.g., Gen 8:1; 19:29; Deut 9:27; Ps 25:6). When people remember God's promises and acts of deliverance, they celebrate the past as present reality (see, e.g., Exod 13:3; Deut 7:18; 1 Chr 16:12; 2 Chr 6:42; Ps 77:11; the eucharistic phrase "in remembrance of me" recalls the same motif). The contemplation of past leaders is a reminder of grace, and thus produces praise of God. The harmony of professed faith and conduct in past leaders is to be reenacted or actualized in the present.

Though introduced somewhat abruptly, the confession to Christ in verse 8 (it has a liturgical ring; see Attridge 1989, 392) provides an important link between verses 7 and 9. Consideration of past leaders who were faithful should lead to a "looking to Jesus" as the ultimate leader and example of faithful endurance (see 12:1-3). The confession expresses the faith of past leaders and what they proclaimed (v. 7). It is not to be surrendered for "strange teachings" (v. 9). To confess Jesus Christ (1 Tim 2:8 speaks of "remembering" Christ in this sense) is to celebrate his constant and unchanging presence by means of which God keeps the promises expressed in verses 5-6.

The author is not asserting that Christ has not been subject to change (rightly, Filson 1967, 31-33). The words of Ps 102:27, cited in 1:12 ("You are the same, and your years will never end."), refer to the eternal rule of the exalted Son. But this eternal Son was subject to change in being made lower than the angels and taking on flesh and blood (2:9-10, 14). Jesus Christ designates one who has *become* the pioneer and perfecter of faith (12:2), but who remains the same in his unchanging faithfulness as heavenly High Priest. Community leaders come and go, like the Old Testament priests (7:23); in past, present (the "today" of salvation; see 1:5; 3:7, 13, 15; 4:7; 5:5), and future, the community can rely on Jesus who "always lives to make intercession for them" (7:25) because he is a "priest forever" (5:6; 7:3, 17, 21, 28). The view that "yesterday, today, and forever" refer to the christological stages of historical existence, exaltation, and eternal intercession (Bruce 1990, 375; similarly Filson 1967, 30-35), or that "yesterday" represents the time when past leaders spoke the truth about Christ, a truth that is to continue "today and forever" (Lane 1991, 530), can be debated.

The confession of praise to the unchanging intercessor is not to be exchanged for false teaching. The language of verse 9a—to be "carried away" as if by wind (cf. Eph 4:14; Jude 12); the adjective "strange"; the reference to "teachings" (the plural is used of those in error in Col 2:22 and 1 Tim 4:1)—suggests a danger posed by heresy, not by minor doctrinal aberrations.

God's grace was operative in and is mediated through Christ (see 2:9; 4:16; 10:29; 12:15; 13:25). Why grace should be contrasted with food is less clear. The NRSV phrase "regulations about food" is somewhat misleading; the text speaks of those who "walk" a path by adhering to certain foods (see, e.g., Eph 2:2, 10 and Col 3:7). The problem is not one of Jewish dietary rules; Old Testament food laws could hardly be called "strange teachings." Even less probable is a situation like that addressed by Paul in 1 Cor 8, 10.

The language of verse 9b is allusive. To "strengthen the heart [sc. oneself] with food" is a Semitic expression for eating (Judg 19:5,

8; Pss 104:15; 105:16). Hebrews uses the expression in a trans-
ferred sense (cf. 1 Thess 3:13; 2 Thess 2:17; Jas 5:8), and with a
different verb to suggest confirmation of inner strength by God (cf.
2:3 where "attested" means "confirmed"; see also 1 Cor 1:6; 2 Cor
1:21; Col 2:7). That foods have not "benefited" people recalls
earlier statements (see 4:2 and esp. 7:18: a cultic regulation proved
ineffectual). The simplest solution to the *crux interpretum* of verse
9 is to read it in connection with 9:9-10: the old sacrificial system
dealt with externals like "food and drink," things that could not
purify the conscience. Only the sacrifice of Christ can purify the
conscience (heart) and mediate heavenly grace (9:14; 10:22; see
Thompson 1982, 144-45, but without the suggestion that Hebrews
is working with a dualistic worldview). "Strange teachings" (v. *9a*)
are any doctrine that detracts from the sufficiency of Christ's
sacrifice in effecting divine grace.

The connection between eating and sacrifice (vv. 10-16), and the
call to follow Christ "outside" (v. 13), may hint at a more than
symbolic meaning for "foods" in verse 9. It is possible that some
in the community found social acceptance and security in continued
participation in other cultic meals (see Attridge 1989, 395). If this
is the case, verse 9 already calls for a break with earthly securities
by reminding the readers that their security lies in the reception of
grace. Taking part in non-Christian cultic meals constitutes a threat
to their existence, denies grace, and means a departure from the
teaching of past leaders (v. 7).

Ignatius seems to be recalling 13:9-10 in *Magn.* 7:2–8:1 when he
urges his readers to "come to one *altar*, to one Jesus Christ. . . . *Do
not be led astray by false doctrines* or by old fables which are
profitless. For if we go on living according to Judaism, we confess
that we have not received *grace*." If Ignatius has read Hebrews
correctly, his specific warning is against sharing a cultic eating with
non-Christian Jews.

10-16: These verses, which also have produced a variety of
interpretations, must be related to the thesis of verse 9: it is by
"eating" from an "altar" that the heart is strengthened by grace.
"We have an altar" is the credal counterpart to "we have such a

high priest" in 8:1. The altar is not any sacrificial table on earth, nor is it the heavenly sanctuary as the prototype of the earthly sanctuary (*pace* Filson 1967, 48-49; Thompson 1982, 146; no altar is mentioned in 8:5 or 9:1-10, 23-24). Analysis of the chiasm in verses 10-16 indicates that verse 10 corresponds to verses 15-16, which speak of sacrifices. The "altar" stands for Christ's sacrificial death within history (v. 12) as the perfect sacrifice that continues to mediate grace in the form of perfect cleansing from sin (9:14; 10:10), something that the sacrificial system of the old covenant could not do.

That old order is referred to in verses 10*b*-11. "Those who officiate [sc. serve] in the tent" are the Levitical priests (see v. 11; 8:4-5; 9:6—the present tense again describes the OT cultus as a backdrop to the new). That they "have no right to eat" from the Christian altar (meant metaphorically, like "tasting" in 6:4-5) recalls the prohibition against Levitical priests eating of the atonement sacrifice (Lev 6:30). The carcasses of the bull and goat whose blood had been brought into the Holy of Holies on Yom Kippur had to be burned outside the sacred area (Exod 29:14; Lev 16:27; Ezek 43:21; cf. Lev 4:12, 21). By speaking of the bodies of "animals" (literally, "living creatures"), and by recalling the action of the high priest in applying the blood, the author hints at the action of the heavenly High Priest in presenting his life-giving blood in the heavenly sanctuary (see 9:12-14, 18-25).

The contrast between "us" and "those" implies that Christians "eat" of a sacrifice that is better than the old sacrifices (see 9:23*b*). Further, just as priests and people were not allowed to eat the sacrifices on Yom Kippur, those who adhere to the old order have no share in the benefits (grace) of the new sacrifice.

The paraphrase of Lev 16:27 in verse 11 placed the phrase "outside the camp" at the end. That phrase becomes the basis of an analogy that sees Christ and his followers belonging to the "outside" (vv. 12-14). Sanctification by his blood (see 9:11-26) was not dependent on Jesus suffering "outside the gate" of Jerusalem (as in John 19:17-20). A lesson is drawn from history. He died outside the *sacred* city (the equivalent to the wilderness camp) to *sanctify* a whole people, making them ritually clean for worship (see 10:10, 14, 29). Those cursed under the Old Testament law were cut off from God's people and executed "outside the camp" (see Lev 10:1-5; 24:14, 23; Num 15:35). The paradox is that the "holy, blameless, undefiled" Jesus (see 7:26) was treated as unclean, yet effected perfect cleansing from the defilement of sin (cf. 2 Cor 5:21; Gal 3:13).

Verses 13-16 draw conclusions from the statements in verses 10-12. Christians who have been sanctified by Christ's blood belong with him on the "outside." To "go out" means to separate from others as a consequence of being made holy (v. 12; cf. Isa 52:11; 2 Cor 6:17; Rev 18:4). It means surrendering earthly security, as did Abraham and Moses (11:8, 26), and sharing the shame and abuse that Jesus endured (12:2-3). The Christian community is characterized not by honor but by shame (see DeSilva 1996). William L. Lane (1991, 543) finds here a "parenetic adaptation of the familiar call to discipleship in terms of cross bearing" (see Matt 10:34-39; 16:24-27; Mark 8:34-38; Luke 14:26-27).

How the readers are to move "outside the camp" is not immediately clear. One proposal is that the author contrasts Christians with the people who, once cleansed, were allowed to return to the camp (Lev 16:26). They belong in the *secular uncleanness of the world*, not in holy places that offer security in cultic performance (see H. Koester 1962, 301). But Christians are a new cultic community, according to Hebrews. To turn 13:13 into an appeal to live in the world is to overlook the text's essential point: separation and the bearing of abuse.

Another solution (see Thompson 1982, 147-50) sees the camp as the earthly sphere. As a pilgrim people, Christians are to renounce all earthly security and follow Christ into *the heavenly sphere*. This interpretation can appeal to verse 14, but turns the eschatology of Hebrews into a dualism. Above all, it fails to give any concrete reality to the appeal in verse 13.

More helpful is a reference to Exod 33:7-8 (see Bruce 1990, 381); those who sought the Lord had to go to the tent of meeting "outside the camp." Similarly, those who seek God now must come to Jesus who was rejected inside the city (13:12). This suggestion does justice to the writer's distinction between sacred and profane spaces and to the reference to Christ's suffering in history, and gives a probable social setting for the community's bearing of abuse for Christ: a *break with the institutions and customs of Judaism,* including common meals (v. 9; thus Westcott 1903, 441-42; Bruce 1990, 381; Filson 1967, 61-66; Lane 1991, 545).

A break with the parent body is the necessary corollary of confessing Christ and approaching him in prayer (4:14-16; 13:8). Those who worship with heavenly beings are a community whose identity is not determined by past earthly ties (12:22-24). Their hope is not set on earthly societal structures—"we have no lasting city" (13:14) is the negative counterpart to "we have an altar" (v. 10). Like the saints of old who went out looking for a better homeland (see 11:8, 10, 14-16, 26-27), Christians are a pilgrim people seeking a "remaining" city (cf. 12:27*b*). That enduring world is "coming" (cf. 2:5) only in the sense that it is still to be inherited (see 12:28). Possibly verse 14 is intended to imply that Jerusalem has lost its redemptive significance in Christian eschatology (see Lane 1991, 547-48). If that is so, we have further evidence that Hebrews was addressed to a diaspora community.

A second conclusion is drawn from the statement that Christians have an altar (v. 10). Two bracketing clauses speak of sacrifices that are God-pleasing (vv. 15*a*, 16*b*); the two inner clauses define the nature of the sacrifices (vv. 15*b*, 16*a*).

The opening phrase, "through him," has a liturgical ring (cf. Col 3:17; 1 Pet 4:11; in *1 Clem.* 61:3; 64; *Mart. Pol.* 14:3 the phrase refers to Jesus as High Priest). It recalls Christ's past sacrifice and present intercession as the basis of access to God. The description of the Christian life as a "sacrifice of praise" is striking. Leviticus 7:12-15 (LXX: 2-5) speaks of the peace offering sacrificed "for a thanksgiving," but the "sacrifice of praise" (as the LXX translates) is material. Also the "sacrifices of praise" in 2 Chr 29:31 (LXX) are material thank offerings. Our writer has borrowed the phrase from the psalms (see 50:14; 107:22; 116:17). Its meaning was probably suggested by Ps 50(LXX: 49):13-14 (the adverbial phrase "continually" may have been suggested by verse 8 of this psalm) where cultic praise is contrasted with animal sacrifice, and is in keeping with other New Testament texts (see Rom 12:1-2; Phil 2:17; 1 Pet 2:5).

In Hos 14:2 praise is called the "fruit of our lips" (for similar expressions see Prov 12:14; 13:2; 18:20). In the thanksgiving psalms, praise often appears as a declaratory confession of God's name and gracious deeds (see, e.g., 7:17; 9:11; 54:6; 75:1; 92:1-2). *Psalms of Solomon* 15:2-3 also links praise with acknowledging God's name as the "fruit of lips" that sing a new psalm (see Lane 1991, 551). Hebrews 13:15 sees the confession to the holy name itself as an act of praise. Rather than referring to God, the name is best taken in a christological sense. (1) God's promises are all enacted through Christ who enables people to approach the divine throne in worship (see "through him" in v. 15a). (2) Verses 10-13 have focused on Jesus as confessed in verse 8. (3) The author has referred to the community's christological confession at three points in the letter (3:1; 4:14; 10:23). His specific point is not merely that the sacrifice of Christ produces praise of God. The very act of confessing Christ is the heart of all worship as praise of God (cf. Phil 2:10-11).

In stating the second aspect of praise, a life of good works (v. 16), the author returns to the language ("do not neglect") and theme of 13:1-6. That praise and thanksgiving are to be matched by ethical actions may have been suggested by Ps 50:23, but a connection between confession, good deeds, and worship has been drawn earlier in the Letter (10:23-25). Doing good includes all acts of kindness for those in need, performed as service to God (see 6:10; 9:14; 12:28; Mark 14:7). Sharing is mentioned as a specific form of doing good. The Greek noun *koinōnia*, translated with a verb in the NRSV, suggests a sharing of material things (see Rom 15:26; 2 Cor 8:4; 9:13; also Acts 2:42-47; a sacramental participation [1 Cor 10:16] or "communion of the Holy Spirit" [2 Cor 13:13] is not meant). The author encourages the continuation of the sharing that the readers have already shown in the past (see 10:33-34).

Since the sacrifice of Christ has already removed the defilement of sin, God does not want animal sacrifices (see 10:5-6) but the offering of a sanctified life in the practice of love (v. 16b; cf. Rom

12:1). This offering is "pleasing to God" (the phrase recalls 12:28; see also 13:21) because it is the response of faith (see 11:5-6).

17-19: The writer returns to the theme of the opening bracket (vv. 7-9). Past leaders are to be remembered; their faith is to be emulated. Present leaders are to be obeyed since they also speak the word of God. To submit to them is to bow to the authority of the word that they speak.

Obedience and submission are required in view of the leaders' function: they are spiritual guardians. They "watch over" the community (the image is appropriate for under-shepherds; see v. 20) in keeping with their duty to remain vigilant in the light of the coming judgment (see Mark 13:33; Luke 21:36; Eph 6:18). Their responsibility to serve others certainly means that they will *have to* give account to God for their ministry (cf. Luke 16:2; Rom 14:12; 1 Cor 3:12-15; 4:2-5). But the statement that "they *will* give account" probably has the obedience of the readers, not of the leaders, in mind. (Cf. *Herm. Vis.* 3.9.10: "Correct one another . . . that I may also give an account of you all to the Lord.") Leaders are to be obeyed as those intent on presenting "souls" (i.e., people destined for eternal life; see 6:19) intact at the final judgment.

Ready obedience will make the leaders' task joyful; grudging compliance will make them sigh or grumble (v. 17c). Calling the latter "unprofitable" (NRSV: "harmful") continues the use of accounting language (cf. "give account" in v. 17b); opposition to leaders will register present and eternal loss.

Perhaps verse 17 reflects tensions between leaders and those who hold "strange teachings" (v. 9; see Lane 1991, 554-55). Significantly, the author identifies himself with the leaders. The plurals in verse 18 (us/we) are not meant in an authorial sense (as in 5:11 and 6:9), since verse 19 reverts to the first-person singular. Prayer for the writer will mean recognition of his status as a leader and acceptance of his instructions. The assertion that all leaders "have a clear conscience" (cf. Paul in 2 Cor 1:12), and their stated desire always to "act" (literally, *behave*) honorably unites them with past leaders whose "way of life" (literally, *behavior*) was recalled in verse 7.

In the writer's own case, prayer is to have a specific focus: speedy restoration to the community (v. 19; see 1 Tim 3:14 for a similar wish). The cause of separation is not stated. He may be hinting at a restoration in the sense of reacceptance, but physical reunion is the obvious intent of his words.

◊ ◊ ◊ ◊

The Letter's concluding block of exhortation calls on the readers to show by their corporate confession and communal life that they belong to a heavenly city. Faithfulness to the truth, attested by past leaders and contained in the confession to Christ, means rejection of error (vv. 7-9). Present leaders are to be respected as those who have a mandate to ensure that the community confesses and lives the truth (vv. 17-19).

Returning to the imagery of the Day of Atonement, the author shows how the sacrifice of Christ is cause both for abandoning all earthly securities and for offering up the new sacrifice of praise (vv. 10-16). Those who embrace the common confession (vv. 9, 15) are "insiders" in terms of their identity as sanctified people of the new covenant (v. 12). But this makes them "outsiders" in terms of their past affiliations and present status in society. To identify with Christ "outside the city" may mean alienation and rejection, but the readers are not merely asked to live with the stigma of confessing Christ. Those without permanent space on earth are assured that they belong to a lasting sacred space: in their worship and in the future inheritance of the heavenly city.

Assertions such as "we have an altar" and "we have a high priest" possibly echo the taunts of non-Christian neighbors who questioned the legitimacy of the Christian religion on the grounds that it possessed no priesthood and no sacrifices. Whether this belongs to the setting of Heb 13 or not, the author asserts that Christians do have an altar and a sacrifice that provide food which, unlike earthly foods (v. 9), does not perish but remains because Christ remains forever (v. 8).

The prayer of *Did.* 10:6 in connection with the *eucharistia,* "Let grace come and let the world pass away," is not far removed from the thought of 12:28 and 13:9. The distinction between those who can and those who cannot eat in 13:10 is matched by a similar emphasis on exclusivity in *Did.* 9:5 and 10:6 (cf. 1 Cor 16:22 in a eucharistic context).

The assertion that the theology of Hebrews excludes any sacramental dimension is questionable. Further sacrifices for atonement from sin are rejected, but 13:9-10 does not rule out the eating of a Christian sacrificial meal. Care must be exercised so as not to interpret Hebrews through Paul, but it is interesting to note that Paul, by analogy, connects the altar of Israel with the table of the Lord (1 Cor 10:18, 21).

Hebrews 13:15, 16 is not explicitly sacramental; the sacrifice of praise refers to the whole of life, not to a liturgical moment. Christological confession also is not limited to sacramental celebration, but the readers may have been reminded of the eucharistic calling on the name of the Lord (1 Cor 1:2; 16:22). Whether the author intended such connections or not, they may also have associated "sharing" (13:16) with the regular expression of fellowship: the breaking of bread (see Acts 2:42, 46).

A Personal Conclusion (13:20-25)

The Letter concludes with a prayer (vv. 20-21), a final appeal (v. 22), personal information (v. 23), greetings, and a short blessing (vv. 24-25)—a pattern found in other New Testament letters (see the table in Attridge 1989, 405). Content and language indicate that these verses are an authentic conclusion, and not added to the letter by a later hand. There are echoes of the body of the letter in references to the "blood of the eternal covenant" and to doing God's "will"; other terms link these verses with those immediately preceding them: "pleasing" (v. 21; see v. 16); "I appeal" (v. 22; the NRSV has "I urge" in v. 19); "leaders" (v. 24; see vv. 7, 17).

The request for prayer in verse 19 was couched in familiar terms; the writer's own prayer for his readers in verses 20-21 is marked by a solemn formality. An opening invocation and doxology frame a prayer that consists of two strophes, each of which (in the Greek) ends with the name Jesus. The first strophe (v. 20) outlines the past action of God that is the basis of the petition for God to act now and in the future (v. 21).

◊ ◊ ◊ ◊

"The God of peace" appears to be a fixed liturgical phrase; it occurs in concluding blessings and prayers in Paul's letters (see Rom 15:33; 16:20; 2 Cor 13:11; Phil 4:9; 1 Thess 5:23). In the context— a prayer that anticipates the end of the worship assembly in which the letter is being read out—"peace" means the wholeness of salvation.

The confession of God as the one "who brought back from the dead our Lord Jesus" also has a formal ring. Though implied earlier (7:16, 24; 9:14), this is the only place in the Letter where Christ's resurrection is explicitly mentioned. As in early credal formulations, God is the active subject of the resurrection (see, e.g., Acts 3:15; Rom 4:24; 1 Cor 6:14; 2 Cor 4:14; for an exception see 1 Thess 4:14). In using the verb "brought back" (not "raised"), the writer reflects the language of the psalms (see 30:3; 71:20). In particular, he is reflecting on Isa 63:11-13 LXX, which asks the question: "Where is he brought up from the sea the shepherd of the sheep, . . . who led Moses with his right hand. . . . He led them through the deep. . . ." Moses was the shepherd of God's people (cf. Ps 77:20) whom God led up from the Red Sea; Christ, who is greater than Moses (3:2-6), was rescued from the abyss of death to rescue others. As the "great shepherd" (cf. John 10:11, 14; 1 Pet 2:25; 5:4; see also the expressions "great high priest" in 4:14; "great priest" in 10:21), Christ fulfills the promise that God, the shepherd of Israel (Ps 23) who "brought up" Israel out of Egypt (see Jer 16:14-15; 23:7-8), would gather a lost people in a final act of rescue (Jer 23:3; Ezek 34:10-16, 23-24).

The statement that God raised Jesus "by the blood of the eternal covenant" becomes less cryptic when seen as an allusion to Zech 9:11: "Because of [i.e., in view of] the blood of my covenant with you, I will set your prisoners free from the waterless pit." God's leading of Jesus up out of the pit of death (for this image see also Pss 30:3; 40:2; 88:4, 6) is proof that God accepted his sacrifice for sin as the basis for a new and permanent covenant.

The expression "eternal covenant" is biblical (cf. Isa 55:3; Jer 32:40; Ezek 37:26), as is also "blood of the covenant" (the phrase from Exod 24:8 was quoted in 9:20 and 10:29). The entire phrase recalls the efficacious power of Christ's sacrifice that has secured an eternal redemption (9:12). By the power of his indestructible life, Christ remains forever as the guarantee of the eternal covenant inaugurated by his death (see 7:21-22).

Christ's resurrection is the basis of the new life of those whom he leads (cf. Rom 6:4; 1 Cor 15:55-58). God who raised Jesus will equip Jesus' followers to do God's will (for Christ's own readiness to do God's will see 10:7). "Everything good" refers not to good deeds themselves (see 13:10; 2 Thess 2:17), but to the gifts of God that are the source of holy living (cf. 9:11; 10:1). God who creates new life (cf. 11:19) continues to produce the evidence of the new life in the Christian community (cf. Phil 2:13). Doing God's will is part of the sacrifice of praise. That is suggested by the phrase, "pleasing in his sight," which recalls the theme of acceptable worship (see 11:4-5; 12:28; 13:16).

Equipment of people with good things "through Jesus Christ" (cf. v. 15) leads to praise of Christ, but the doxology at the end of verse 21 more naturally refers to God who was invoked at the beginning of verse 20, and who has been the main subject in the two halves of the prayer. Other New Testament prayers for, or assurances of, God's strength conclude with similar doxologies and an "Amen" (see Rom 16:27; Eph 3:14-21; Phil 4:19-20; 1 Pet 5:10-11).

A final appeal (v. 22), using the same verb as in verse 19, addresses the readers in familiar fashion as "brothers" (cf. 3:1, 12; 10:19). The plea to "bear with" the letter's message carries no sharpness (by contrast, see 2 Cor 11:1, 4, 19-20). Its description as brief is probably an epistolary convention (cf. 1 Pet 5:12; Ign. *Rom.* 8:2; Ign. *Pol.* 7:3; *Barn.* 1:5), like the author's occasional comment that he could say much more (see 5:11; 9:5; 11:32). There is a play on words as the author *appeals* for patience in listening to his message of *appeal,* though "word of exhortation" seems to have been a standard term for sermonic exposition of the Scriptures in hellenistic synagogues (see Acts 13:15; 2 Macc 15:8-11; cf. 1 Pet 5:12).

The Timothy mentioned is obviously well known to the readers (v. 23). He is almost certainly the man found by Paul on his journeys (see Acts 16:1; 2 Tim 1:5), the faithful companion and pupil whom Paul also called "our brother" (2 Cor 1:1; cf. Col 1:1). A special affinity with Timothy, son of a Jewish mother and a Greek father (Acts 16:1-3), would help to explain the author's fusion of Jewish Christian thought with hellenistic expression. It is natural to assume that Timothy has been "set free" from prison, but the verb could simply mean that he has departed or been "sent away" from some place (see Acts 13:3; 15:30, 33; 28:25). Whatever the facts, the writer hopes soon to be united with Timothy, so that a joint reunion with the readers can take place. Meanwhile, this Letter must suffice.

In greeting the leaders and saints the author is not distinguishing between clergy and laity. Special recognition of leaders again signals support of the local leadership (see 13:17-18), but the mention of leaders with "all" the saints places the emphasis on unity. Whether the Letter and greetings are to be passed on to other house-churches is not clear (cf. Col 4:16; 1 Thess 5:27). The writer probably wishes absent members of the church to be included in the expression of Christian fellowship.

Greetings are extended on behalf of "those from Italy," but their identity and present location remain unclear. That they are sending greetings home *to* Italy is more probable than that they are with the writer in Italy, though early copyists added "written from Italy/Rome" at the end of Hebrews. This probability is supported but not proved by the phrase "from Italy" in Acts 18:2.

Though the Greek word for grace *(charis)* is similar to the verb with which secular letters often concluded *(chaire* meant something like our modern "Cheers!"), the blessing with God's grace at the end of most New Testament letters is more than a formality. "Grace be with all of you"—the wording is the same as in Titus 3:15—is a liturgical blessing. Like all blessings, it is a performative word assuring the readers that they are recipients of the grace that comes from the past and present work of the High Priest (see 2:9; 4:16;

10:29; 12:15; 13:9). The final "Amen" is missing in some manuscripts. If original, it is an apt ending for a letter that claims to teach the truth finally revealed in Christ (cf. 1:2).

◊ ◊ ◊ ◊

The call to worship, as an expression of confident faith, is sounded at the end of the Letter. The writer begins his concluding lines with prayer and ends them with blessing. He encloses his finale with liturgical references to the great gifts of peace and grace (vv. 20, 25). The prayer in verses 20-21 recalls the central message of the Letter, reminding the readers that they are a new covenant people, sanctified by Christ's blood. As the one led from death by God, Jesus is now their great leader also in worship (cf. 8:1). He leads into God's presence for continual sprinkling with the cleansing blood so that God's people can be renewed for their own sacrifice: a life of praise and good works.

These last verses are proof of the writer's pastoral heart. Concerned for the integrity of the reader's faith and practice, for their own unity, and for continued fellowship with himself, he could have simply issued harsh warnings and threats of divine punishment. Instead, his "word of exhortation" becomes a word of comfort. God provides "everything good" in Christ, surrounding people with peace and grace. That will ensure that they live God-pleasing lives.

SELECT BIBLIOGRAPHY

SELECT WORKS ON HEBREWS
(BOTH CITED AND NOT CITED)

Aune, D. E. 1991. "Heracles and Christ: Heracles Imagery in the Christology of Early Christianity." In *Greeks, Romans, and Christians: Essays in Honour of Abraham J. Malherbe*, edited by D. L. Balch, E. Ferguson, and W. A. Meeks, 3-19. Minneapolis: Fortress.

Bligh, John. 1966. *Chiastic Analysis of the Epistle to the Hebrews*. Oxford: Clarendon.

Cody, Aelred. 1960. *Heavenly Sanctuary and Liturgy in the Epistle to the Hebrews*. St. Meinrad, IN: Grail.

Cosby, Michael R. 1988. *The Rhetorical Composition and Function of Hebrews 11*. Macon, GA: Mercer University Press.

D'Angelo, Mary Rose. 1979. *Moses in the Letter to the Hebrews*. SBLDS 42. Missoula, MT: Scholars Press.

Demarest, Bruce. 1976. *A History of Interpretation of Hebrews 7:1-10 from the Reformation to the Present*. Tübingen: Mohr-Siebeck.

DeSilva, David A. 1996. *Despising Shame: Honor Discourse and Community Maintenance in the Epistle to the Hebrews*. SBLDS 152. Atlanta: Scholars Press.

Dey, Lala K. 1975. *The Intermediary World and Patterns of Perfection in Philo and Hebrews*. SBLDS 25. Missoula, MT: Scholars Press.

Dunnill, John. 1992. *Covenant and Sacrifice in the Letter to the Hebrews*. SNTSMS 75. Cambridge: Cambridge University Press.

Elliott, John H. 1981. *A Home for the Homeless: A Sociological Exegesis of 1 Peter and Its Situation and Strategy*. Philadelphia: Fortress.

Filson, Floyd V. 1967. *"Yesterday": A Study of Hebrews in the Light of Chapter 13*. London: SCM.

Fuller, R. H. 1995. "Hebrews." In *The General Letters: Hebrews, James, 1-2 Peter, Jude, 1-3 John*. Proclamation Commentaries, edited by Gerhard Krodel. Minneapolis: Fortress.

Greer, Rowan. 1973. *The Captain of Our Salvation: A Study in the Patristic Exegesis of Hebrews*. Tübingen: Mohr-Siebeck.

Guthrie, George H. 1994. *The Structure of Hebrews: A Text-Linguistic Analysis.* NovTSup 73. Leiden: E. J. Brill.

Hoppins, Ruth. 1969. *Priscilla, Author of the Epistle to the Hebrews, and Other Essays.* Jericho, NY: Exposition.

Horton, Fred L. 1976. *The Melchizedek Tradition: A Critical Examination of the Sources to the Fifth Century AD and in the Epistle to the Hebrews.* SNTSMS 30. Cambridge: Cambridge University Press.

Hughes, Graham. 1979. *Hebrews and Hermeneutics: The Epistle to the Hebrews as a New Testament Example of Biblical Interpretation.* SNTSMS 38. Cambridge: Cambridge University Press.

Hurst, L. D. 1990. *The Epistle to the Hebrews: Its Background of Thought.* SNTSMS 65. Cambridge: Cambridge University Press.

Isaacs, Marie E. 1992. *Sacred Space: An Approach to the Theology of the Epistle to the Hebrews.* JSNTSup 73. Sheffield: JSOT.

Käsemann, Ernst. 1984. *The Wandering People of God: An Investigation of the Letter to the Hebrews.* Minneapolis: Augsburg. Translated by Roy A. Harrisville and Irving L. Sandberg from the 2nd edition (1957) of the original German, *Das wandernde Gottesvolk.*

Kennedy, George A. 1984. *New Testament Interpretation Through Rhetorical Criticism.* Chapel Hill: University of North Carolina Press.

Kistemaker, Simon J. 1981. *The Psalm Citations in the Epistle to the Hebrews.* Amsterdam: G. van Soest.

Koester, Craig R. 1994. "The Epistle to the Hebrews in Recent Study." *CR:BS* 2:123-45.

Koester, Helmut. 1962. " 'Outside the Camp': Hebrews 13:9-14." *HTR* 55:299-315.

Lehne, Susanne. 1990. *The New Covenant in Hebrews.* JSNTSup 44. Sheffield: JSOT.

Lindars, Barnabas. 1989. "The Rhetorical Structure of Hebrews." *NTS* 35:382-408.

————. 1991. *Theology of the Letter to the Hebrews.* New Testament Theology Series. Cambridge: Cambridge University Press.

Lussier, E. 1975. *Christ's Priesthood According to the Epistle to the Hebrews.* Collegeville, MN: Liturgical Press.

Mack, Burton L. 1990. *Rhetoric and the New Testament.* Guides to Biblical Scholarship. Minneapolis: Fortress.

Manson, William. 1951. *The Epistle to the Hebrews: An Historical and Theological Reconsideration.* London: Hodder & Stoughton.

National Association of Baptist Professors of Religion, and Dale F. Leschert. 1995. *Hermeneutical Foundations of Hebrews: A Study in the*

Validity of the Epistle's Interpretation of Some Core Citations from the Psalms. Lewiston, NY: Edwin Mellen.

Neyrey, J. H. 1991. " 'Without Beginning of Days or End of Life' (Hebrews 7:3): Topos for a True Deity." *CBQ* 53:439-55.

Pearson, Birger A. 1990. *Gnosticism, Judaism, and Egyptian Christianity.* Minneapolis: Fortress.

Perkins, Pheme. 1993. *Gnosticism and the New Testament.* Minneapolis: Fortress.

Peterson, David. 1982. *Hebrews and Perfection.* SNTSMS 47. Cambridge: Cambridge University Press.

Pfitzner, Victor C. 1967. *Paul and the Agon Motif: Traditional Athletic Imagery in the Pauline Literature.* NovTSup 18. Leiden: E. J. Brill.

Pursiful, Darrell. J. 1993. *The Cultic Motif in the Spirituality of the Book of Hebrews.* Lewiston, NY: Edwin Mellen.

Sabourin, Leopold. 1973. *Priesthood: A Comparative Study.* Leiden: E. J. Brill.

Scholer, John M. 1991. *Proleptic Priests: Priesthood in the Epistle to the Hebrews.* JSNTSup 49. Sheffield: JSOT.

Selwyn, E. G. 1947. *The First Epistle of Peter.* London: Macmillan.

Smith, Jerome. 1969. *A Priest Forever: A Study of Typology and Eschatology in Hebrews.* London: Sheed and Ward.

Sowers, Sidney G. 1965. *The Hermeneutics of Philo and Hebrews: A Comparison of the Interpretation of the Old Testament in Philo Judaeus and the Epistle to the Hebrews.* Zürich: EVZ-Verlag.

Swetnam, J. 1981. *Jesus and Isaac: A Study of the Epistle to the Hebrews in the Light of the Aqedah.* AnBib 94. Rome: Pontifical Biblical Institute.

————. 1989. "Christology and Eucharist in the Epistle to the Hebrews." *Bib* 70:74-95.

Synge, F. C. 1959. *Hebrews and the Scriptures.* London: SPCK.

Thompson, James W. 1982. *The Beginnings of Christian Philosophy: The Epistle to the Hebrews.* CBQMS 13. Washington, DC: Catholic Biblical Association.

van der Horst, P. W. 1990. "Sarah's Seminal Emission: Hebrews 11:11 in the Light of Ancient Embryology." In *Greeks, Romans, and Christians: Essays in Honour of Abraham J. Malherbe,* edited by D. L. Balch, E. Ferguson, and W. A. Meeks, 287-302. Minneapolis: Fortress.

Vanhoye, Albert. 1964. *A Structured Translation of the Epistle to the Hebrews.* Translated by J. Swetnam. Rome: Pontifical Biblical Institute.

————. 1977. *Our Priest Is Christ: The Doctrine of the Epistle to the Hebrews.* Rome: Biblical Institute Press.

————. 1989. *Structure and Message of the Epistle to the Hebrews.* Subsidia Biblica 12. Rome: Pontifical Biblical Institute.

Williamson, R. 1970. *Philo and the Epistle to the Hebrews.* Leiden: E. J. Brill.

Wills, L. 1984. "The Form of the Sermon in Hellenistic Judaism and Early Christianity." *HTR* 77:277-99.

COMMENTARIES (BOTH CITED AND NOT CITED)

Attridge, Harold W. 1989. *The Epistle to the Hebrews.* Hermeneia. Philadelphia: Fortress. — A scholarly analysis of the Greek text, rich in nonbiblical material. Also accessible to nonspecialists since text-critical issues are kept separate from the main text, and all Greek words referred to are translated.

Braun, H. 1984. *An die Hebräer.* HNT 14. Tübingen: Mohr-Siebeck. — A work full of textual and philological detail in a famous German commentary series, but for specialized study only.

Bruce, F. F. 1990. *The Epistle to the Hebrews.* NICNT. Grand Rapids, MI: Eerdmans. — For many years the standard English commentary on Hebrews, the 1964 edition has been revised in view of more recent studies. All Greek words appearing in the main text are transliterated and explained.

Buchanan, George W., trans. 1972. *To the Hebrews.* AB 36. Garden City, NY: Doubleday. — Less helpful to the general reader because of some rather idiosyncratic interpretations, Buchanan sees the whole letter as a homiletic midrash (sermonic commentary) on Psalm 110, addressed to Jewish Christians in Jerusalem.

Casey, Juliana. 1900. *Hebrews.* New Testament Message 18. Wilmington, DE: Michael Glazier. — Essay-format rather than verse-by-verse commentary. A good starting point for students wanting to become familiar with the terrain of Hebrews.

Ellingworth, Paul. 1991. *The Epistle to the Hebrews.* Epworth Commentaries. London: Epworth. — A popular, nontechnical commentary based on the Revised English Bible.

————. 1993. *The Epistle to the Hebrews: A Commentary on the Greek Text.* NIGTC. Grand Rapids, MI: Eerdmans. — One of the more important recent commentaries. Offers detailed analysis of the Greek text. Full of linguistic data and exegetical options, but not so helpful in summarizing the letter's distinctive message.

Grässer, Erich. 1990–93. *An die Hebräer.* EKKNT 17.1-2. Zürich: Benziger Verlag; Neukirchen-Vluyn: Neukirchener Verlag. — A Protestant contribution to a well-respected series that brings together Catholic and Protestant scholarship.

Guthrie, Donald. 1983. *The Letter to the Hebrews.* TNTC 15. Downers Grove, IL: InterVarsity. — Full of textual data without becoming technical. All Greek words in the main text are transliterated and explained.

Hughes, Philip E. 1987. *Commentary on Hebrews.* Grand Rapids, MI: Eerdmans. — Though based on an analysis of the Greek text, this commentary is sometimes expository rather than exegetical. Accessible to the nonspecialist.

Kistemaker, Simon J. 1984. *Exposition of the Epistle to the Hebrews.* Grand Rapids, MI: Baker. — Scholarly, but expository rather than exegetical. Easy to follow for the general reader since textual minutiae are kept to a minimum.

Lane, William L. 1991. *Hebrews 1–8; 9–13.* WBC 47A; 47B. Dallas: Word. — Like that of Spicq, a massive work that offers the best recent commentary, and one that can be used by nonspecialists. It combines appreciation of the distinctive literary and rhetorical character of Hebrews, careful analysis of the text, and helpful reconstruction of its historical setting. Like most recent commentators, Lane sees Hebrews as written to wavering Jewish Christians in Rome.

Long, Thomas G. 1997. *Hebrews.* Interpretation. Louisville: Westminster/John Knox. — This latest addition to a popular series could not be consulted for this commentary.

Moffatt, James. 1924. *A Critical and Exegetical Commentary on the Epistle to the Hebrews.* ICC. Edinburgh: T. & T. Clark. — Now dated, but full of textual insight and masterfully written. Requires a very good knowledge of Greek. A foundational work in English scholarship.

Montefiore, Hugh W. 1964. *A Commentary on the Epistle to the Hebrews.* HNTC. New York: Harper. — Written in clear English and open to the nonspecialist despite many references to ancient and contemporary literature.

Pfitzner, Victor C. 1979. *Hebrews.* Chi Rho Commentary. Adelaide: Lutheran Publishing House. — Popular presentation, reflecting problems of the text but aimed also at edificatory reading.

Riggenbach, Eduard. 1922. *Der Brief an die Hebräer.* KNT 14. Leipzig: Deichert. Wuppertal: Brockhaus. 1987. — A classic in German Protestant literature by a scholar whose insights have often stood the test of later scholarship.

Smith, Robert H. 1984. *Hebrews*. ACNT. Minneapolis: Augsburg. — A popular presentation, very readable and succinct. Endnotes indicate scholarly discussion.

Spicq, Ceslas. 1952–53. *L'Épître aux Hébreux*. 2 vols. Paris: Gabalda. — A massive work by a Catholic scholar that has gained the stature of a classic.

Weiss, Hans-Friedrich. 1991. *Der Brief an die Hebräer*. MeyerK 13. Göttingen: Vandenhoeck & Ruprecht. — Protestant scholarship in one of the best-known German commentary series (replacing the earlier volume by Otto Michel).

Westcott, Brooke Foss. 1903. *The Epistle to the Hebrews*. 3rd ed., London: Macmillan. — Technical and now superseded, but those able to handle Greek can still consult Westcott's introduction and comments, in the form of notes, with profit.

Wilson, R. McClellan. 1987. *Hebrews*. NCB. Grand Rapids, MI: Eerdmans. — Scholarly references are packed into the main text, but generally do not detract from readability.

INDEX